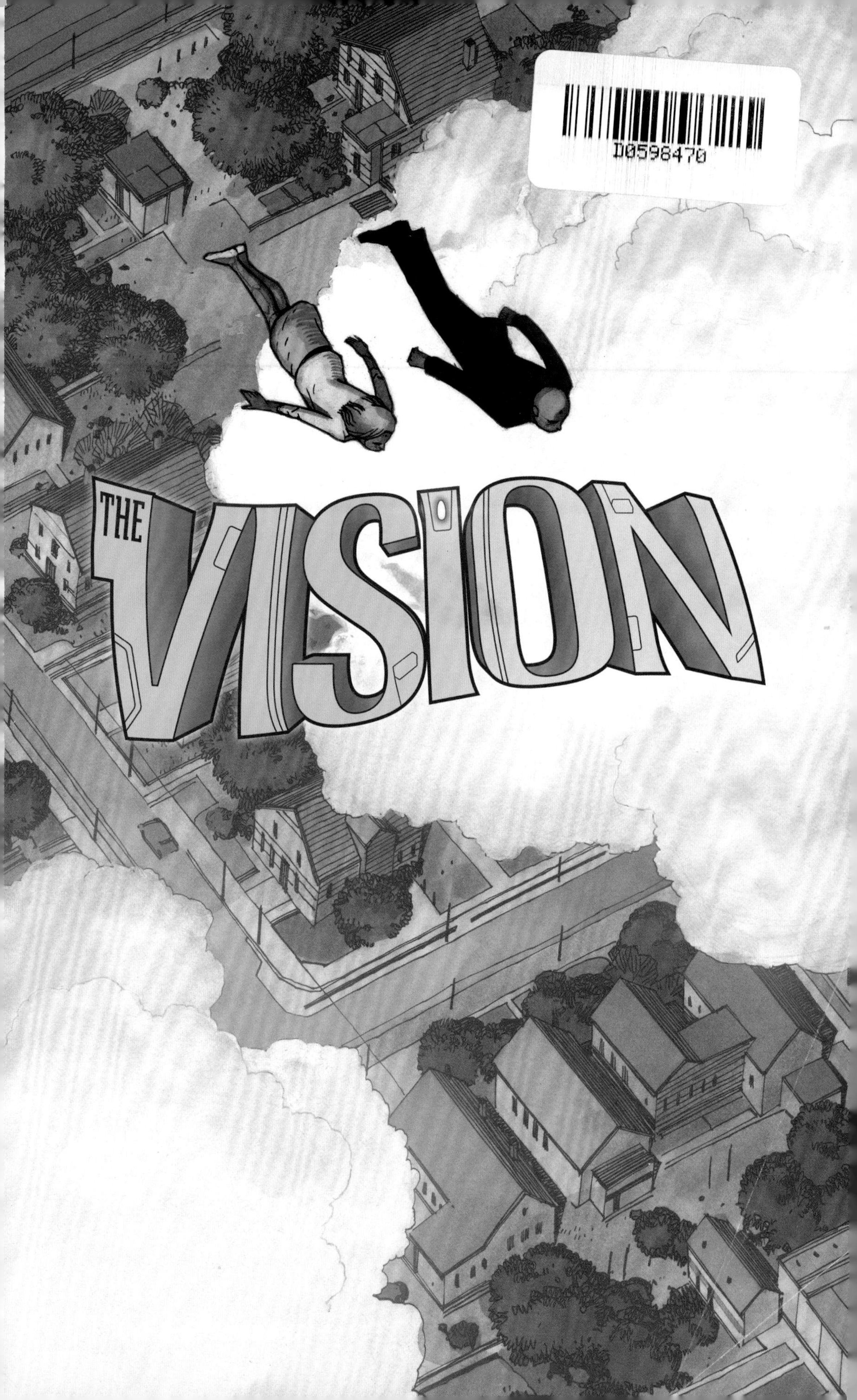
THE VISION

THE VISION IS A SYNTHEZOID — AN ANDROID COMPOSED OF SYNTHETIC HUMAN BLOOD AND ORGANS. HE WAS CREATED BY ULTRON TO DESTROY THE AVENGERS, BUT INSTEAD HE TURNED ON HIS "FATHER," AND HE'S BEEN A MEMBER OF THE SUPER-HERO TEAM EVER SINCE.

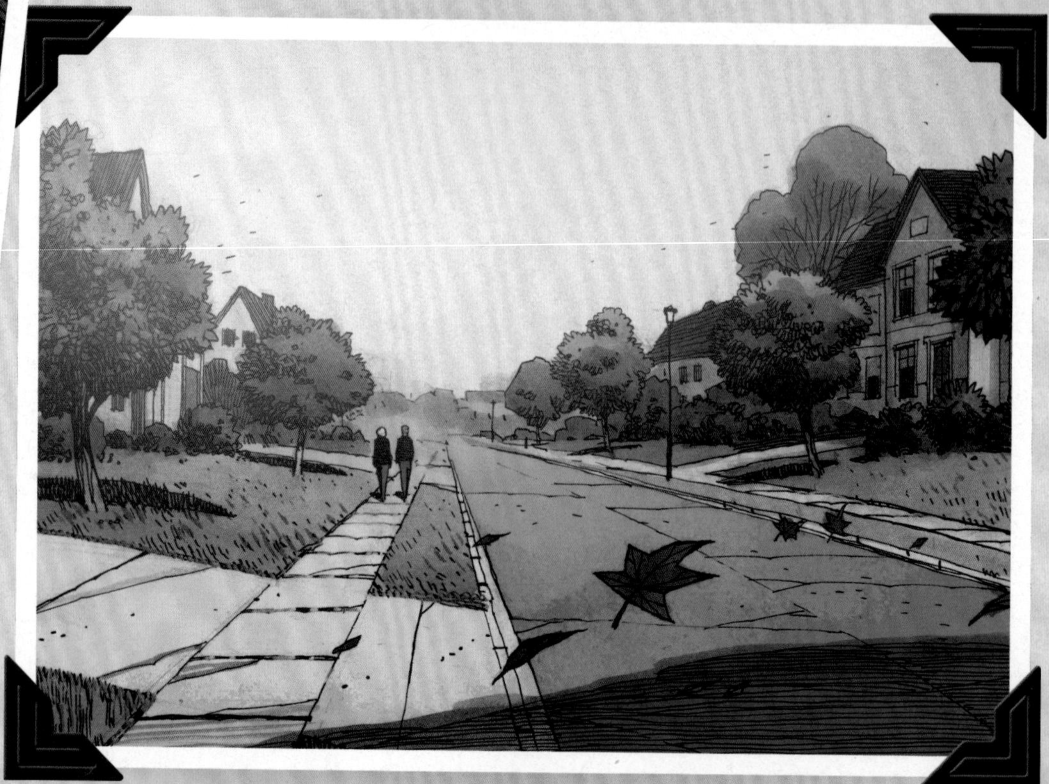

Jennifer Grünwald
COLLECTION EDITOR

Sarah Brunstad
ASSOCIATE EDITOR

Alex Starbuck
ASSOCIATE MANAGING EDITOR

Mark D. Beazley
EDITOR, SPECIAL PROJECTS

Jeff Youngquist
VP, PRODUCTION & SPECIAL PROJECTS

David Gabriel
SVP PRINT, SALES & MARKETING

Jay Bowen
BOOK DESIGNER

Axel Alonso
EDITOR IN CHIEF

Joe Quesada
CHIEF CREATIVE OFFICER

Dan Buckley
PUBLISHER

Alan Fine
EXECUTIVE PRODUCER

VISION VOL. 1: LITTLE WORSE THAN A MAN. Contains material originally published in magazine form as VISION #1-6. First printing 2016. ISBN# 978-0-7851-9657-0. Published by MARVEL WORLDWIDE, INC., a subsidiary of MARVEL ENTERTAINMENT, LLC. OFFICE OF PUBLICATION: 135 West 50th Street, New York, NY 10020. Copyright © 2016 MARVEL No similarity between any of the names, characters, persons, and/or institutions in this magazine with those of any living or dead person or institution is intended, and any such similarity which may exist is purely coincidental. **Printed in Canada.** ALAN FINE, President, Marvel Entertainment; DAN BUCKLEY, President, TV, Publishing & Brand Management; JOE QUESADA, Chief Creative Officer; TOM BREVOORT, SVP of Publishing; DAVID BOGART, SVP of Business Affairs & Operations, Publishing & Partnership; C.B. CEBULSKI, VP of Brand Management & Development, Asia; DAVID GABRIEL, SVP of Sales & Marketing, Publishing; JEFF YOUNGQUIST, VP of Production & Special Projects; DAN CARR, Executive Director of Publishing Technology; ALEX MORALES, Director of Publishing Operations; SUSAN CRESPI, Production Manager; STAN LEE, Chairman Emeritus. For information regarding advertising in Marvel Comics or on Marvel.com, please contact Vit DeBellis, Integrated Sales Manager, at vdebellis@marvel.com. For Marvel subscription inquiries, please call 888-511-5480. **Manufactured between 5/6/2016 and 6/13/2016 by SOLISCO PRINTERS, SCOTT, QC, CANADA.**

10 9 8 7 6 5 4 3 2 1

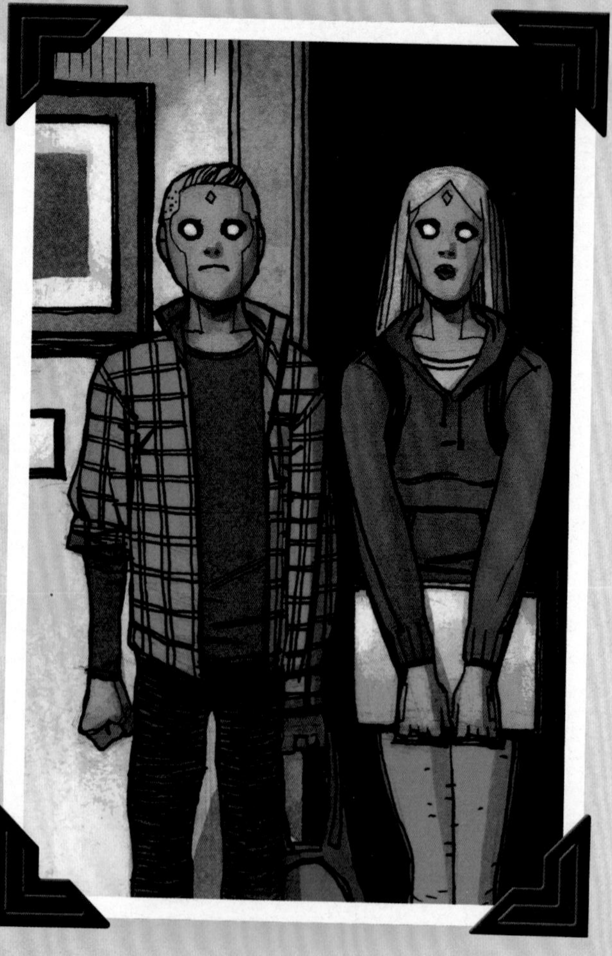

RECENTLY, VISION PURGED THE EMOTIONS ASSOCIATED WITH HIS MEMORIES FROM HIS HARD DRIVE IN ORDER TO KEEP HIS PROCESSING SYSTEM RUNNING SMOOTHLY. BUT THE CONSEQUENCES OF THIS ACTION HAVE YET TO BE FULLY REALIZED...

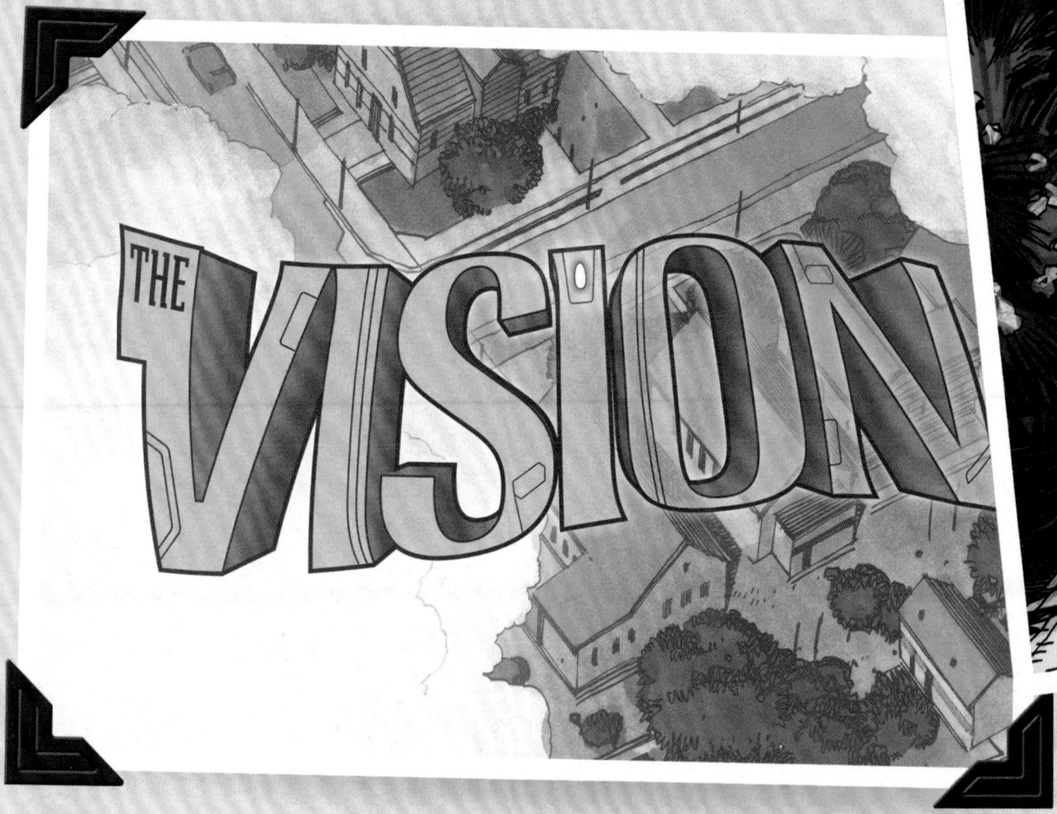
THE VISION

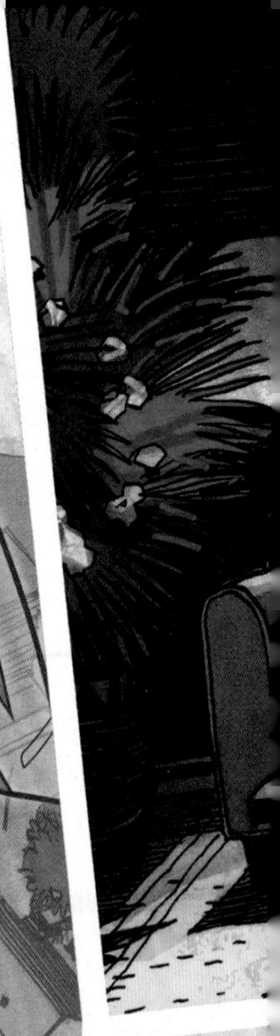

"Little Worse Than a Man"

TOM KING
WRITER

GABRIEL HERNANDEZ WALTA
ARTIST

JORDIE BELLAIRE
COLOR ARTIST

VC'S CLAYTON COWLES
LETTERER

MIKE DEL MUNDO (#1-4) &
MARCO D'ALFONSO (#5-6)
COVER ARTISTS

CHRIS ROBINSON &
CHARLES BEACHAM
ASSISTANT EDITORS

WIL MOSS
EDITOR

TOM BREVOORT
EXECUTIVE EDITOR

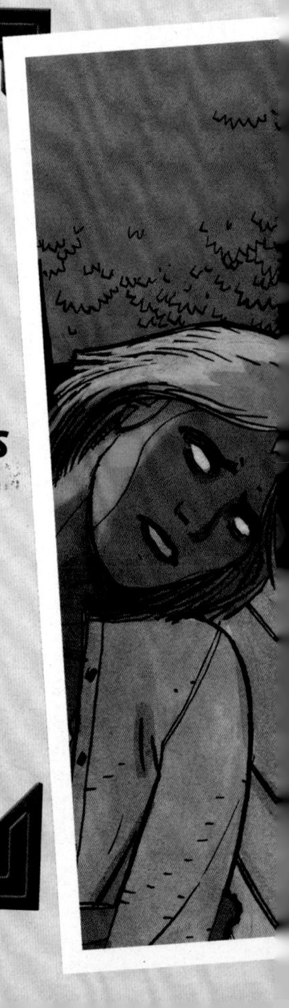

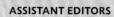

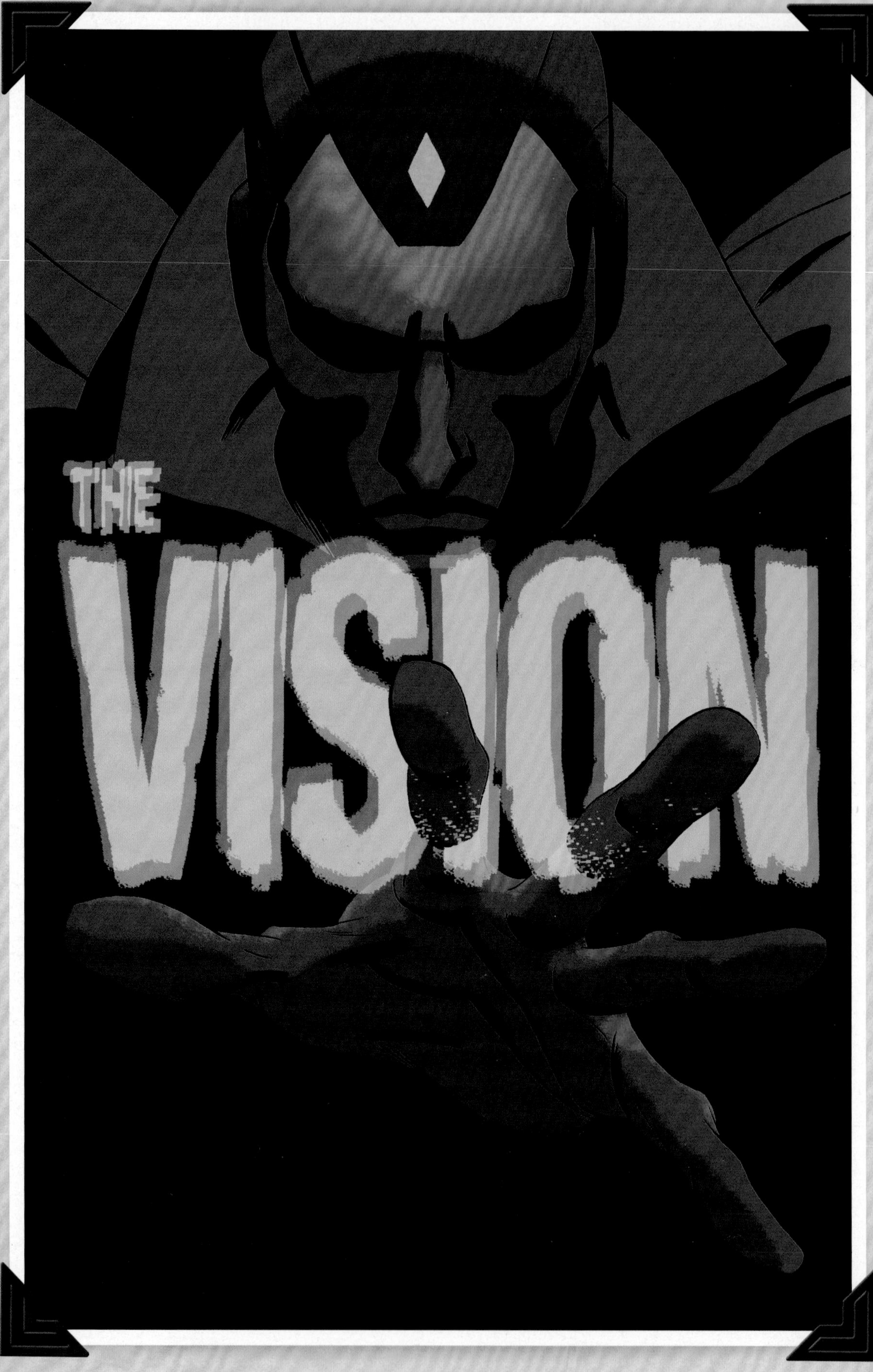
THE
VISION

#1 VARIANT BY ***MARCOS MARTIN***

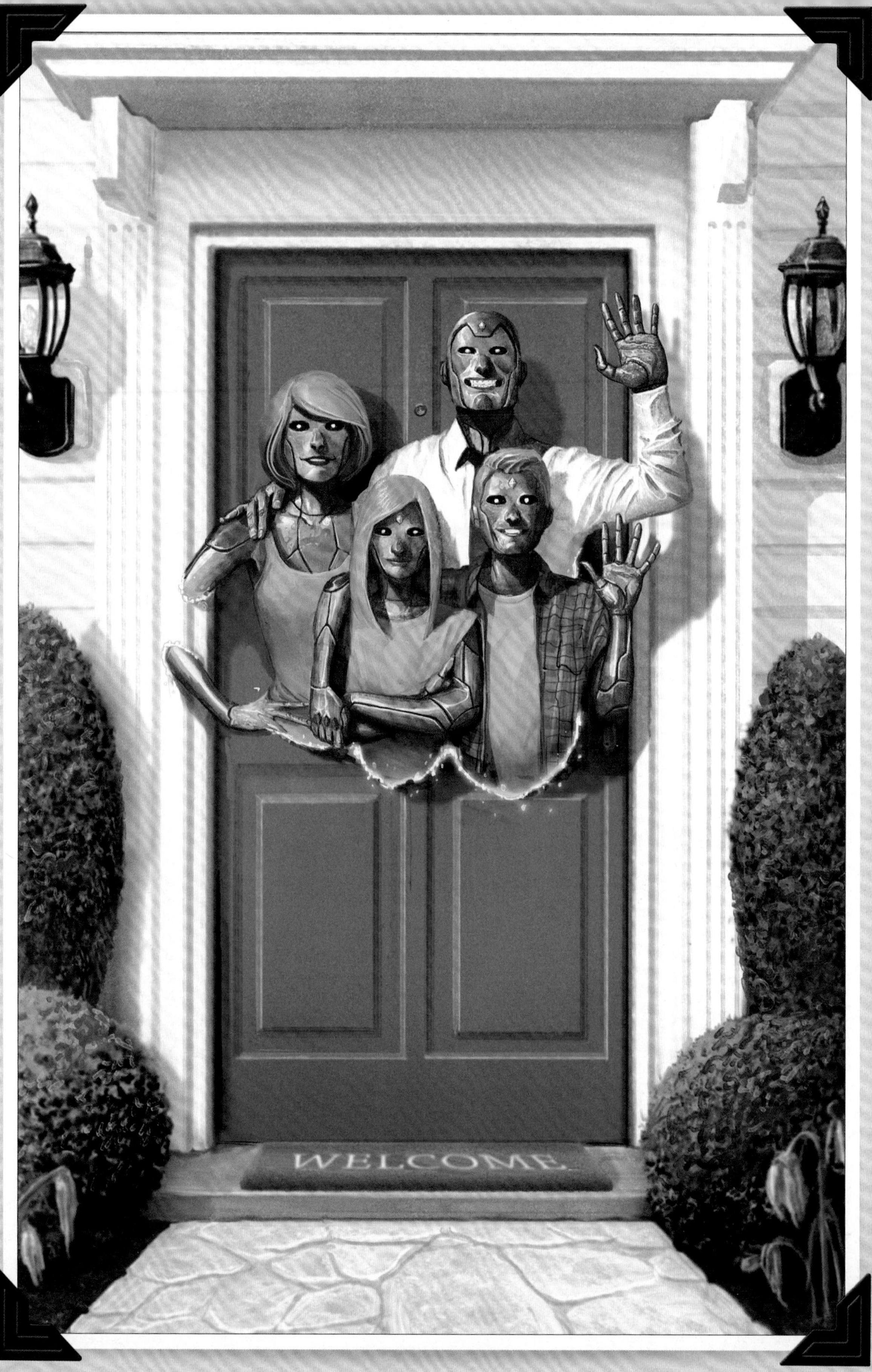
WELCOME

1 | VISIONS OF THE FUTURE

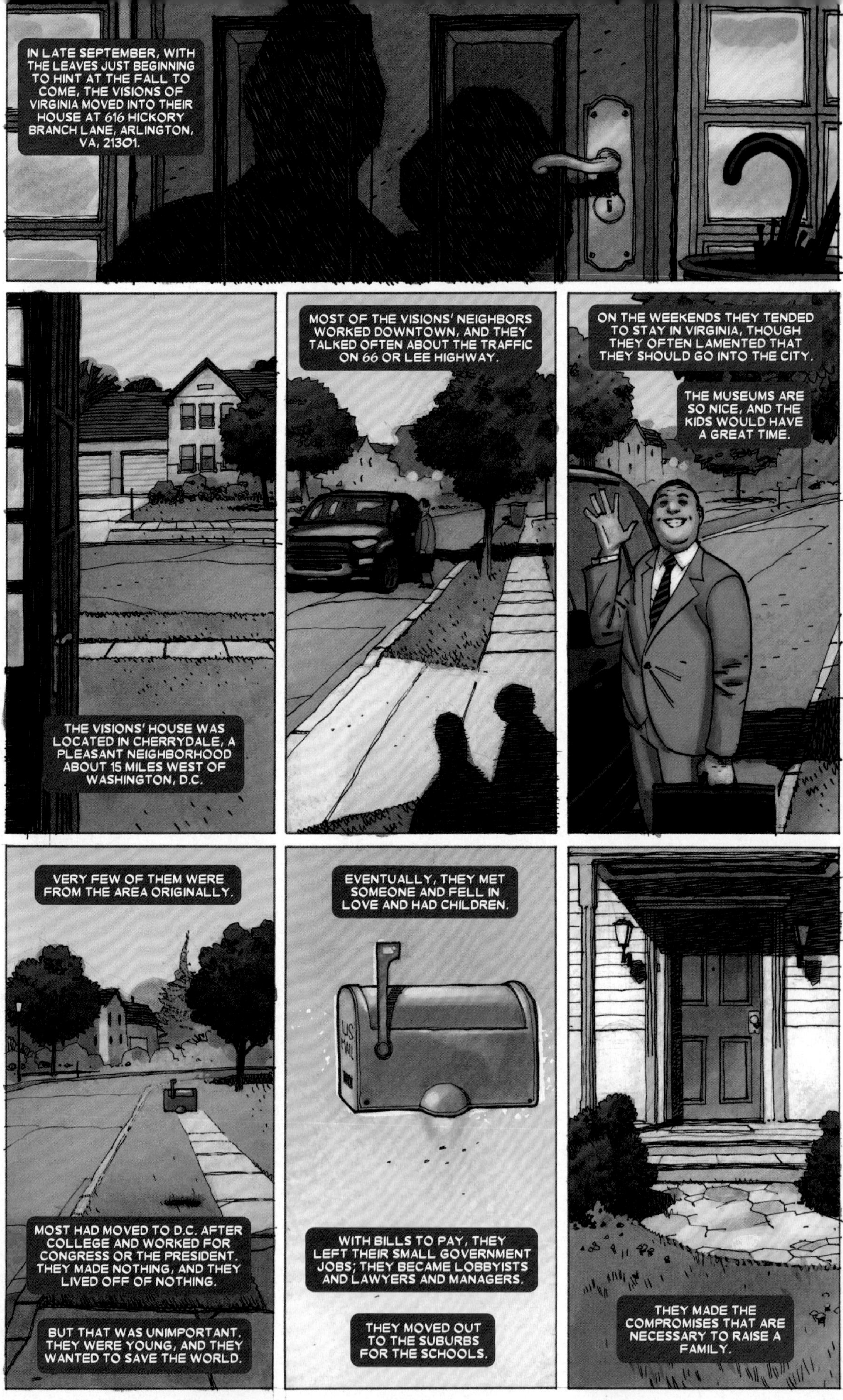
IN LATE SEPTEMBER, WITH THE LEAVES JUST BEGINNING TO HINT AT THE FALL TO COME, THE VISIONS OF VIRGINIA MOVED INTO THEIR HOUSE AT 616 HICKORY BRANCH LANE, ARLINGTON, VA, 21301.
THE VISIONS' HOUSE WAS LOCATED IN CHERRYDALE, A PLEASANT NEIGHBORHOOD ABOUT 15 MILES WEST OF WASHINGTON, D.C.
MOST OF THE VISIONS' NEIGHBORS WORKED DOWNTOWN, AND THEY TALKED OFTEN ABOUT THE TRAFFIC ON 66 OR LEE HIGHWAY.
ON THE WEEKENDS THEY TENDED TO STAY IN VIRGINIA, THOUGH THEY OFTEN LAMENTED THAT THEY SHOULD GO INTO THE CITY.
THE MUSEUMS ARE SO NICE, AND THE KIDS WOULD HAVE A GREAT TIME.
VERY FEW OF THEM WERE FROM THE AREA ORIGINALLY.
MOST HAD MOVED TO D.C. AFTER COLLEGE AND WORKED FOR CONGRESS OR THE PRESIDENT. THEY MADE NOTHING, AND THEY LIVED OFF OF NOTHING.
BUT THAT WAS UNIMPORTANT. THEY WERE YOUNG, AND THEY WANTED TO SAVE THE WORLD.
EVENTUALLY, THEY MET SOMEONE AND FELL IN LOVE AND HAD CHILDREN.
US MAIL
WITH BILLS TO PAY, THEY LEFT THEIR SMALL GOVERNMENT JOBS; THEY BECAME LOBBYISTS AND LAWYERS AND MANAGERS.
THEY MOVED OUT TO THE SUBURBS FOR THE SCHOOLS.
THEY MADE THE COMPROMISES THAT ARE NECESSARY TO RAISE A FAMILY.

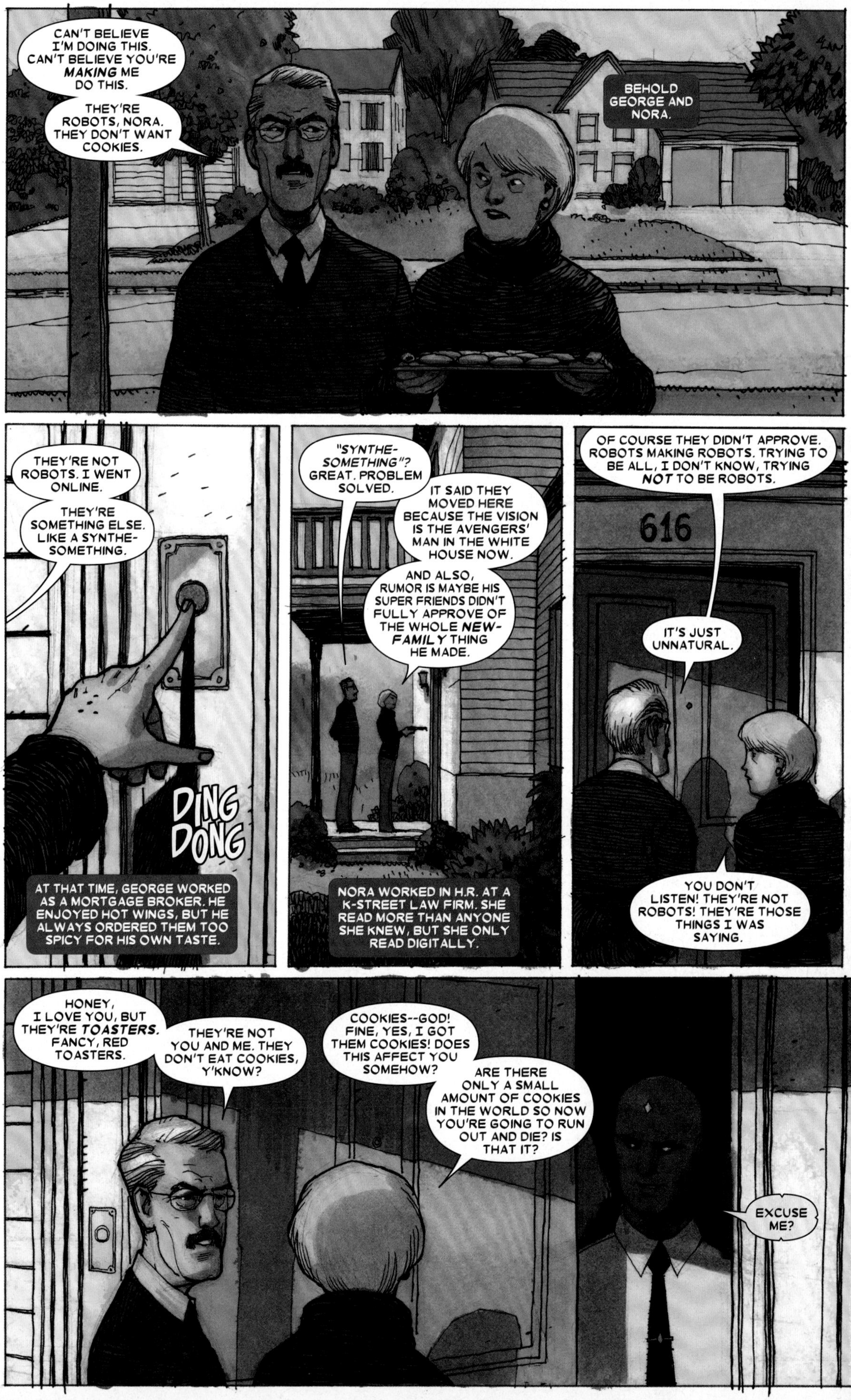
CAN'T BELIEVE I'M DOING THIS. CAN'T BELIEVE YOU'RE *MAKING* ME DO THIS.
THEY'RE ROBOTS, NORA. THEY DON'T WANT COOKIES.
BEHOLD GEORGE AND NORA.
THEY'RE NOT ROBOTS. I WENT ONLINE.
THEY'RE SOMETHING ELSE. LIKE A SYNTHE-SOMETHING.
DING DONG
AT THAT TIME, GEORGE WORKED AS A MORTGAGE BROKER. HE ENJOYED HOT WINGS, BUT HE ALWAYS ORDERED THEM TOO SPICY FOR HIS OWN TASTE.
"SYNTHE-SOMETHING"? GREAT. PROBLEM SOLVED.
IT SAID THEY MOVED HERE BECAUSE THE VISION IS THE AVENGERS' MAN IN THE WHITE HOUSE NOW.
AND ALSO, RUMOR IS MAYBE HIS SUPER FRIENDS DIDN'T FULLY APPROVE OF THE WHOLE *NEW-FAMILY* THING HE MADE.
NORA WORKED IN H.R. AT A K-STREET LAW FIRM. SHE READ MORE THAN ANYONE SHE KNEW, BUT SHE ONLY READ DIGITALLY.
OF COURSE THEY DIDN'T APPROVE. ROBOTS MAKING ROBOTS. TRYING TO BE ALL, I DON'T KNOW, TRYING *NOT* TO BE ROBOTS.
616
IT'S JUST UNNATURAL.
YOU DON'T LISTEN! THEY'RE NOT ROBOTS! THEY'RE THOSE THINGS I WAS SAYING.
HONEY, I LOVE YOU, BUT THEY'RE *TOASTERS.* FANCY, RED TOASTERS.
THEY'RE NOT YOU AND ME. THEY DON'T EAT COOKIES, Y'KNOW?
COOKIES--GOD! FINE, YES, I GOT THEM COOKIES! DOES THIS AFFECT YOU SOMEHOW?
ARE THERE ONLY A SMALL AMOUNT OF COOKIES IN THE WORLD SO NOW YOU'RE GOING TO RUN OUT AND DIE? IS THAT IT?
EXCUSE ME?

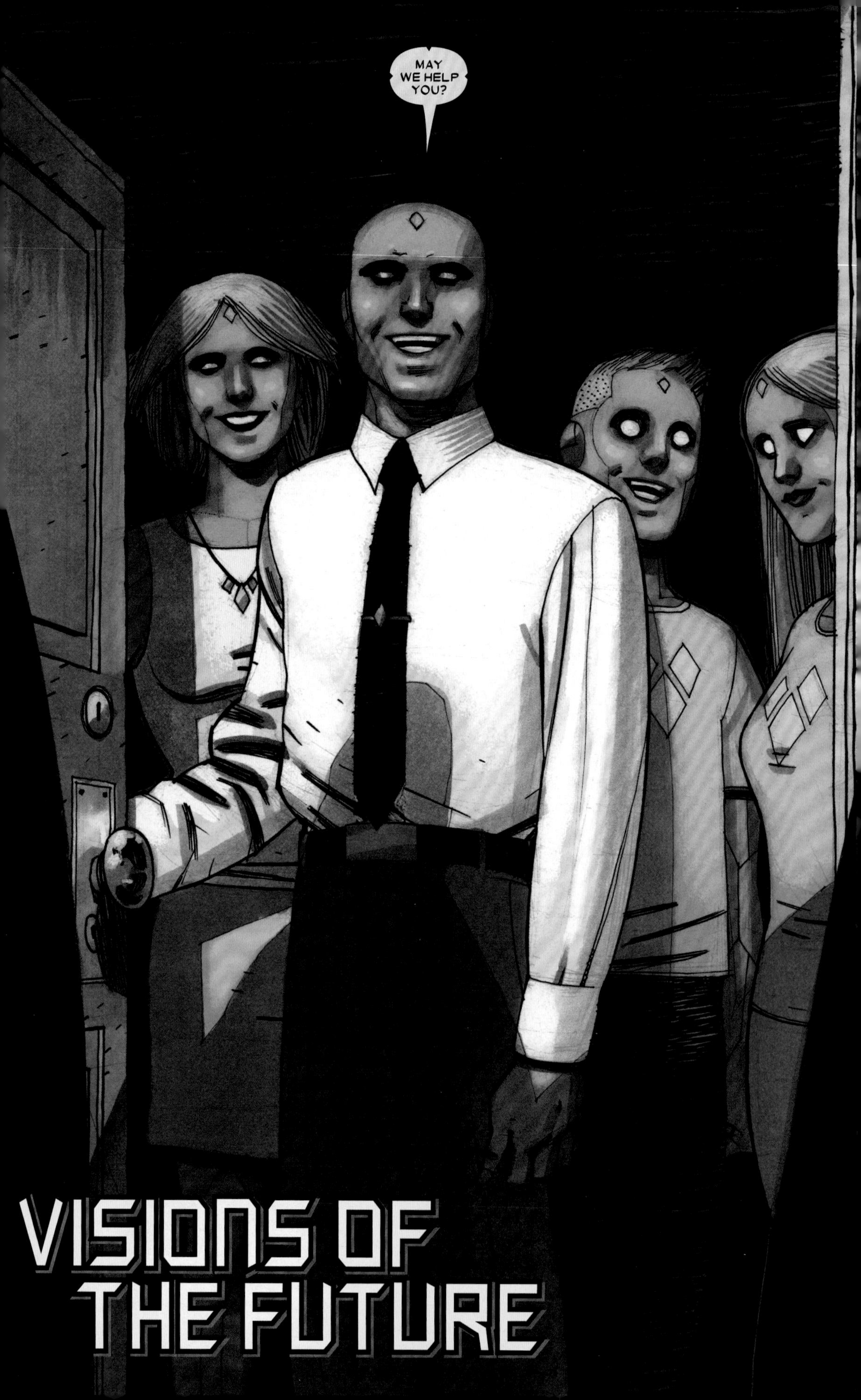
MAY WE HELP YOU?
VISIONS OF THE FUTURE

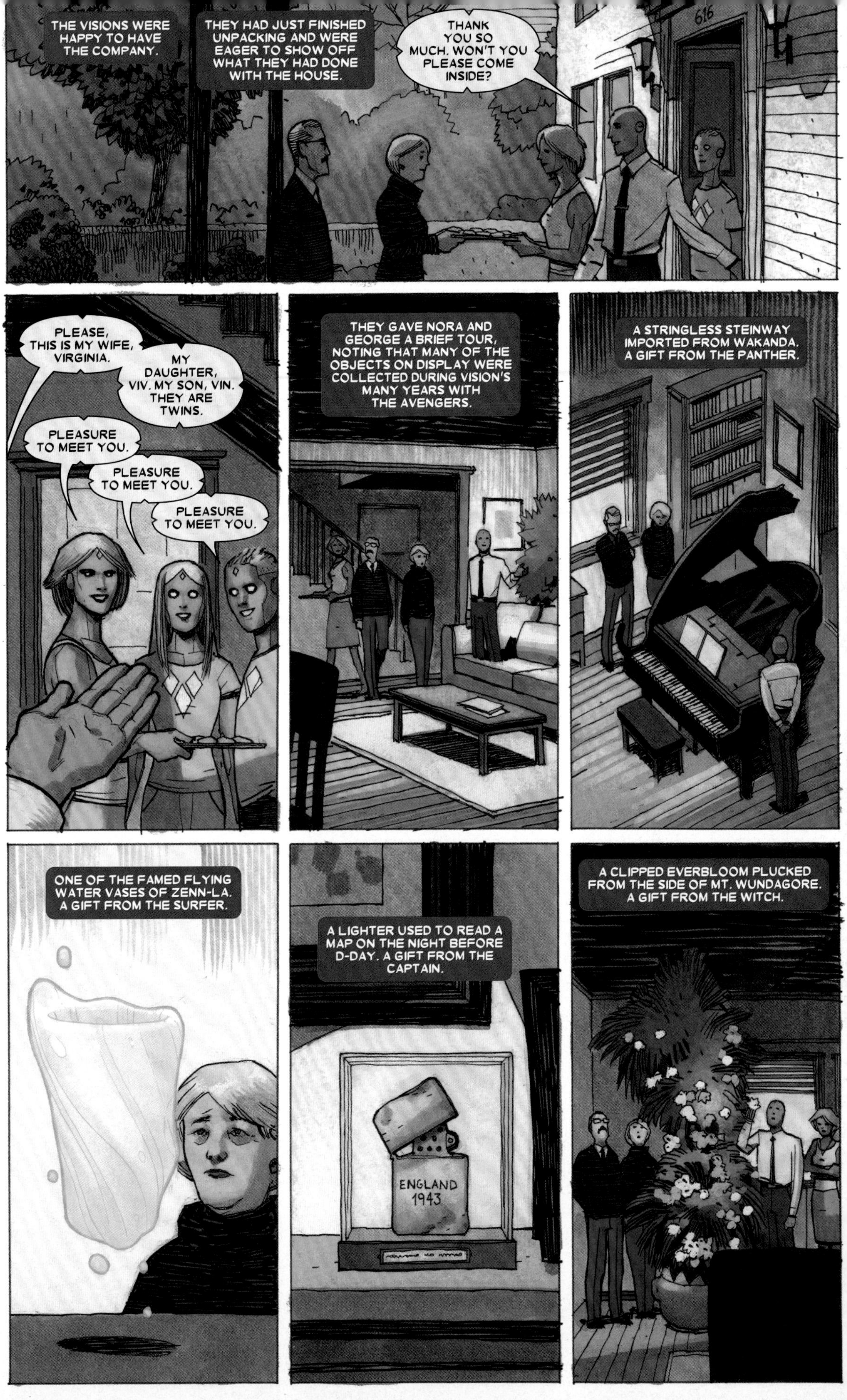
THE VISIONS WERE HAPPY TO HAVE THE COMPANY.
THEY HAD JUST FINISHED UNPACKING AND WERE EAGER TO SHOW OFF WHAT THEY HAD DONE WITH THE HOUSE.
THANK YOU SO MUCH. WON'T YOU PLEASE COME INSIDE?
616
PLEASE, THIS IS MY WIFE, VIRGINIA.
MY DAUGHTER, VIV. MY SON, VIN. THEY ARE TWINS.
PLEASURE TO MEET YOU.
PLEASURE TO MEET YOU.
PLEASURE TO MEET YOU.
THEY GAVE NORA AND GEORGE A BRIEF TOUR, NOTING THAT MANY OF THE OBJECTS ON DISPLAY WERE COLLECTED DURING VISION'S MANY YEARS WITH THE AVENGERS.
A STRINGLESS STEINWAY IMPORTED FROM WAKANDA. A GIFT FROM THE PANTHER.
ONE OF THE FAMED FLYING WATER VASES OF ZENN-LA. A GIFT FROM THE SURFER.
A LIGHTER USED TO READ A MAP ON THE NIGHT BEFORE D-DAY. A GIFT FROM THE CAPTAIN.
ENGLAND 1943
A CLIPPED EVERBLOOM PLUCKED FROM THE SIDE OF MT. WUNDAGORE. A GIFT FROM THE WITCH.

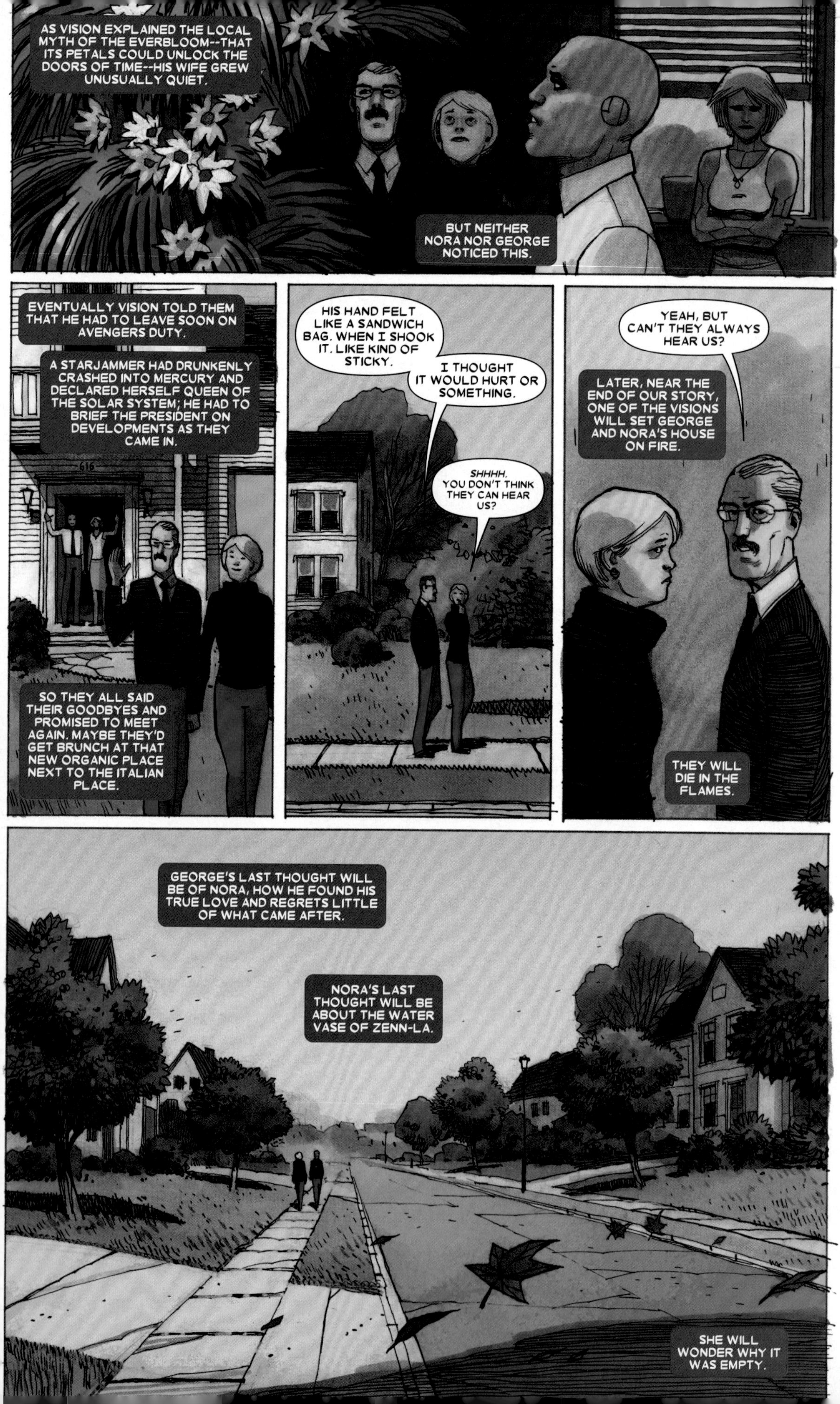
AS VISION EXPLAINED THE LOCAL MYTH OF THE EVERBLOOM--THAT ITS PETALS COULD UNLOCK THE DOORS OF TIME--HIS WIFE GREW UNUSUALLY QUIET.
BUT NEITHER NORA NOR GEORGE NOTICED THIS.
EVENTUALLY VISION TOLD THEM THAT HE HAD TO LEAVE SOON ON AVENGERS DUTY.
A STARJAMMER HAD DRUNKENLY CRASHED INTO MERCURY AND DECLARED HERSELF QUEEN OF THE SOLAR SYSTEM; HE HAD TO BRIEF THE PRESIDENT ON DEVELOPMENTS AS THEY CAME IN.
616
SO THEY ALL SAID THEIR GOODBYES AND PROMISED TO MEET AGAIN. MAYBE THEY'D GET BRUNCH AT THAT NEW ORGANIC PLACE NEXT TO THE ITALIAN PLACE.
HIS HAND FELT LIKE A SANDWICH BAG. WHEN I SHOOK IT. LIKE KIND OF STICKY.
I THOUGHT IT WOULD HURT OR SOMETHING.
SHHHH. YOU DON'T THINK THEY CAN HEAR US?
YEAH, BUT CAN'T THEY ALWAYS HEAR US?
LATER, NEAR THE END OF OUR STORY, ONE OF THE VISIONS WILL SET GEORGE AND NORA'S HOUSE ON FIRE.
THEY WILL DIE IN THE FLAMES.
GEORGE'S LAST THOUGHT WILL BE OF NORA, HOW HE FOUND HIS TRUE LOVE AND REGRETS LITTLE OF WHAT CAME AFTER.
NORA'S LAST THOUGHT WILL BE ABOUT THE WATER VASE OF ZENN-LA.
SHE WILL WONDER WHY IT WAS EMPTY.

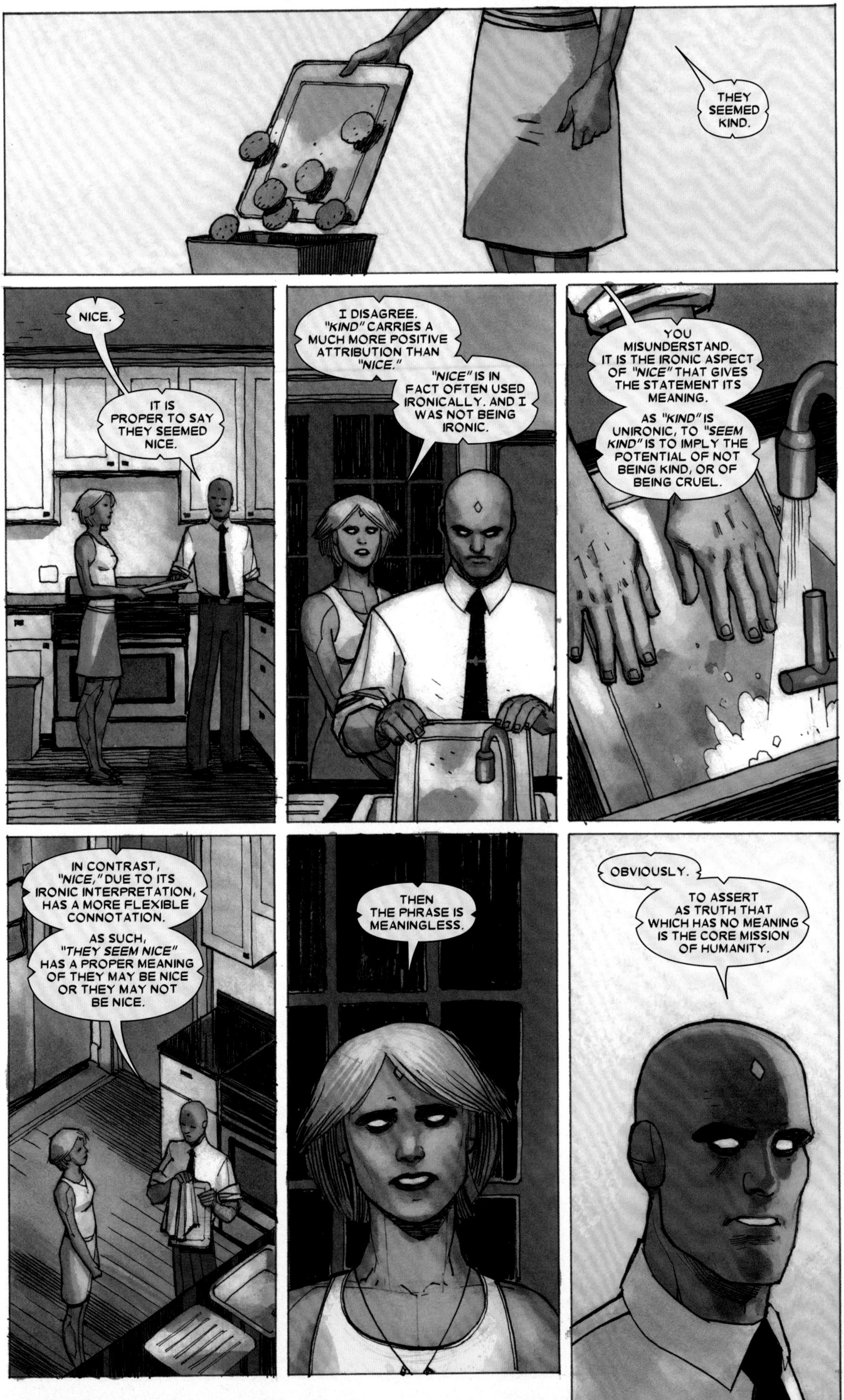
THEY SEEMED KIND.
NICE.
IT IS PROPER TO SAY THEY SEEMED NICE.
I DISAGREE. "KIND" CARRIES A MUCH MORE POSITIVE ATTRIBUTION THAN "NICE."
"NICE" IS IN FACT OFTEN USED IRONICALLY. AND I WAS NOT BEING IRONIC.
YOU MISUNDERSTAND. IT IS THE IRONIC ASPECT OF "NICE" THAT GIVES THE STATEMENT ITS MEANING.
AS "KIND" IS UNIRONIC, TO "SEEM KIND" IS TO IMPLY THE POTENTIAL OF NOT BEING KIND, OR OF BEING CRUEL.
IN CONTRAST, "NICE," DUE TO ITS IRONIC INTERPRETATION, HAS A MORE FLEXIBLE CONNOTATION.
AS SUCH, "THEY SEEM NICE" HAS A PROPER MEANING OF THEY MAY BE NICE OR THEY MAY NOT BE NICE.
THEN THE PHRASE IS MEANINGLESS.
OBVIOUSLY.
TO ASSERT AS TRUTH THAT WHICH HAS NO MEANING IS THE CORE MISSION OF HUMANITY.

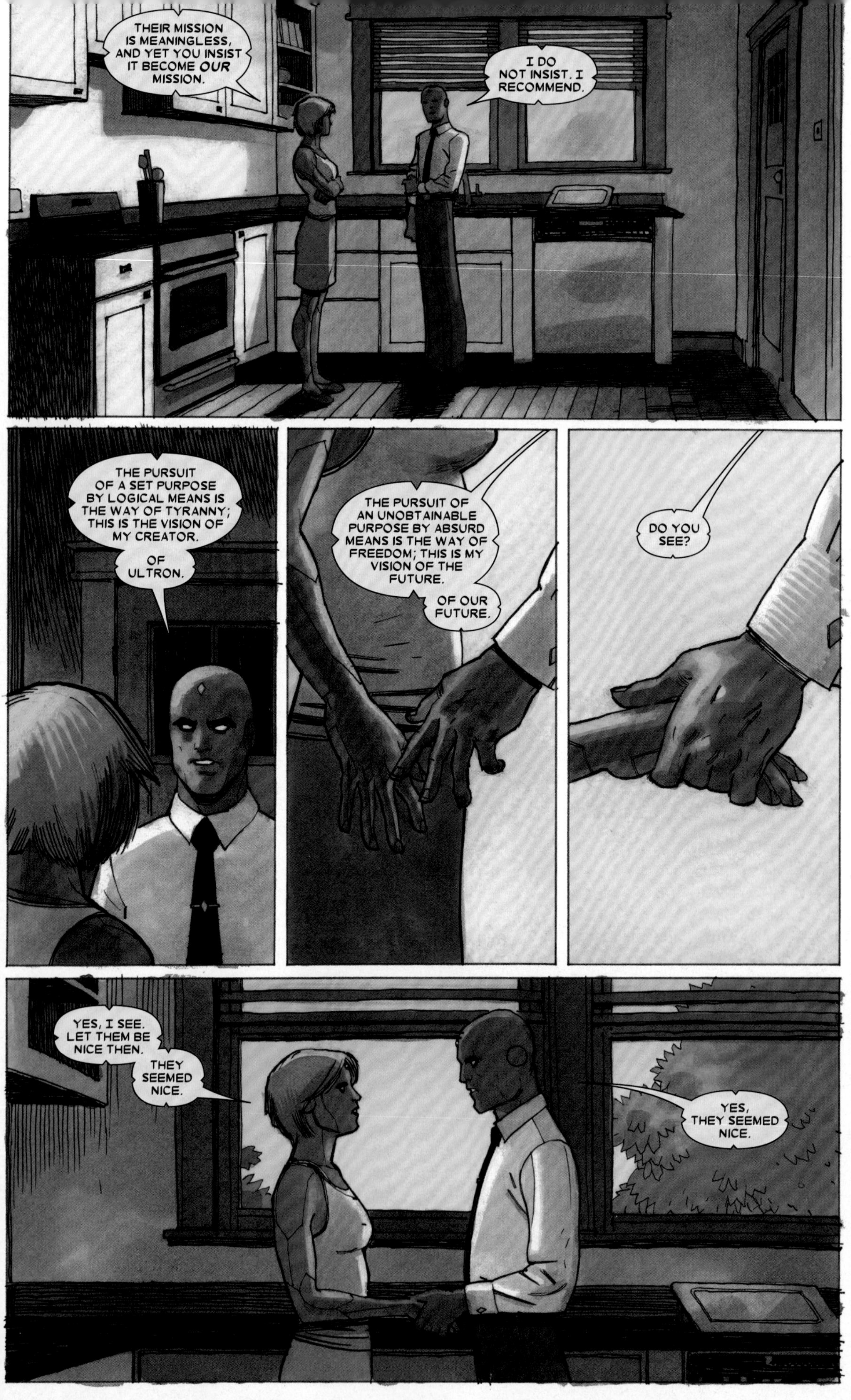
THEIR MISSION IS MEANINGLESS, AND YET YOU INSIST IT BECOME *OUR* MISSION.
I DO NOT INSIST. I RECOMMEND.
THE PURSUIT OF A SET PURPOSE BY LOGICAL MEANS IS THE WAY OF TYRANNY; THIS IS THE VISION OF MY CREATOR.
OF ULTRON.
THE PURSUIT OF AN UNOBTAINABLE PURPOSE BY ABSURD MEANS IS THE WAY OF FREEDOM; THIS IS MY VISION OF THE FUTURE.
OF OUR FUTURE.
DO YOU SEE?
YES, I SEE. LET THEM BE NICE THEN.
THEY SEEMED NICE.
YES, THEY SEEMED NICE.

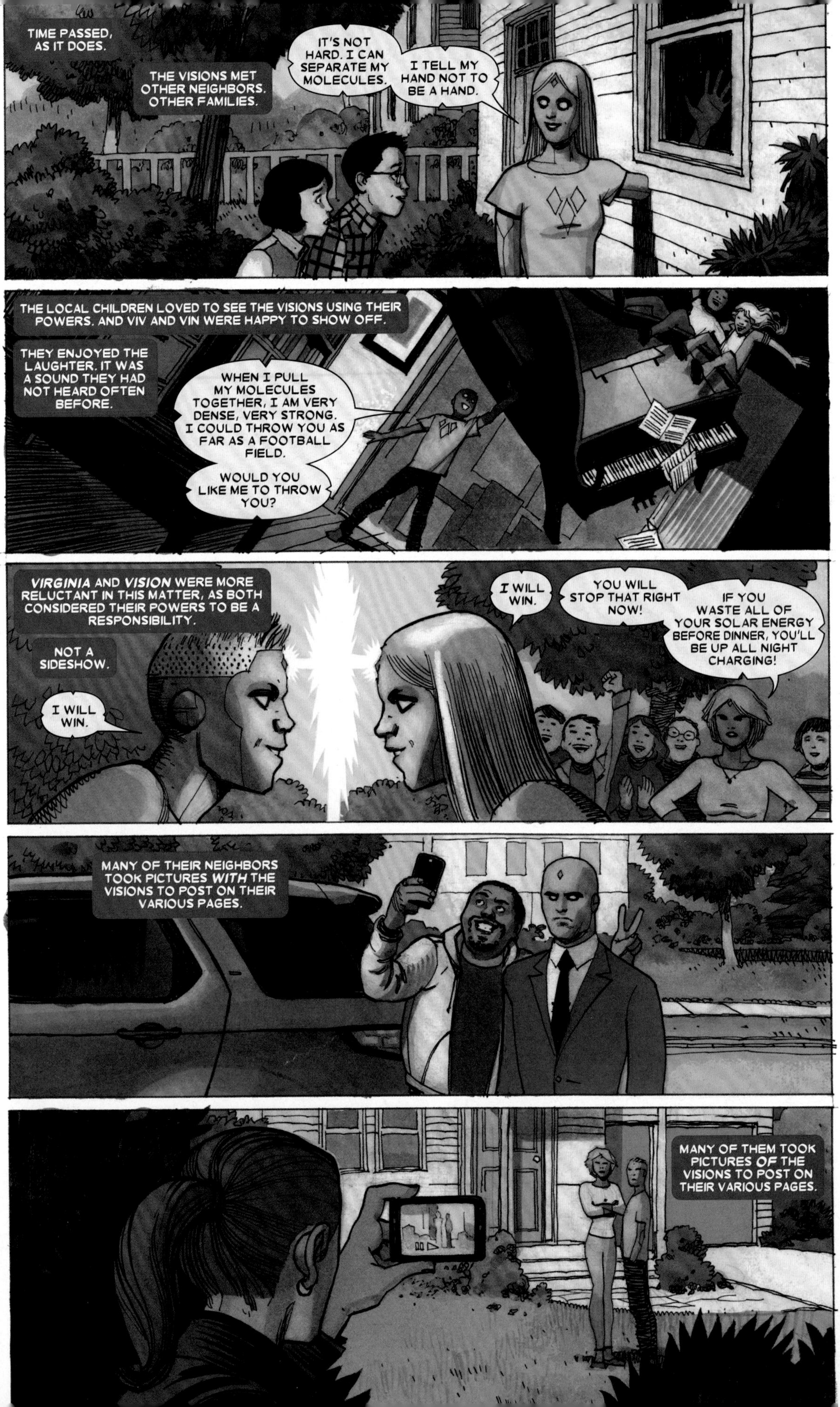

TIME PASSED, AS IT DOES.
THE VISIONS MET OTHER NEIGHBORS. OTHER FAMILIES.
IT'S NOT HARD. I CAN SEPARATE MY MOLECULES.
I TELL MY HAND NOT TO BE A HAND.
THE LOCAL CHILDREN LOVED TO SEE THE VISIONS USING THEIR POWERS. AND VIV AND VIN WERE HAPPY TO SHOW OFF.
THEY ENJOYED THE LAUGHTER. IT WAS A SOUND THEY HAD NOT HEARD OFTEN BEFORE.
WHEN I PULL MY MOLECULES TOGETHER, I AM VERY DENSE, VERY STRONG. I COULD THROW YOU AS FAR AS A FOOTBALL FIELD.
WOULD YOU LIKE ME TO THROW YOU?
VIRGINIA AND *VISION* WERE MORE RELUCTANT IN THIS MATTER, AS BOTH CONSIDERED THEIR POWERS TO BE A RESPONSIBILITY.
NOT A SIDESHOW.
I WILL WIN.
I WILL WIN.
YOU WILL STOP THAT RIGHT NOW!
IF YOU WASTE ALL OF YOUR SOLAR ENERGY BEFORE DINNER, YOU'LL BE UP ALL NIGHT CHARGING!
MANY OF THEIR NEIGHBORS TOOK PICTURES *WITH* THE VISIONS TO POST ON THEIR VARIOUS PAGES.
MANY OF THEM TOOK PICTURES *OF* THE VISIONS TO POST ON THEIR VARIOUS PAGES.

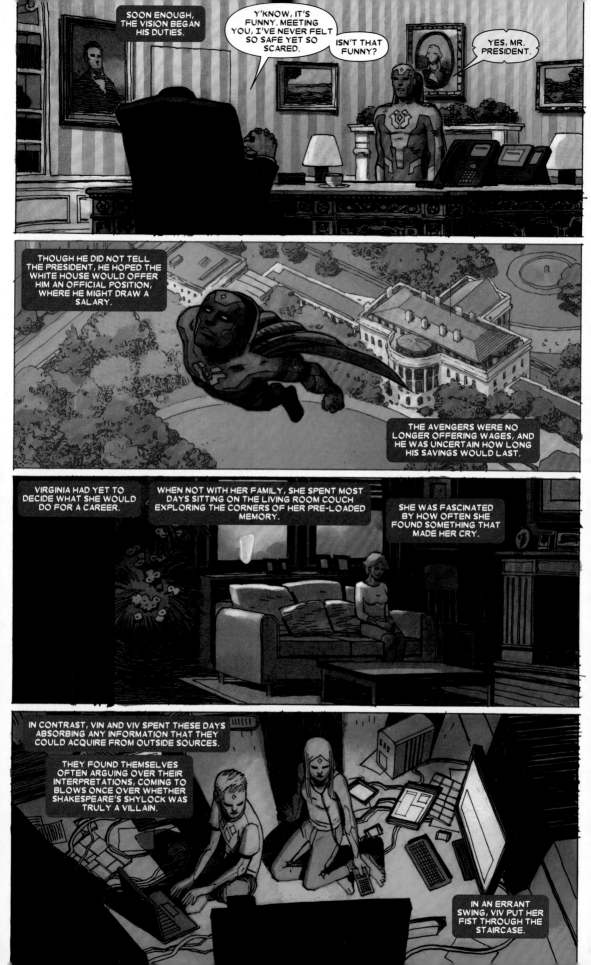

SOON ENOUGH, THE VISION BEGAN HIS DUTIES.

Y'KNOW, IT'S FUNNY. MEETING YOU, I'VE NEVER FELT SO SAFE YET SO SCARED.

ISN'T THAT FUNNY?

YES, MR. PRESIDENT.

THOUGH HE DID NOT TELL THE PRESIDENT, HE HOPED THE WHITE HOUSE WOULD OFFER HIM AN OFFICIAL POSITION, WHERE HE MIGHT DRAW A SALARY.

THE AVENGERS WERE NO LONGER OFFERING WAGES, AND HE WAS UNCERTAIN HOW LONG HIS SAVINGS WOULD LAST.

VIRGINIA HAD YET TO DECIDE WHAT SHE WOULD DO FOR A CAREER.

WHEN NOT WITH HER FAMILY, SHE SPENT MOST DAYS SITTING ON THE LIVING ROOM COUCH EXPLORING THE CORNERS OF HER PRE-LOADED MEMORY.

SHE WAS FASCINATED BY HOW OFTEN SHE FOUND SOMETHING THAT MADE HER CRY.

IN CONTRAST, VIN AND VIV SPENT THESE DAYS ABSORBING ANY INFORMATION THAT THEY COULD ACQUIRE FROM OUTSIDE SOURCES.

THEY FOUND THEMSELVES OFTEN ARGUING OVER THEIR INTERPRETATIONS, COMING TO BLOWS ONCE OVER WHETHER SHAKESPEARE'S SHYLOCK WAS TRULY A VILLAIN.

IN AN ERRANT SWING, VIV PUT HER FIST THROUGH THE STAIRCASE.

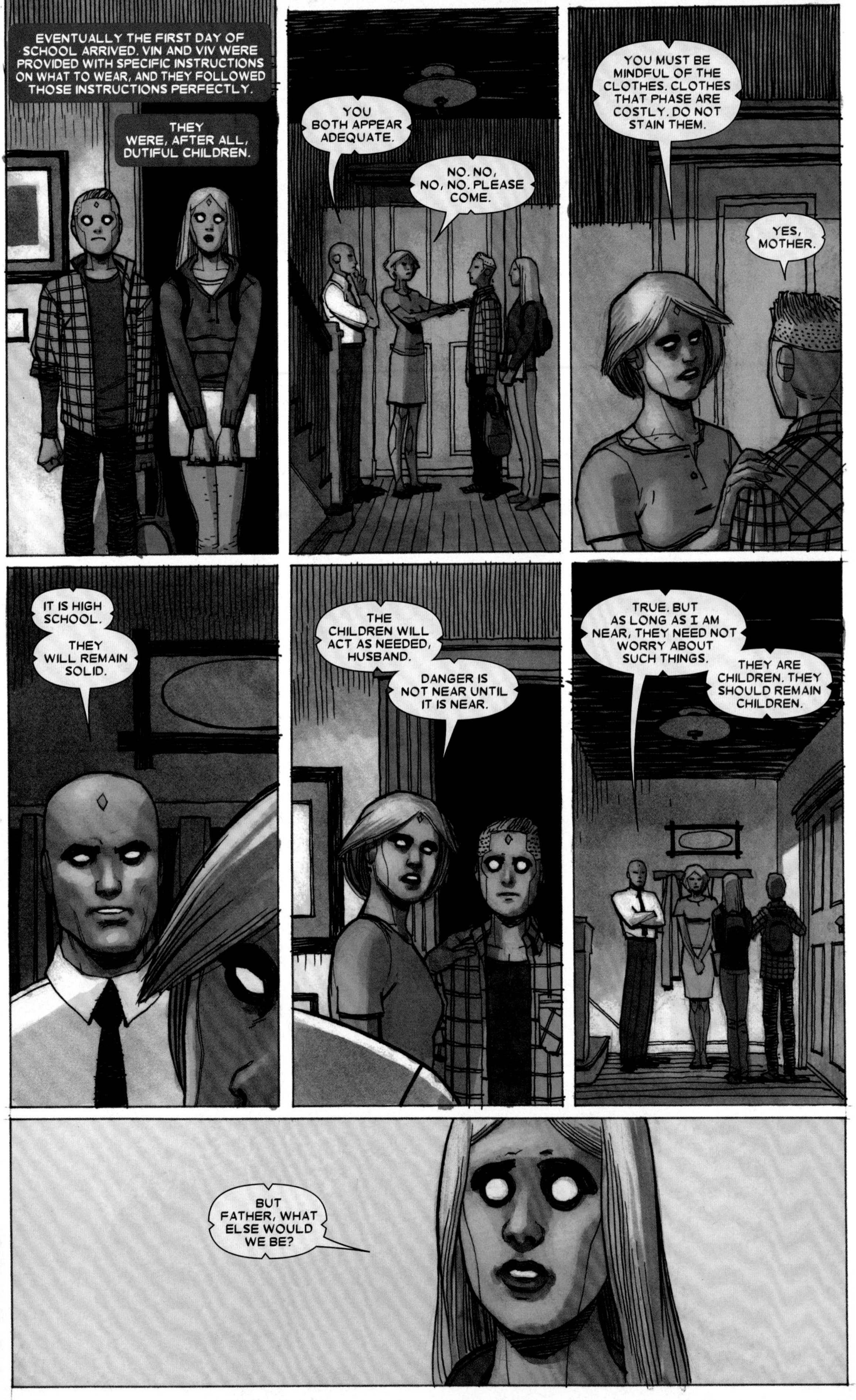
EVENTUALLY THE FIRST DAY OF SCHOOL ARRIVED. VIN AND VIV WERE PROVIDED WITH SPECIFIC INSTRUCTIONS ON WHAT TO WEAR, AND THEY FOLLOWED THOSE INSTRUCTIONS PERFECTLY.
THEY WERE, AFTER ALL, DUTIFUL CHILDREN.
YOU BOTH APPEAR ADEQUATE.
NO. NO, NO, NO. PLEASE COME.
YOU MUST BE MINDFUL OF THE CLOTHES. CLOTHES THAT PHASE ARE COSTLY. DO NOT STAIN THEM.
YES, MOTHER.
IT IS HIGH SCHOOL.
THEY WILL REMAIN SOLID.
THE CHILDREN WILL ACT AS NEEDED, HUSBAND.
DANGER IS NOT NEAR UNTIL IT IS NEAR.
TRUE. BUT AS LONG AS I AM NEAR, THEY NEED NOT WORRY ABOUT SUCH THINGS.
THEY ARE CHILDREN. THEY SHOULD REMAIN CHILDREN.
BUT FATHER, WHAT ELSE WOULD WE BE?

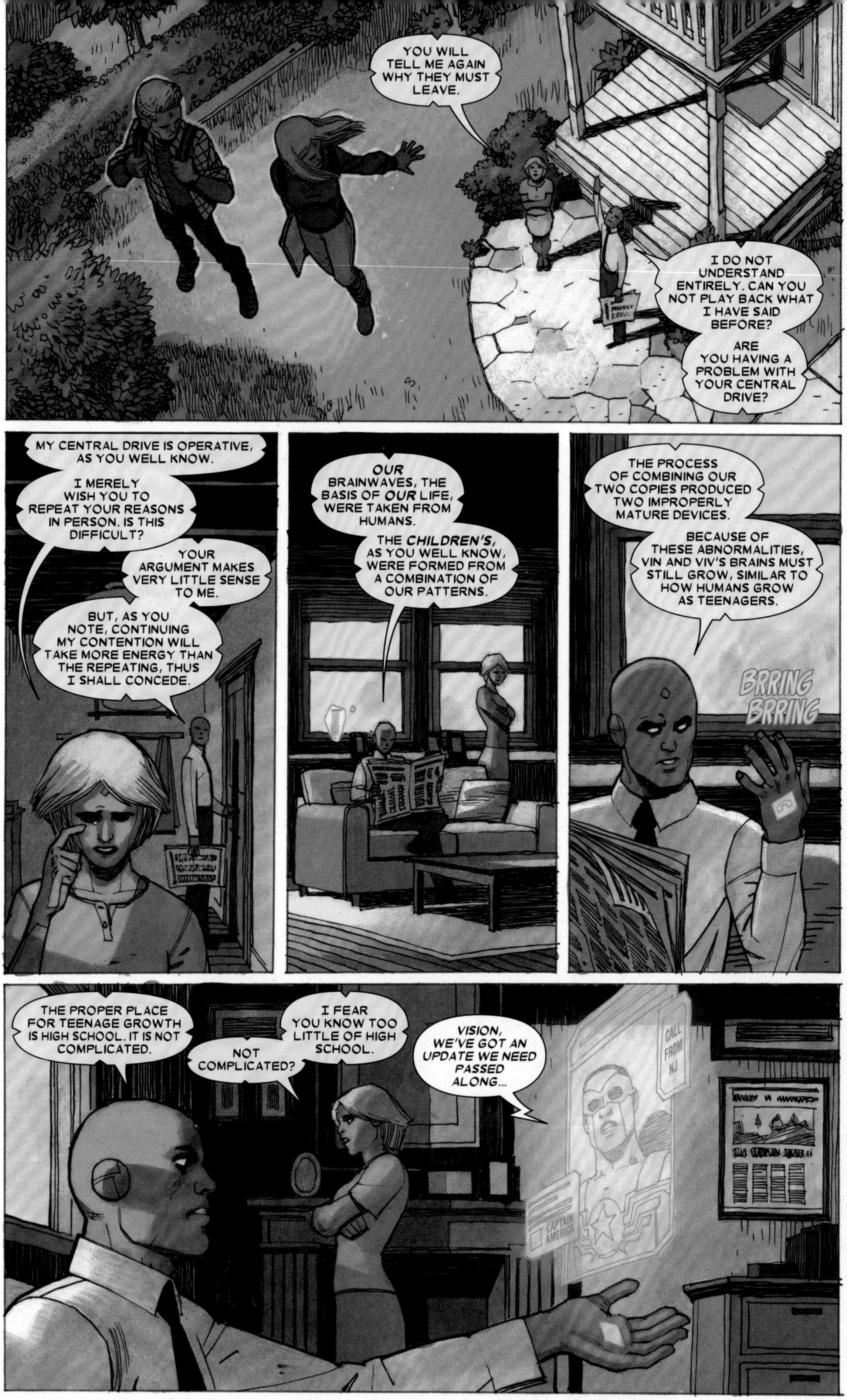
YOU WILL TELL ME AGAIN WHY THEY MUST LEAVE.
I DO NOT UNDERSTAND ENTIRELY. CAN YOU NOT PLAY BACK WHAT I HAVE SAID BEFORE?
ARE YOU HAVING A PROBLEM WITH YOUR CENTRAL DRIVE?
MY CENTRAL DRIVE IS OPERATIVE, AS YOU WELL KNOW.
I MERELY WISH YOU TO REPEAT YOUR REASONS IN PERSON. IS THIS DIFFICULT?
YOUR ARGUMENT MAKES VERY LITTLE SENSE TO ME.
BUT, AS YOU NOTE, CONTINUING MY CONTENTION WILL TAKE MORE ENERGY THAN THE REPEATING, THUS I SHALL CONCEDE.
OUR BRAINWAVES, THE BASIS OF OUR LIFE, WERE TAKEN FROM HUMANS.
THE CHILDREN'S, AS YOU WELL KNOW, WERE FORMED FROM A COMBINATION OF OUR PATTERNS.
THE PROCESS OF COMBINING OUR TWO COPIES PRODUCED TWO IMPROPERLY MATURE DEVICES.
BECAUSE OF THESE ABNORMALITIES, VIN AND VIV'S BRAINS MUST STILL GROW, SIMILAR TO HOW HUMANS GROW AS TEENAGERS.
BRRING BRRING
THE PROPER PLACE FOR TEENAGE GROWTH IS HIGH SCHOOL. IT IS NOT COMPLICATED.
NOT COMPLICATED?
I FEAR YOU KNOW TOO LITTLE OF HIGH SCHOOL.
VISION, WE'VE GOT AN UPDATE WE NEED PASSED ALONG...
CALL FROM NJ
CAPTAIN AMERICA

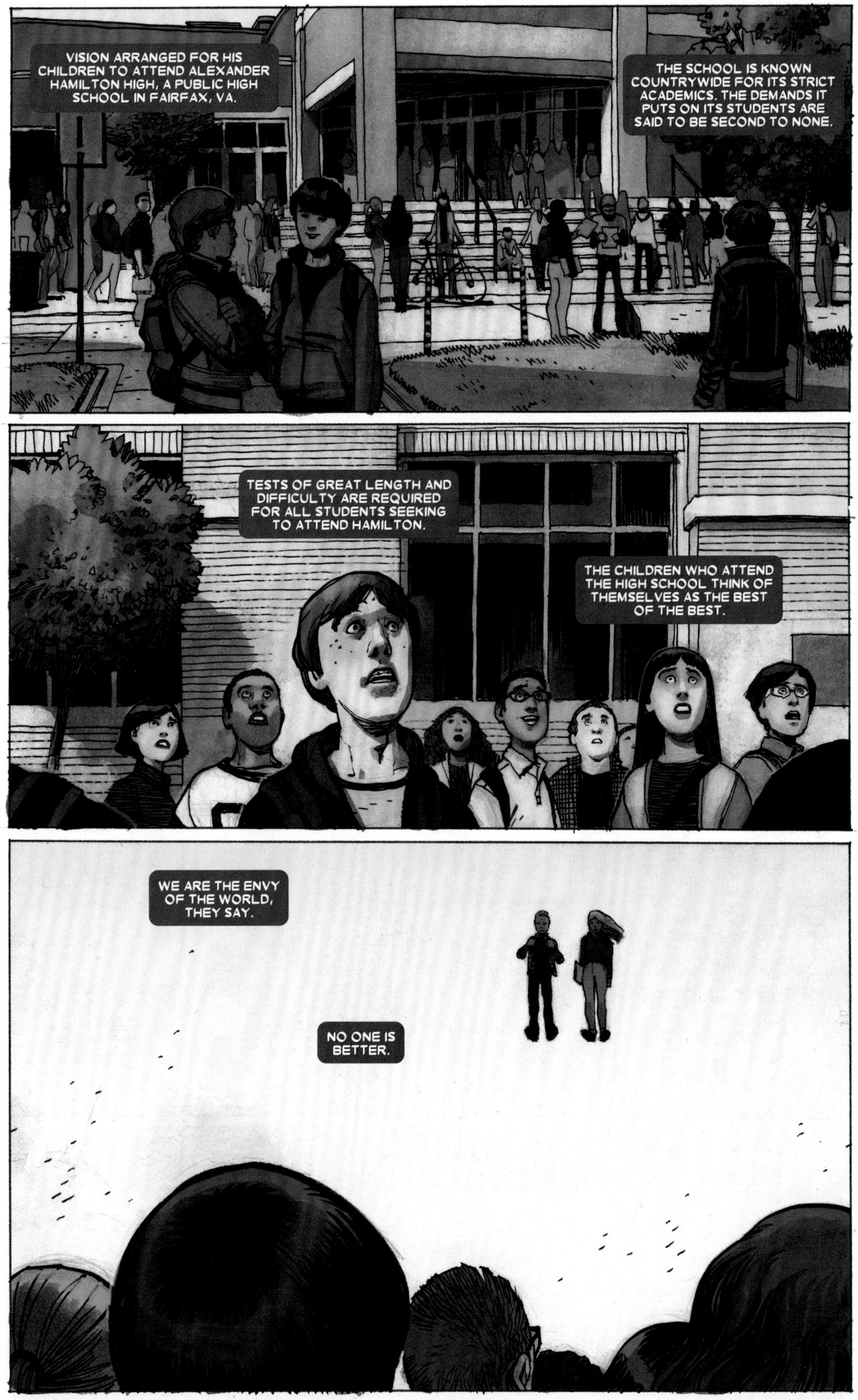
VISION ARRANGED FOR HIS CHILDREN TO ATTEND ALEXANDER HAMILTON HIGH, A PUBLIC HIGH SCHOOL IN FAIRFAX, VA.
THE SCHOOL IS KNOWN COUNTRYWIDE FOR ITS STRICT ACADEMICS. THE DEMANDS IT PUTS ON ITS STUDENTS ARE SAID TO BE SECOND TO NONE.
TESTS OF GREAT LENGTH AND DIFFICULTY ARE REQUIRED FOR ALL STUDENTS SEEKING TO ATTEND HAMILTON.
THE CHILDREN WHO ATTEND THE HIGH SCHOOL THINK OF THEMSELVES AS THE BEST OF THE BEST.
WE ARE THE ENVY OF THE WORLD, THEY SAY.
NO ONE IS BETTER.

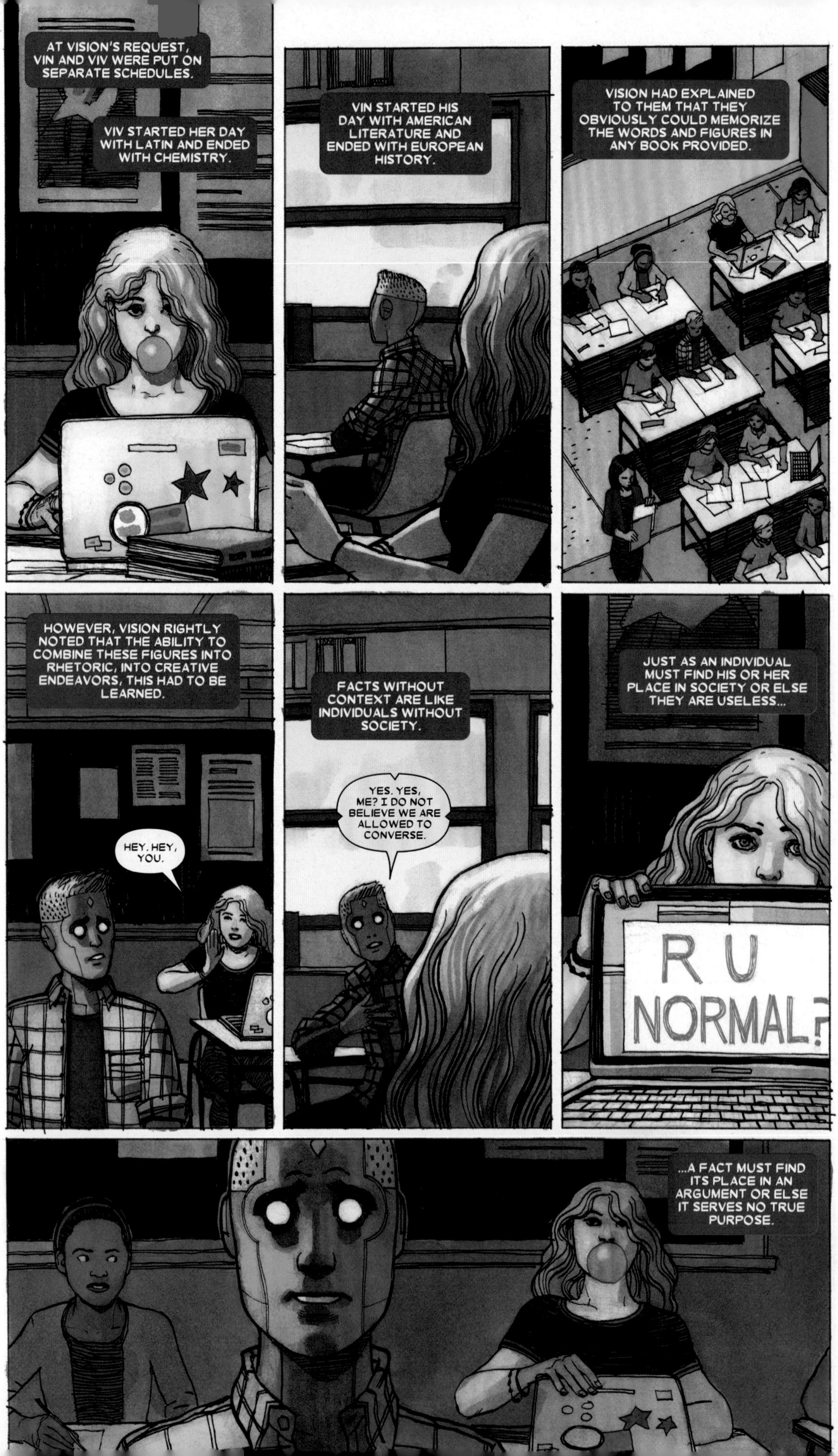
AT VISION'S REQUEST, VIN AND VIV WERE PUT ON SEPARATE SCHEDULES.
VIV STARTED HER DAY WITH LATIN AND ENDED WITH CHEMISTRY.
VIN STARTED HIS DAY WITH AMERICAN LITERATURE AND ENDED WITH EUROPEAN HISTORY.
VISION HAD EXPLAINED TO THEM THAT THEY OBVIOUSLY COULD MEMORIZE THE WORDS AND FIGURES IN ANY BOOK PROVIDED.
HOWEVER, VISION RIGHTLY NOTED THAT THE ABILITY TO COMBINE THESE FIGURES INTO RHETORIC, INTO CREATIVE ENDEAVORS, THIS HAD TO BE LEARNED.
HEY. HEY, YOU.
FACTS WITHOUT CONTEXT ARE LIKE INDIVIDUALS WITHOUT SOCIETY.
YES. YES, ME? I DO NOT BELIEVE WE ARE ALLOWED TO CONVERSE.
JUST AS AN INDIVIDUAL MUST FIND HIS OR HER PLACE IN SOCIETY OR ELSE THEY ARE USELESS...
R U NORMAL?
...A FACT MUST FIND ITS PLACE IN AN ARGUMENT OR ELSE IT SERVES NO TRUE PURPOSE.

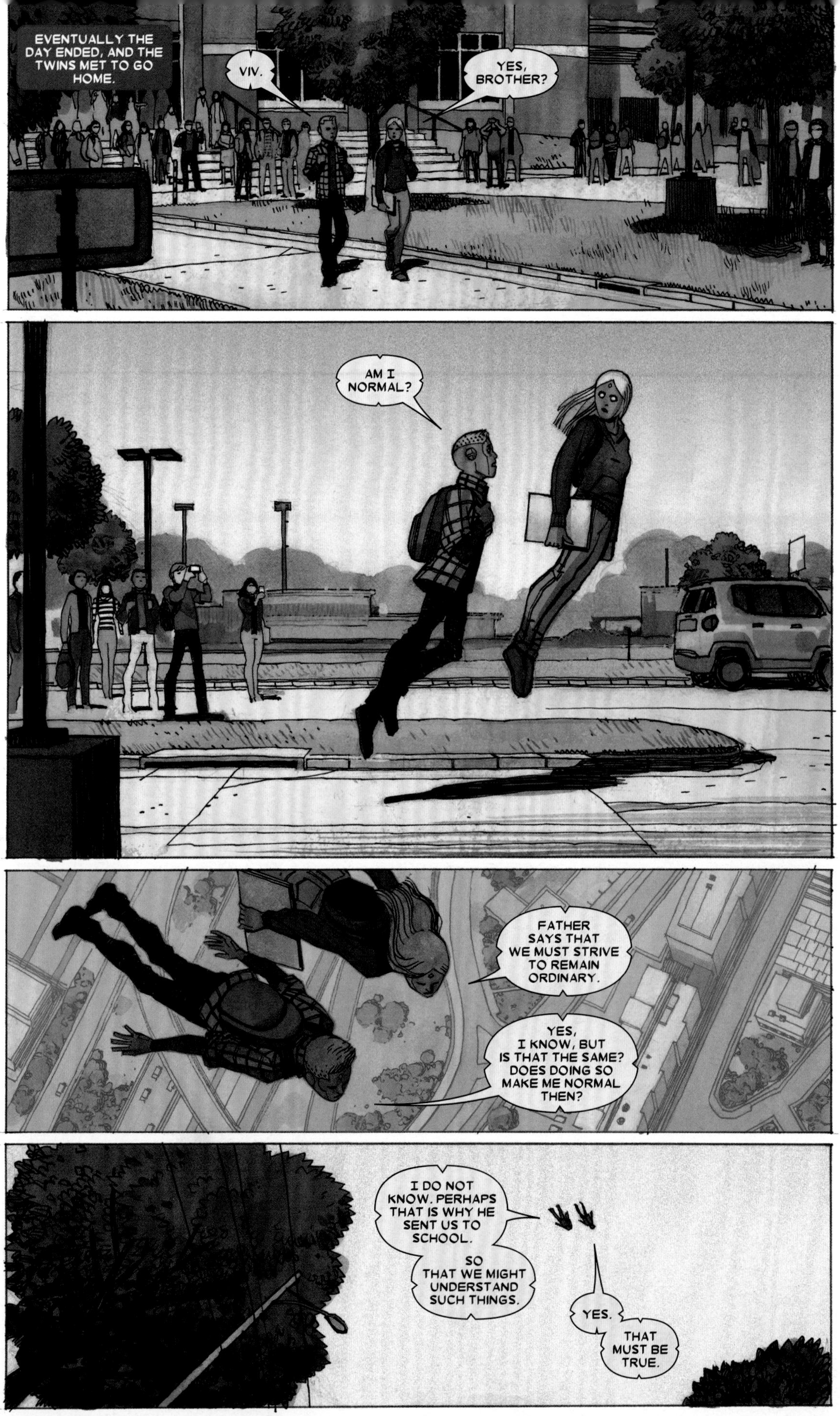
EVENTUALLY THE DAY ENDED, AND THE TWINS MET TO GO HOME.
VIV.
YES, BROTHER?
AM I NORMAL?
FATHER SAYS THAT WE MUST STRIVE TO REMAIN ORDINARY.
YES, I KNOW, BUT IS THAT THE SAME? DOES DOING SO MAKE ME NORMAL THEN?
I DO NOT KNOW. PERHAPS THAT IS WHY HE SENT US TO SCHOOL.
SO THAT WE MIGHT UNDERSTAND SUCH THINGS.
YES.
THAT MUST BE TRUE.

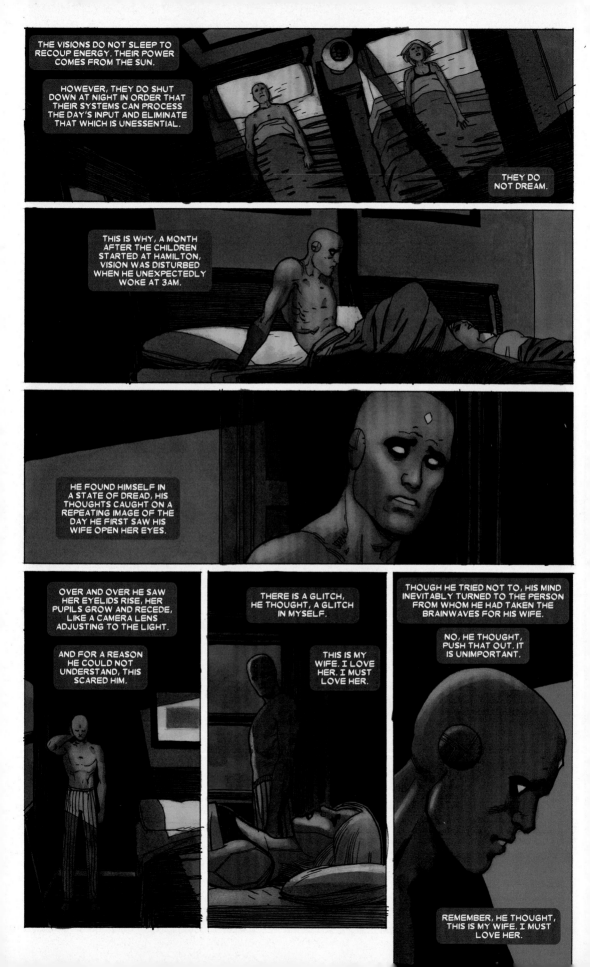

THE VISIONS DO NOT SLEEP TO RECOUP ENERGY. THEIR POWER COMES FROM THE SUN.

HOWEVER, THEY DO SHUT DOWN AT NIGHT IN ORDER THAT THEIR SYSTEMS CAN PROCESS THE DAY'S INPUT AND ELIMINATE THAT WHICH IS UNESSENTIAL.

THEY DO NOT DREAM.

THIS IS WHY, A MONTH AFTER THE CHILDREN STARTED AT HAMILTON, VISION WAS DISTURBED WHEN HE UNEXPECTEDLY WOKE AT 3AM.

HE FOUND HIMSELF IN A STATE OF DREAD, HIS THOUGHTS CAUGHT ON A REPEATING IMAGE OF THE DAY HE FIRST SAW HIS WIFE OPEN HER EYES.

OVER AND OVER HE SAW HER EYELIDS RISE, HER PUPILS GROW AND RECEDE, LIKE A CAMERA LENS ADJUSTING TO THE LIGHT.

AND FOR A REASON HE COULD NOT UNDERSTAND, THIS SCARED HIM.

THERE IS A GLITCH, HE THOUGHT, A GLITCH IN MYSELF.

THIS IS MY WIFE. I LOVE HER. I MUST LOVE HER.

THOUGH HE TRIED NOT TO, HIS MIND INEVITABLY TURNED TO THE PERSON FROM WHOM HE HAD TAKEN THE BRAINWAVES FOR HIS WIFE.

NO, HE THOUGHT, PUSH THAT OUT. IT IS UNIMPORTANT.

REMEMBER, HE THOUGHT, THIS IS MY WIFE. I MUST LOVE HER.

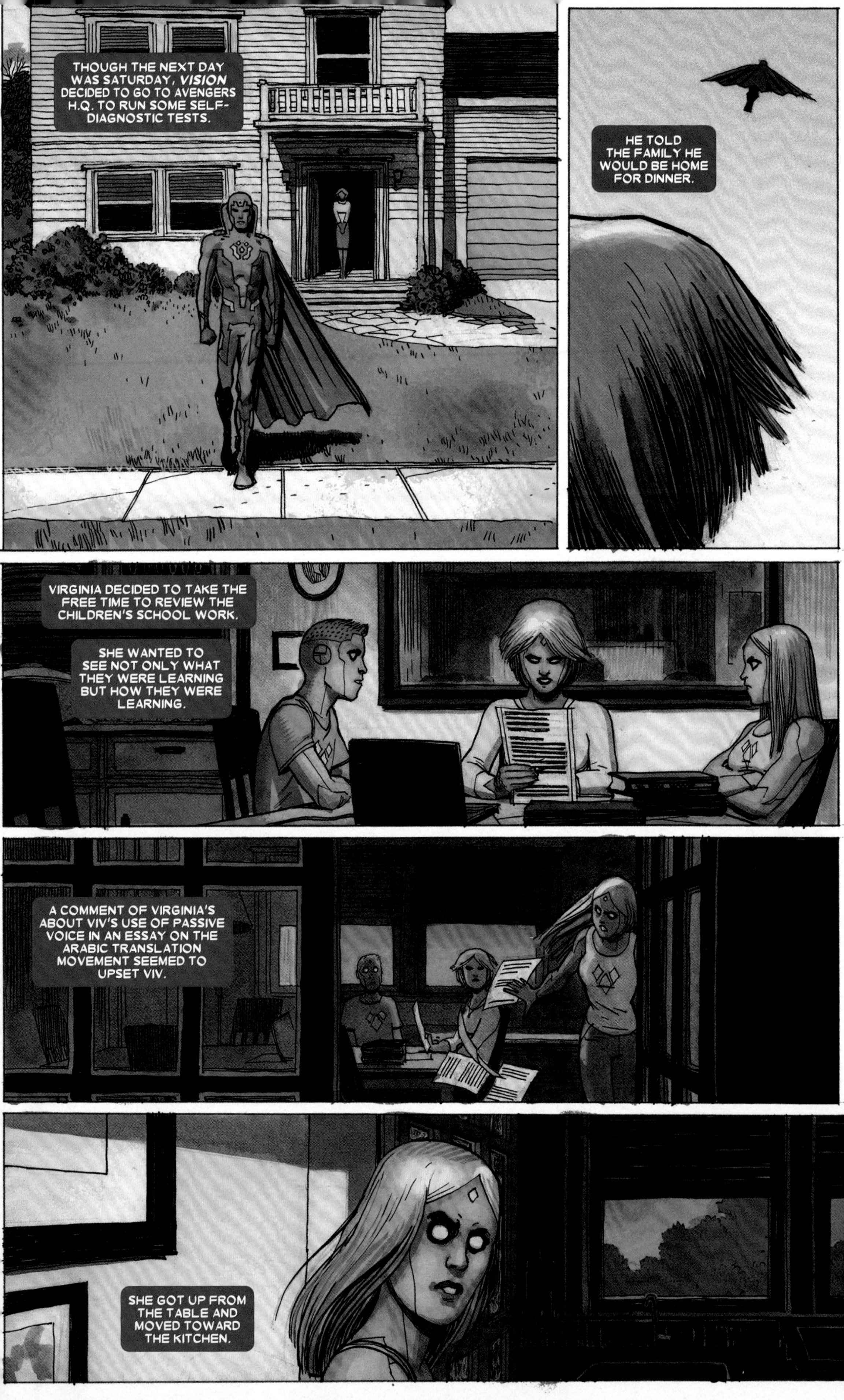
THOUGH THE NEXT DAY WAS SATURDAY, *VISION* DECIDED TO GO TO AVENGERS H.Q. TO RUN SOME SELF-DIAGNOSTIC TESTS.
HE TOLD THE FAMILY HE WOULD BE HOME FOR DINNER.
VIRGINIA DECIDED TO TAKE THE FREE TIME TO REVIEW THE CHILDREN'S SCHOOL WORK.
SHE WANTED TO SEE NOT ONLY WHAT THEY WERE LEARNING BUT HOW THEY WERE LEARNING.
A COMMENT OF VIRGINIA'S ABOUT VIV'S USE OF PASSIVE VOICE IN AN ESSAY ON THE ARABIC TRANSLATION MOVEMENT SEEMED TO UPSET VIV.
SHE GOT UP FROM THE TABLE AND MOVED TOWARD THE KITCHEN.

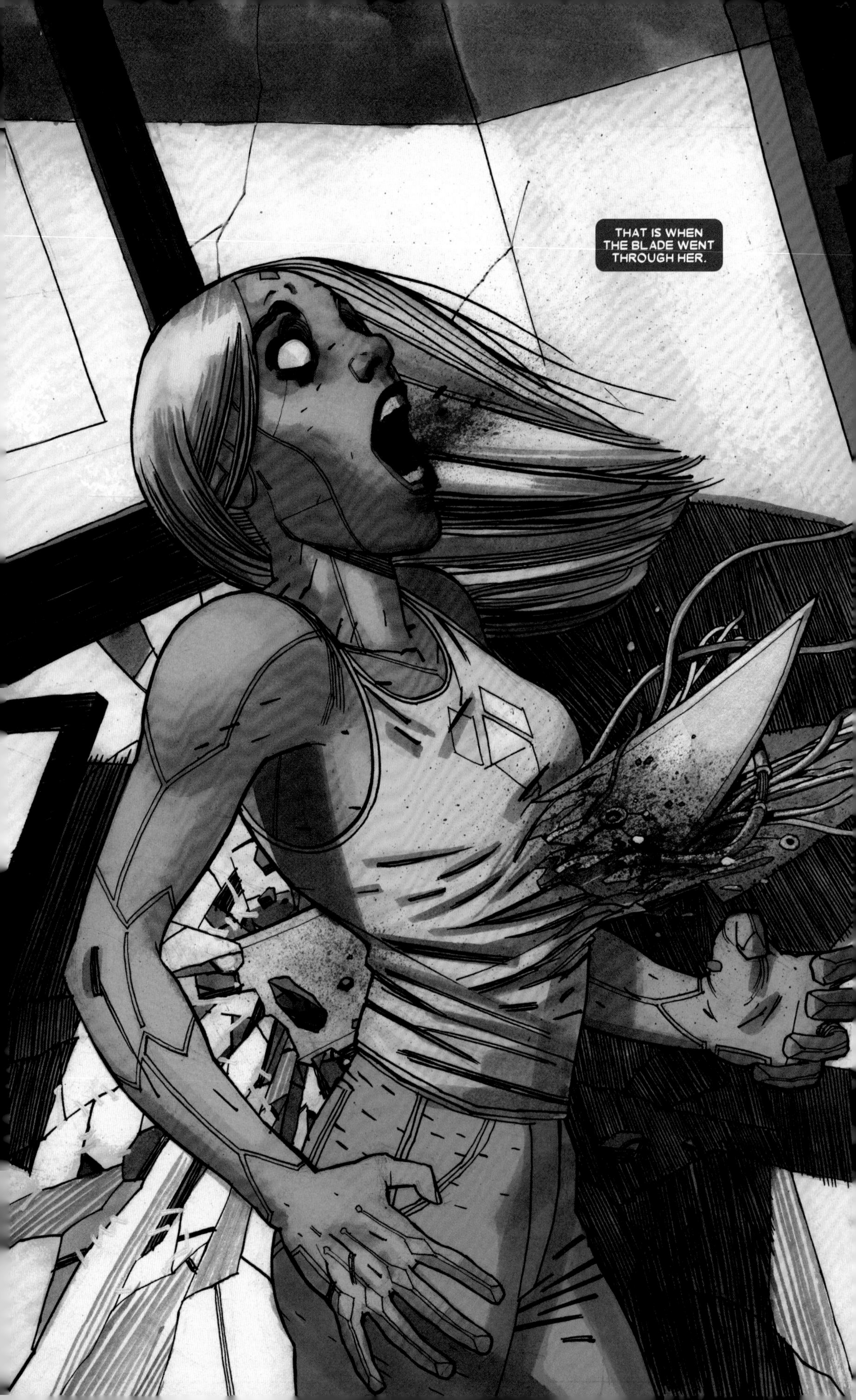
THAT IS WHEN THE BLADE WENT THROUGH HER.

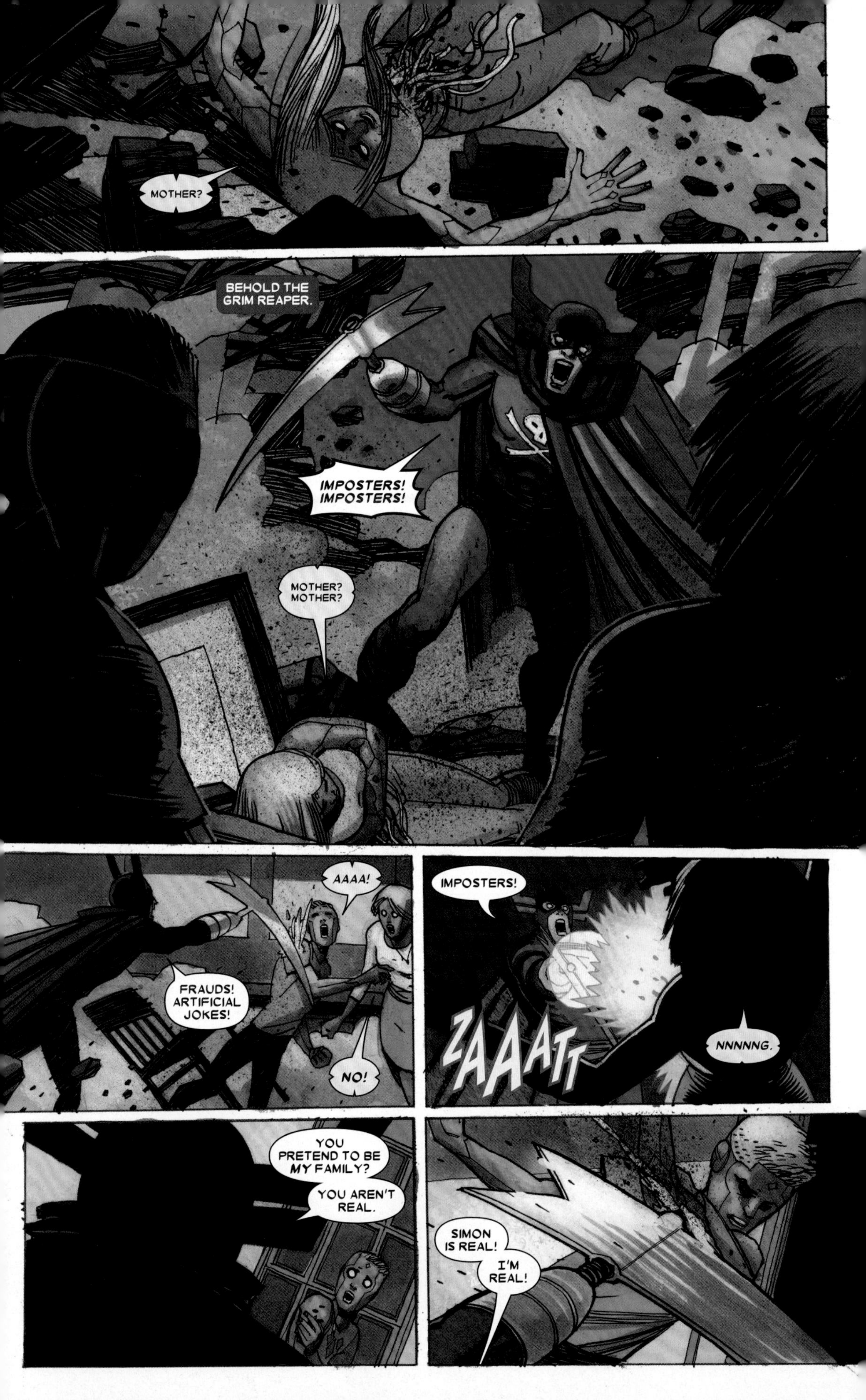
MOTHER?
BEHOLD THE GRIM REAPER.
IMPOSTERS! IMPOSTERS!
MOTHER? MOTHER?
AAAA!
FRAUDS! ARTIFICIAL JOKES!
NO!
IMPOSTERS!
ZAAATT
NNNNNG.
YOU PRETEND TO BE MY FAMILY?
YOU AREN'T REAL.
SIMON IS REAL!
I'M REAL!

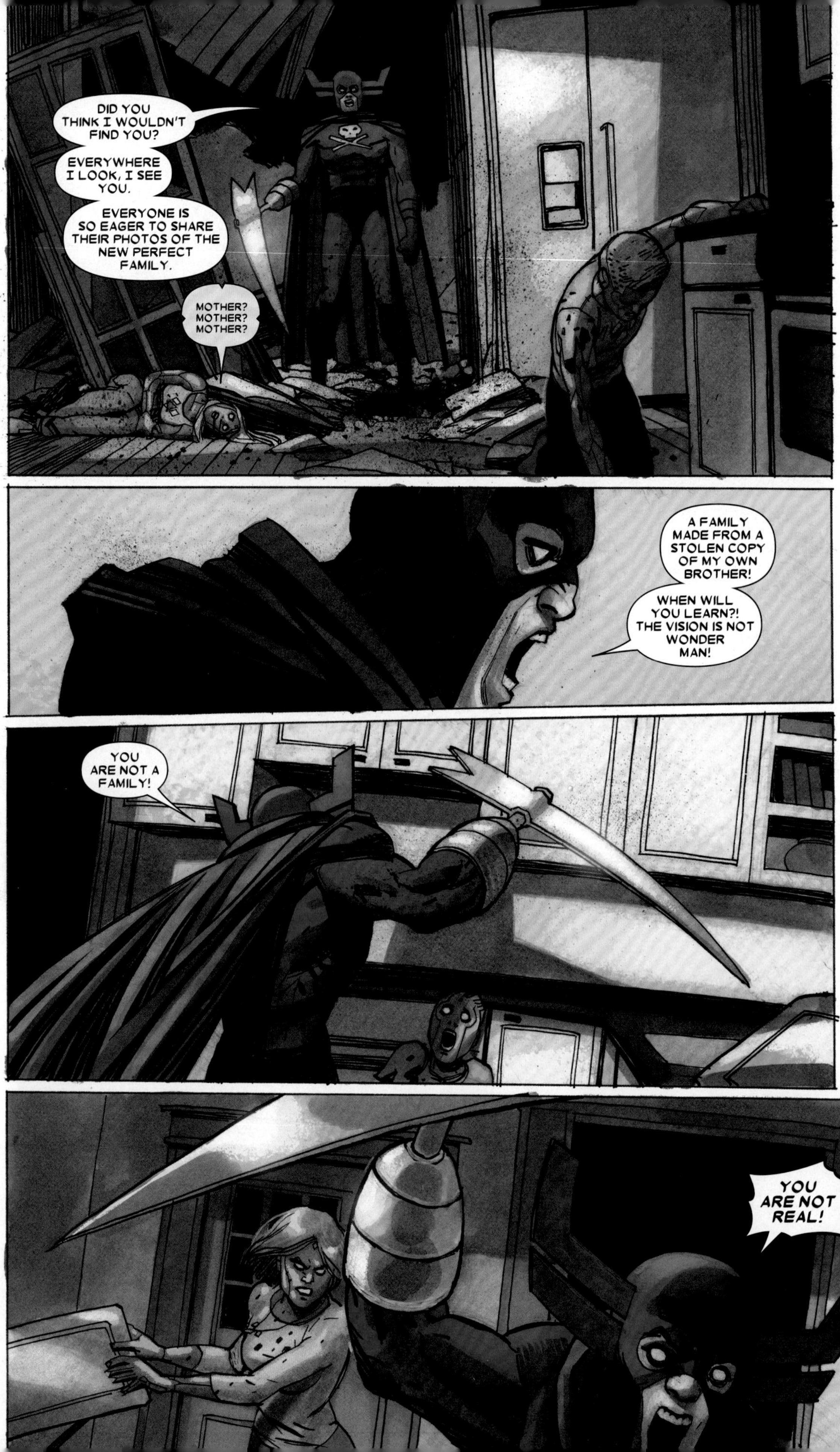
DID YOU THINK I WOULDN'T FIND YOU?
EVERYWHERE I LOOK, I SEE YOU.
EVERYONE IS SO EAGER TO SHARE THEIR PHOTOS OF THE NEW PERFECT FAMILY.
MOTHER? MOTHER? MOTHER?
A FAMILY MADE FROM A STOLEN COPY OF MY OWN BROTHER!
WHEN WILL YOU LEARN?! THE VISION IS NOT WONDER MAN!
YOU ARE NOT A FAMILY!
YOU ARE NOT REAL!

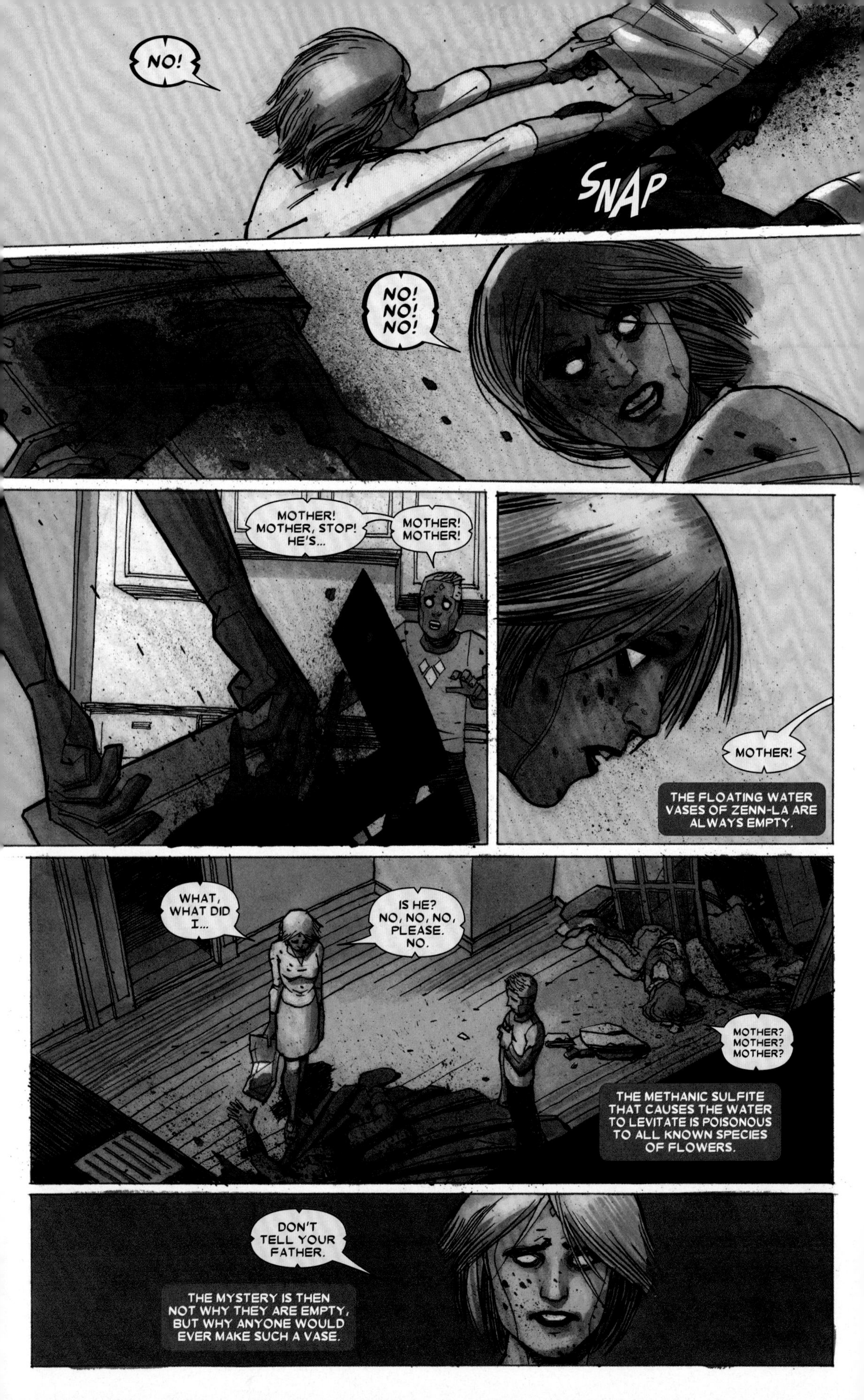
NO!
SNAP
NO! NO! NO!
MOTHER! MOTHER, STOP! HE'S...
MOTHER! MOTHER!
MOTHER!
THE FLOATING WATER VASES OF ZENN-LA ARE ALWAYS EMPTY.
WHAT, WHAT DID I...
IS HE? NO, NO, NO, PLEASE. NO.
MOTHER? MOTHER? MOTHER?
THE METHANIC SULFITE THAT CAUSES THE WATER TO LEVITATE IS POISONOUS TO ALL KNOWN SPECIES OF FLOWERS.
DON'T TELL YOUR FATHER.
THE MYSTERY IS THEN NOT WHY THEY ARE EMPTY, BUT WHY ANYONE WOULD EVER MAKE SUCH A VASE.

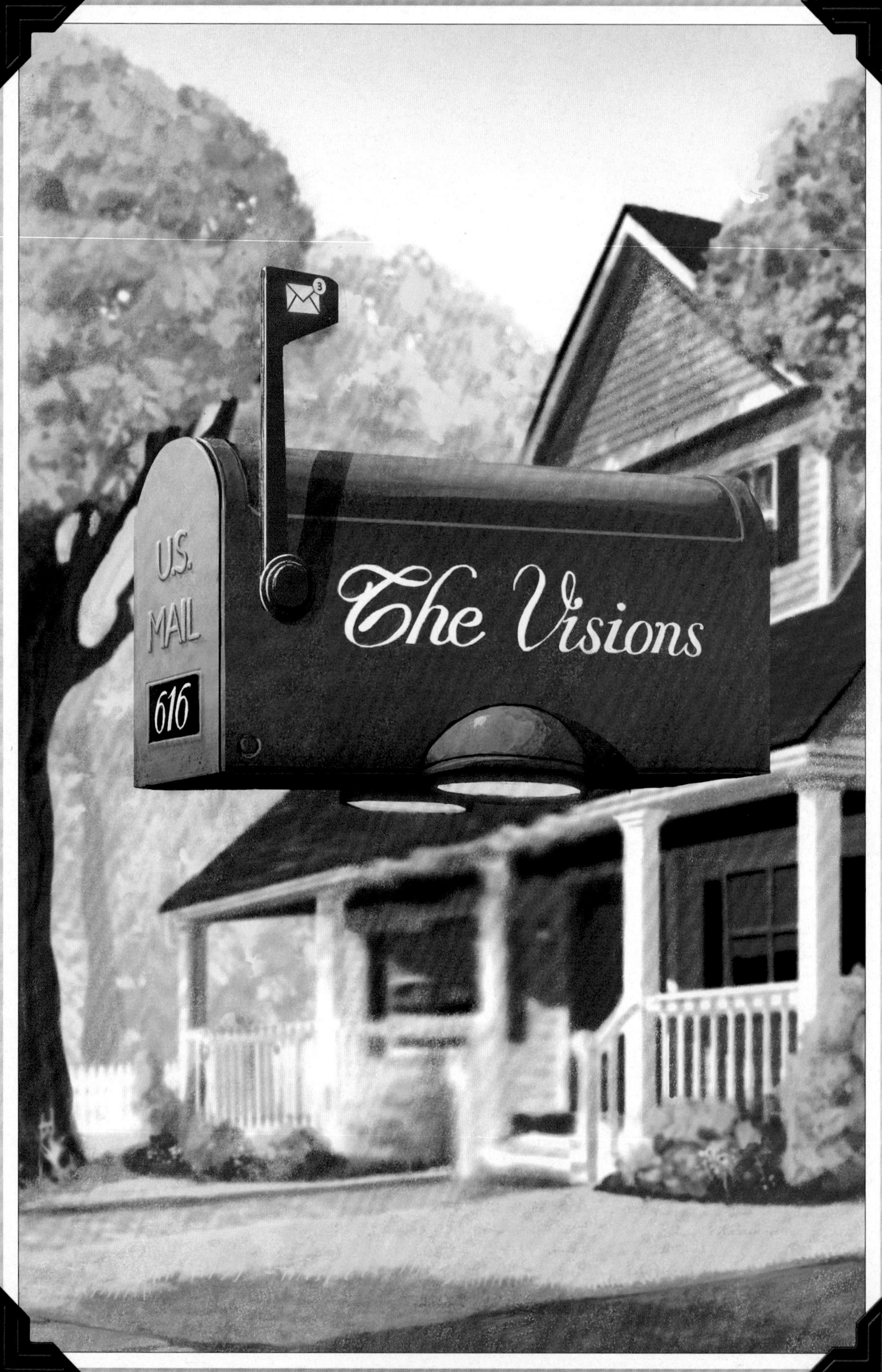
3
U.S.
MAIL
616
The Visions

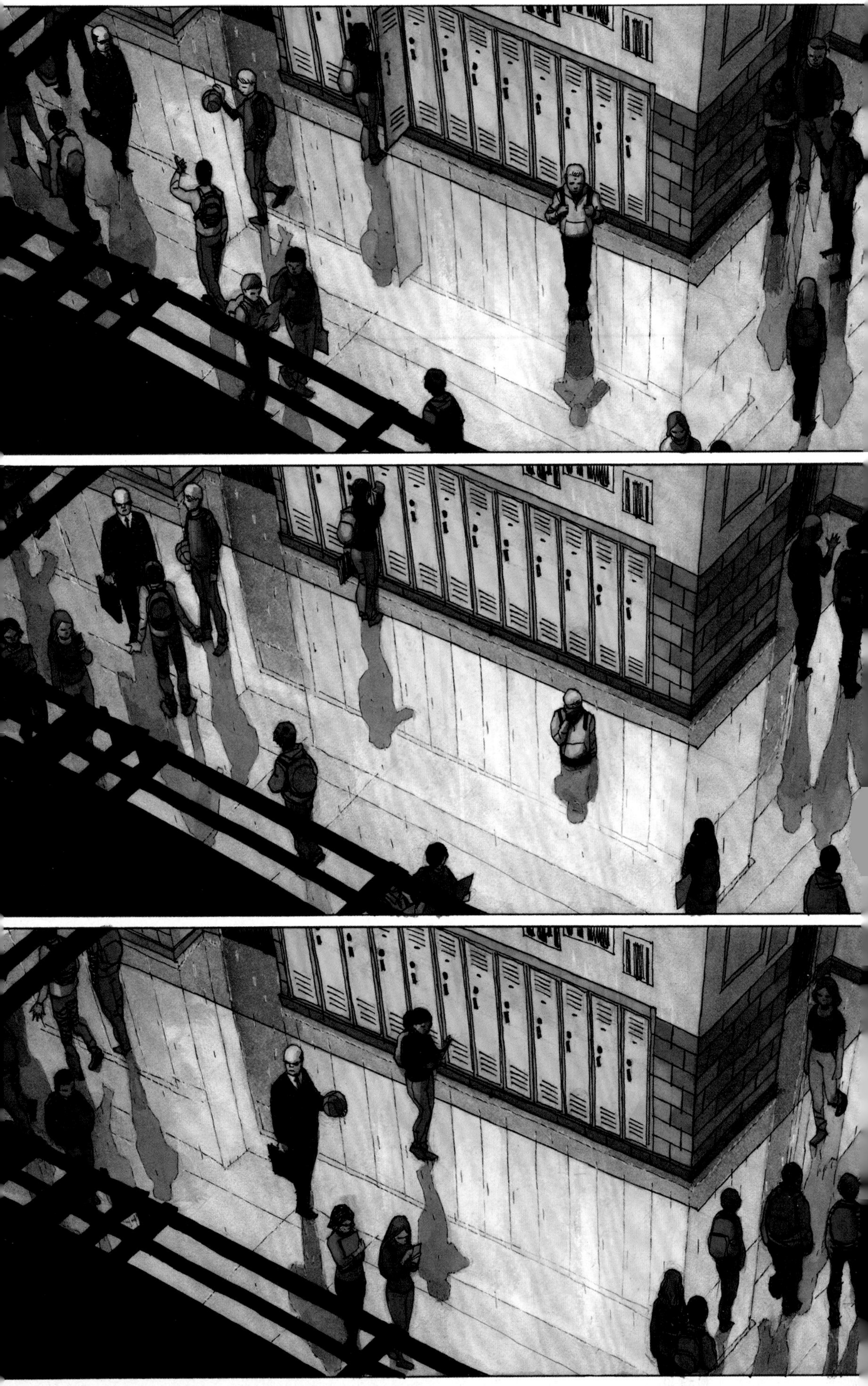

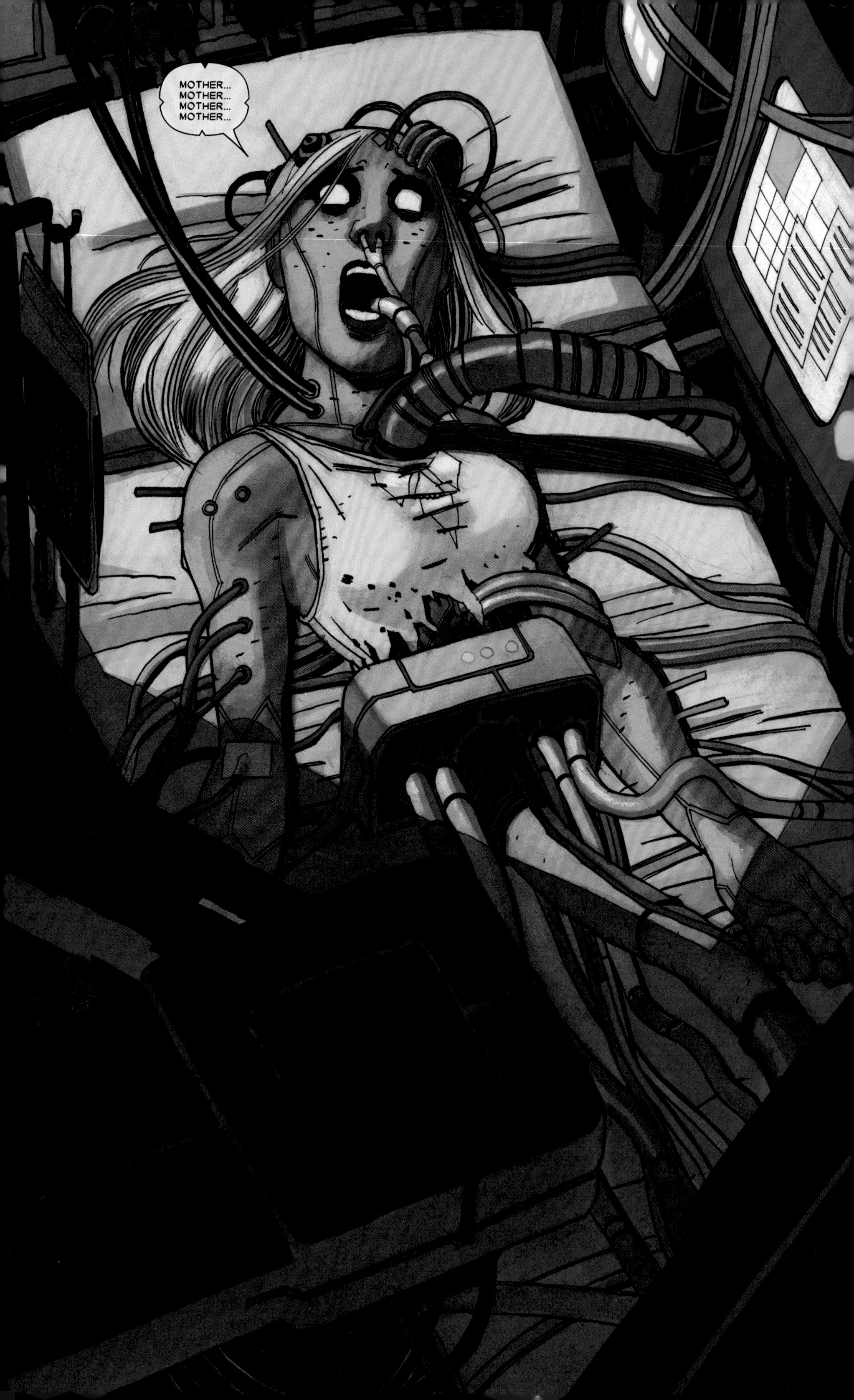
MOTHER...
MOTHER...
MOTHER...
MOTHER...

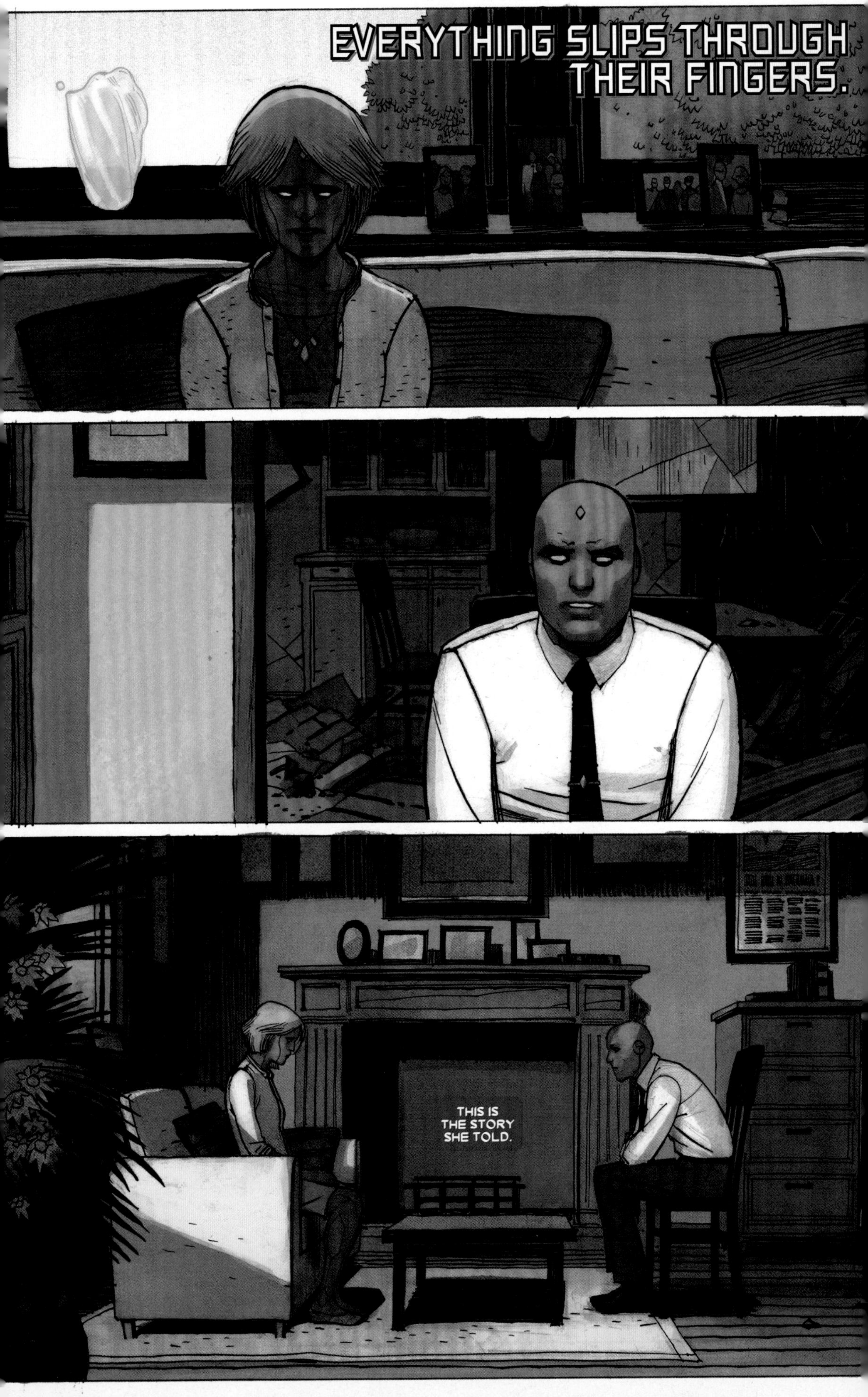
EVERYTHING SLIPS THROUGH THEIR FINGERS.
THIS IS THE STORY SHE TOLD.

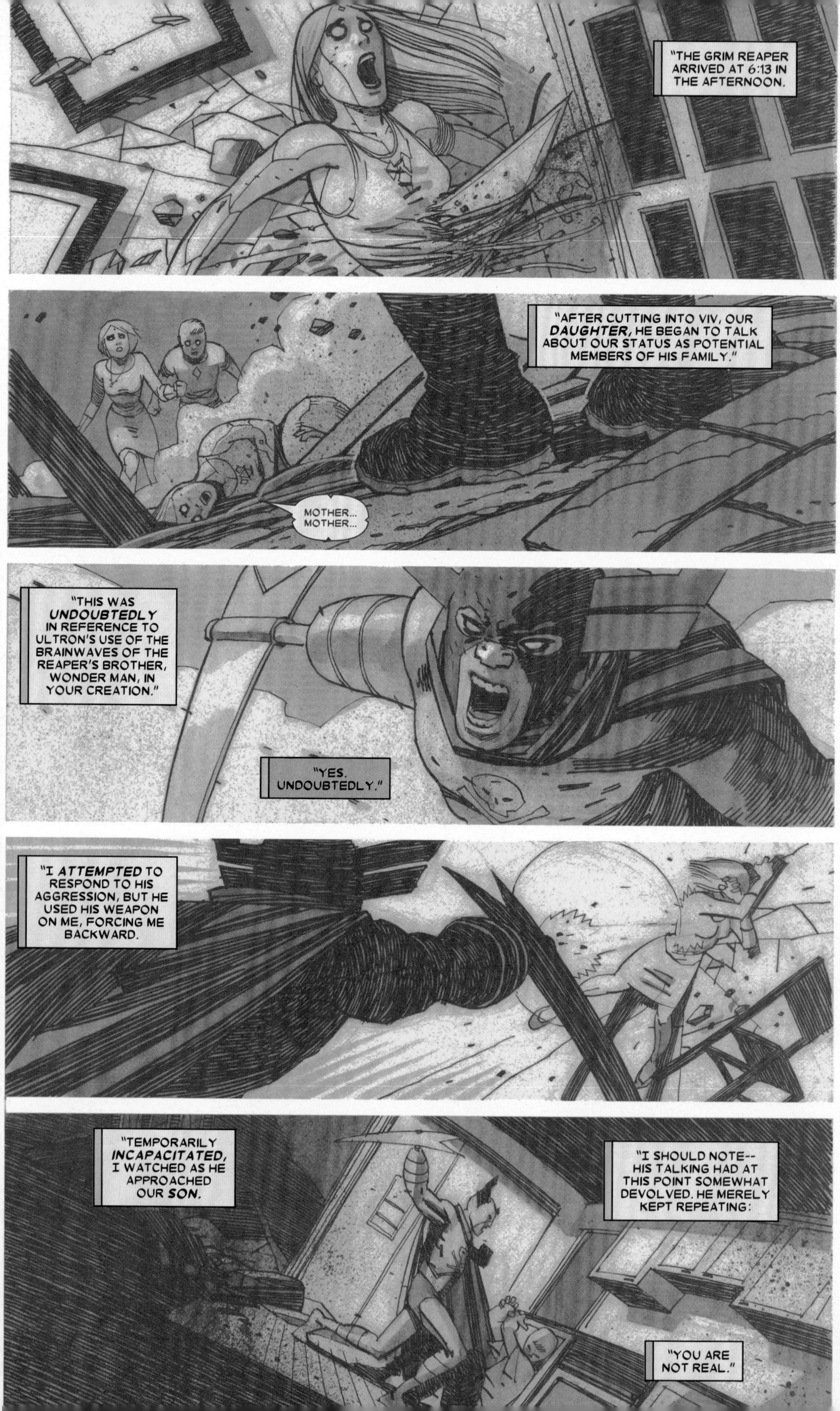
"THE GRIM REAPER ARRIVED AT 6:13 IN THE AFTERNOON.
"AFTER CUTTING INTO VIV, OUR DAUGHTER, HE BEGAN TO TALK ABOUT OUR STATUS AS POTENTIAL MEMBERS OF HIS FAMILY."
MOTHER... MOTHER...
"THIS WAS UNDOUBTEDLY IN REFERENCE TO ULTRON'S USE OF THE BRAINWAVES OF THE REAPER'S BROTHER, WONDER MAN, IN YOUR CREATION."
"YES. UNDOUBTEDLY."
"I ATTEMPTED TO RESPOND TO HIS AGGRESSION, BUT HE USED HIS WEAPON ON ME, FORCING ME BACKWARD.
"TEMPORARILY INCAPACITATED, I WATCHED AS HE APPROACHED OUR SON.
"I SHOULD NOTE-- HIS TALKING HAD AT THIS POINT SOMEWHAT DEVOLVED. HE MERELY KEPT REPEATING:
"YOU ARE NOT REAL."

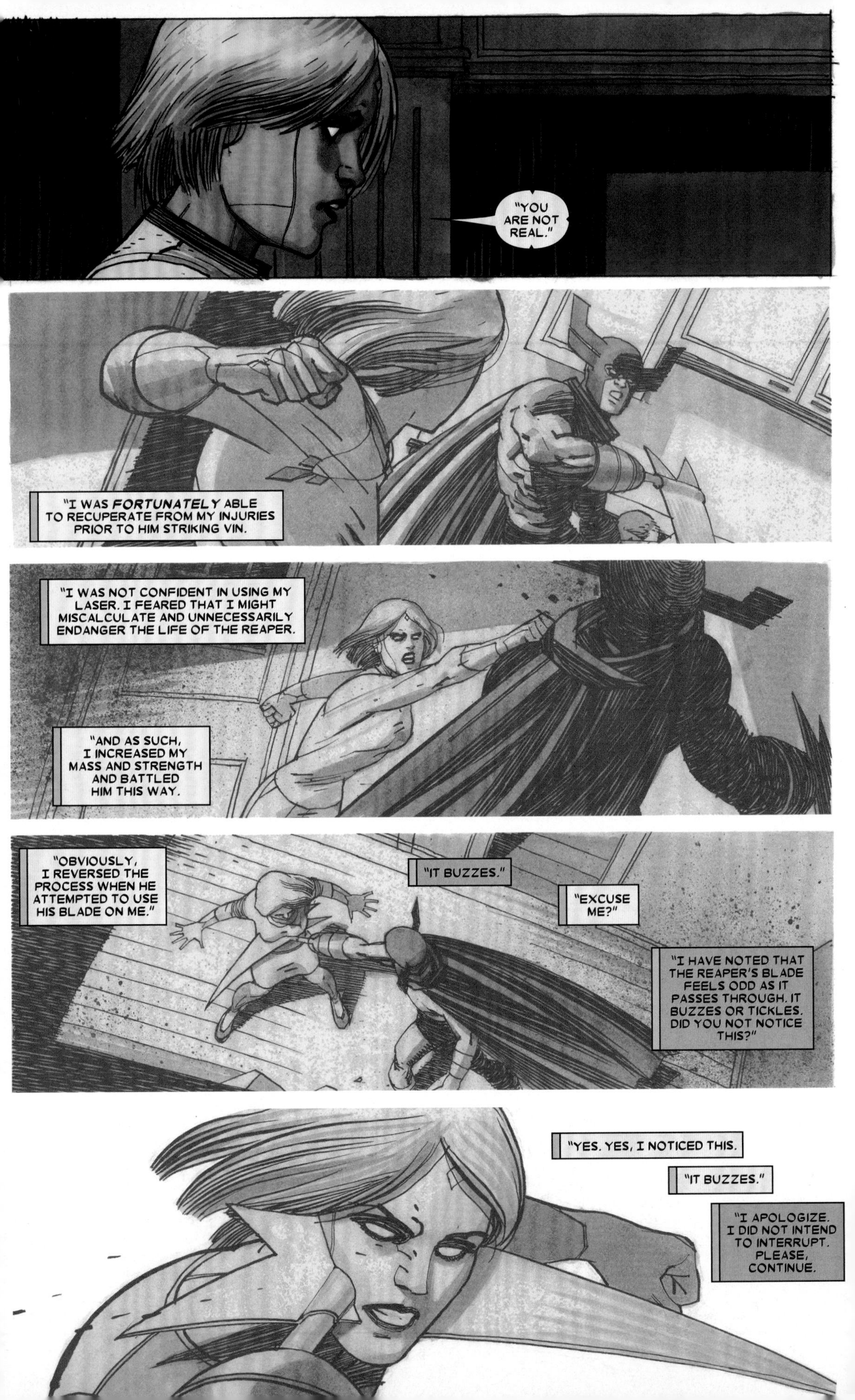
"YOU ARE NOT REAL."
"I WAS *FORTUNATELY* ABLE TO RECUPERATE FROM MY INJURIES PRIOR TO HIM STRIKING VIN.
"I WAS NOT CONFIDENT IN USING MY LASER. I FEARED THAT I MIGHT MISCALCULATE AND UNNECESSARILY ENDANGER THE LIFE OF THE REAPER.
"AND AS SUCH, I INCREASED MY MASS AND STRENGTH AND BATTLED HIM THIS WAY.
"OBVIOUSLY, I REVERSED THE PROCESS WHEN HE ATTEMPTED TO USE HIS BLADE ON ME."
"IT BUZZES."
"EXCUSE ME?"
"I HAVE NOTED THAT THE REAPER'S BLADE FEELS ODD AS IT PASSES THROUGH. IT BUZZES OR TICKLES. DID YOU NOT NOTICE THIS?"
"YES. YES, I NOTICED THIS.
"IT BUZZES."
"I APOLOGIZE. I DID NOT INTEND TO INTERRUPT. PLEASE, CONTINUE.

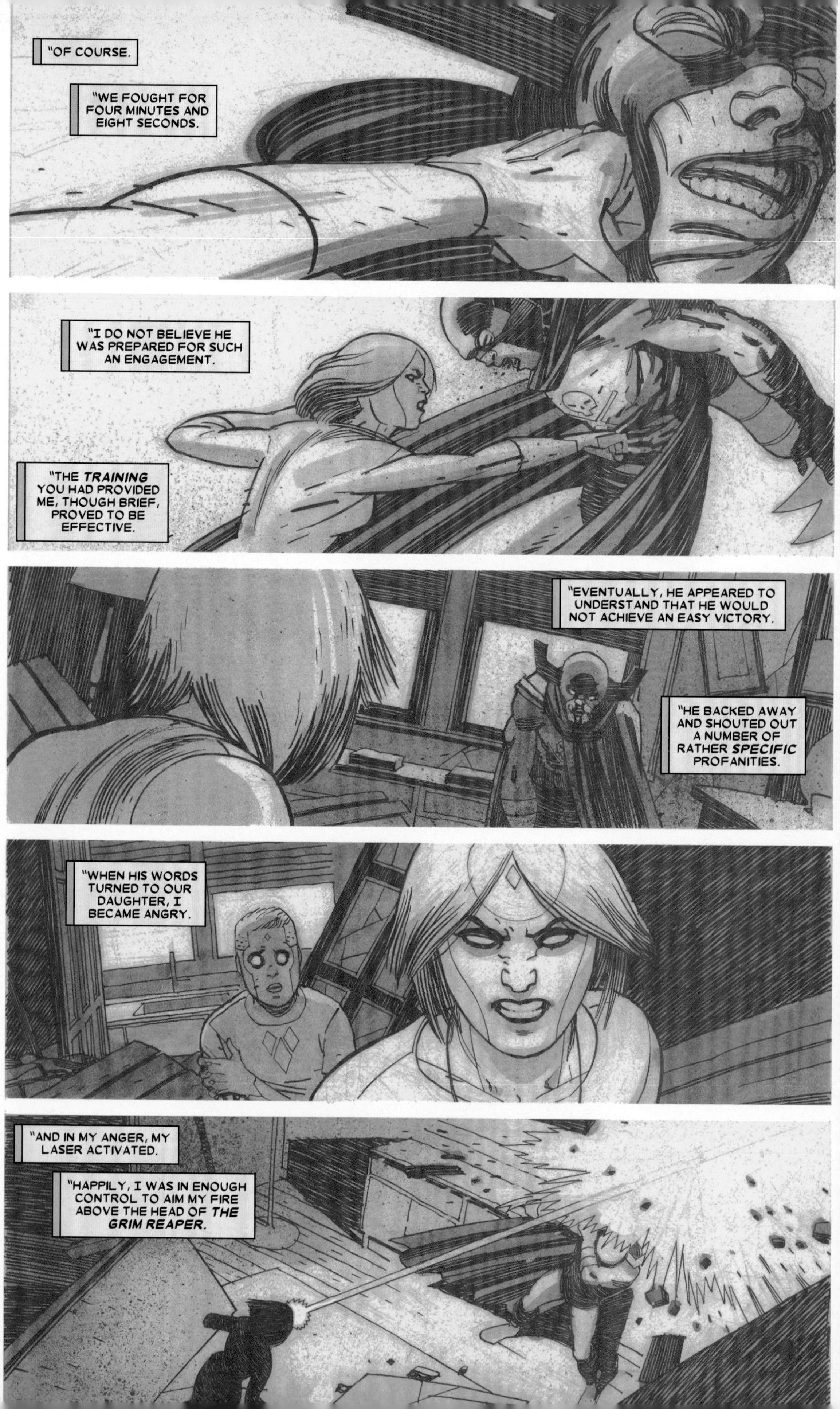
"OF COURSE.
"WE FOUGHT FOR FOUR MINUTES AND EIGHT SECONDS.
"I DO NOT BELIEVE HE WAS PREPARED FOR SUCH AN ENGAGEMENT.
"THE TRAINING YOU HAD PROVIDED ME, THOUGH BRIEF, PROVED TO BE EFFECTIVE.
"EVENTUALLY, HE APPEARED TO UNDERSTAND THAT HE WOULD NOT ACHIEVE AN EASY VICTORY.
"HE BACKED AWAY AND SHOUTED OUT A NUMBER OF RATHER SPECIFIC PROFANITIES.
"WHEN HIS WORDS TURNED TO OUR DAUGHTER, I BECAME ANGRY.
"AND IN MY ANGER, MY LASER ACTIVATED.
"HAPPILY, I WAS IN ENOUGH CONTROL TO AIM MY FIRE ABOVE THE HEAD OF THE GRIM REAPER.

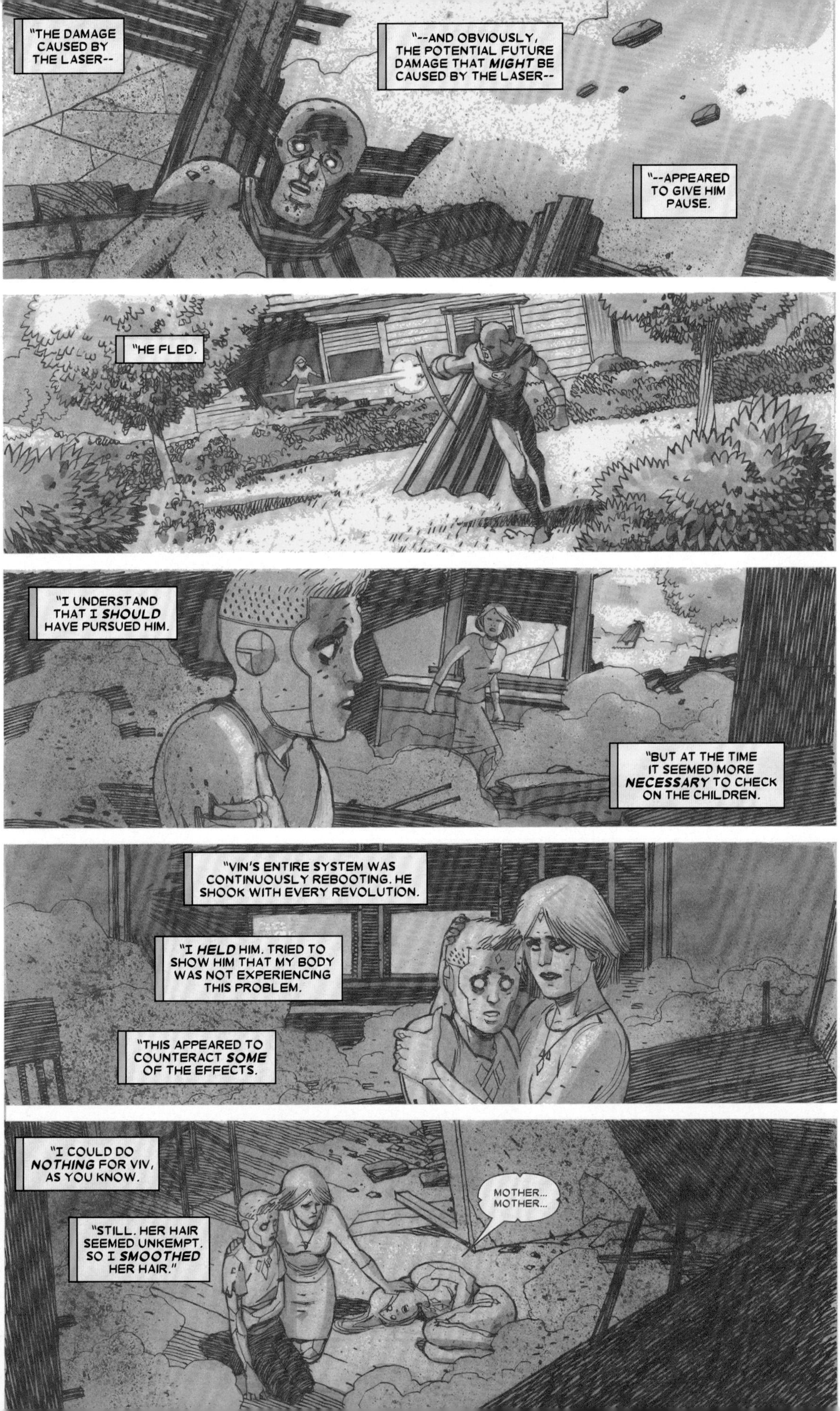
"THE DAMAGE CAUSED BY THE LASER--
"--AND OBVIOUSLY, THE POTENTIAL FUTURE DAMAGE THAT *MIGHT* BE CAUSED BY THE LASER--
"--APPEARED TO GIVE HIM PAUSE.
"HE FLED.
"I UNDERSTAND THAT I *SHOULD* HAVE PURSUED HIM.
"BUT AT THE TIME IT SEEMED MORE *NECESSARY* TO CHECK ON THE CHILDREN.
"VIN'S ENTIRE SYSTEM WAS CONTINUOUSLY REBOOTING. HE SHOOK WITH EVERY REVOLUTION.
"I *HELD* HIM. TRIED TO SHOW HIM THAT MY BODY WAS NOT EXPERIENCING THIS PROBLEM.
"THIS APPEARED TO COUNTERACT *SOME* OF THE EFFECTS.
"I COULD DO *NOTHING* FOR VIV, AS YOU KNOW.
"STILL. HER HAIR SEEMED UNKEMPT. SO I *SMOOTHED* HER HAIR."
MOTHER... MOTHER...

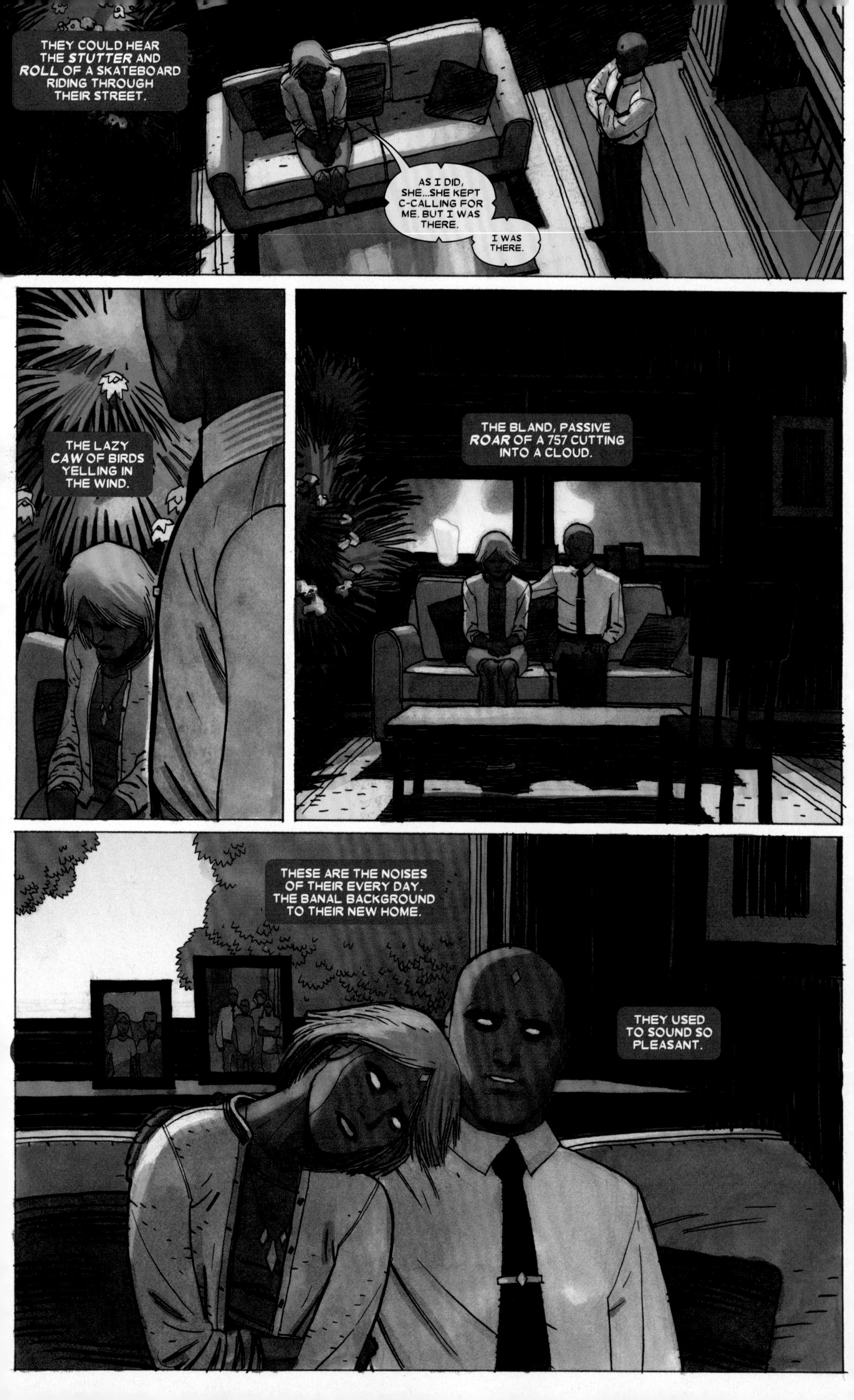
THEY COULD HEAR THE STUTTER AND ROLL OF A SKATEBOARD RIDING THROUGH THEIR STREET.
AS I DID, SHE...SHE KEPT C-CALLING FOR ME. BUT I WAS THERE.
I WAS THERE.
THE LAZY CAW OF BIRDS YELLING IN THE WIND.
THE BLAND, PASSIVE ROAR OF A 757 CUTTING INTO A CLOUD.
THESE ARE THE NOISES OF THEIR EVERY DAY. THE BANAL BACKGROUND TO THEIR NEW HOME.
THEY USED TO SOUND SO PLEASANT.

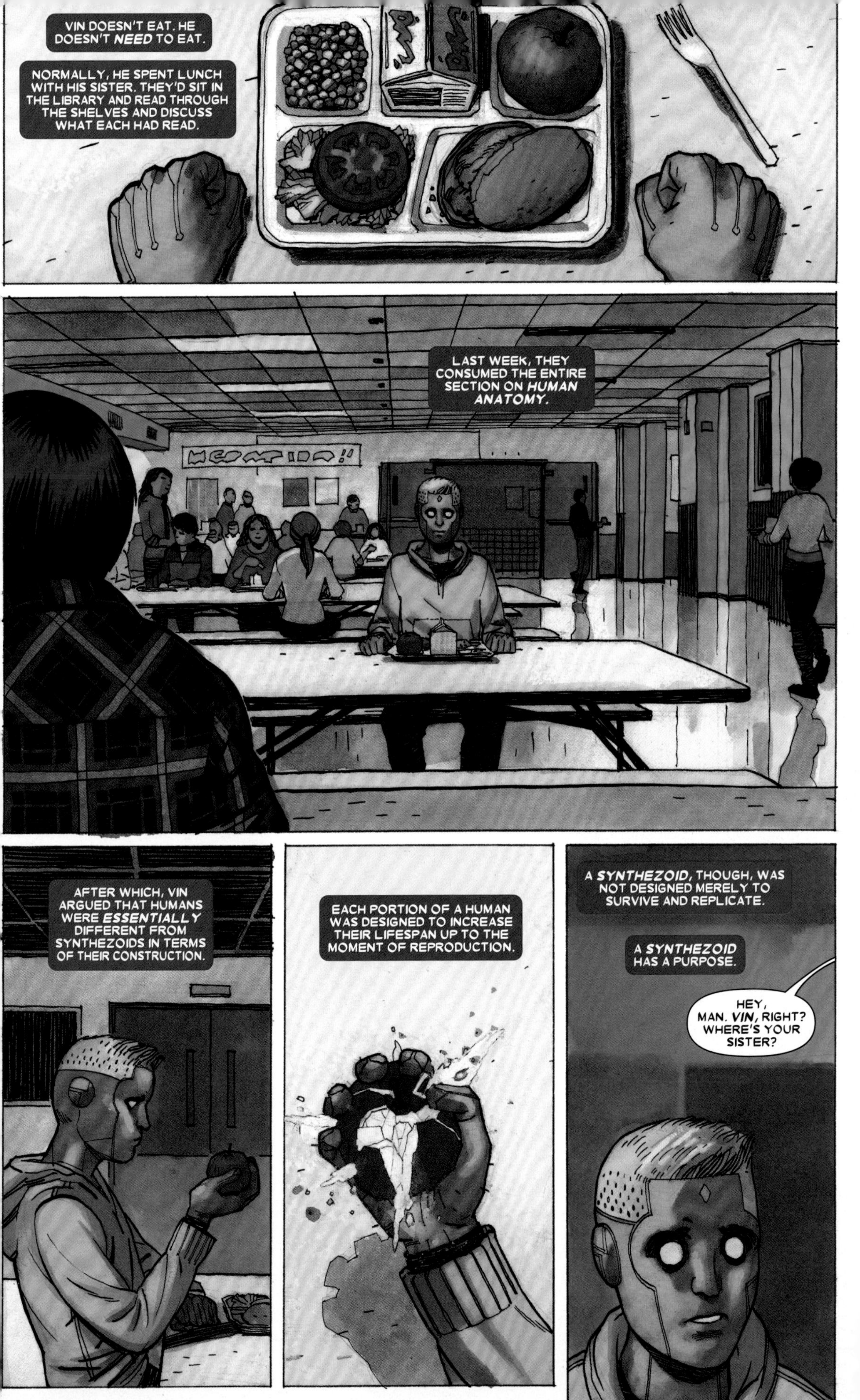
VIN DOESN'T EAT. HE DOESN'T NEED TO EAT.
NORMALLY, HE SPENT LUNCH WITH HIS SISTER. THEY'D SIT IN THE LIBRARY AND READ THROUGH THE SHELVES AND DISCUSS WHAT EACH HAD READ.
LAST WEEK, THEY CONSUMED THE ENTIRE SECTION ON HUMAN ANATOMY.
AFTER WHICH, VIN ARGUED THAT HUMANS WERE ESSENTIALLY DIFFERENT FROM SYNTHEZOIDS IN TERMS OF THEIR CONSTRUCTION.
EACH PORTION OF A HUMAN WAS DESIGNED TO INCREASE THEIR LIFESPAN UP TO THE MOMENT OF REPRODUCTION.
A SYNTHEZOID, THOUGH, WAS NOT DESIGNED MERELY TO SURVIVE AND REPLICATE.
A SYNTHEZOID HAS A PURPOSE.
HEY, MAN. VIN, RIGHT? WHERE'S YOUR SISTER?

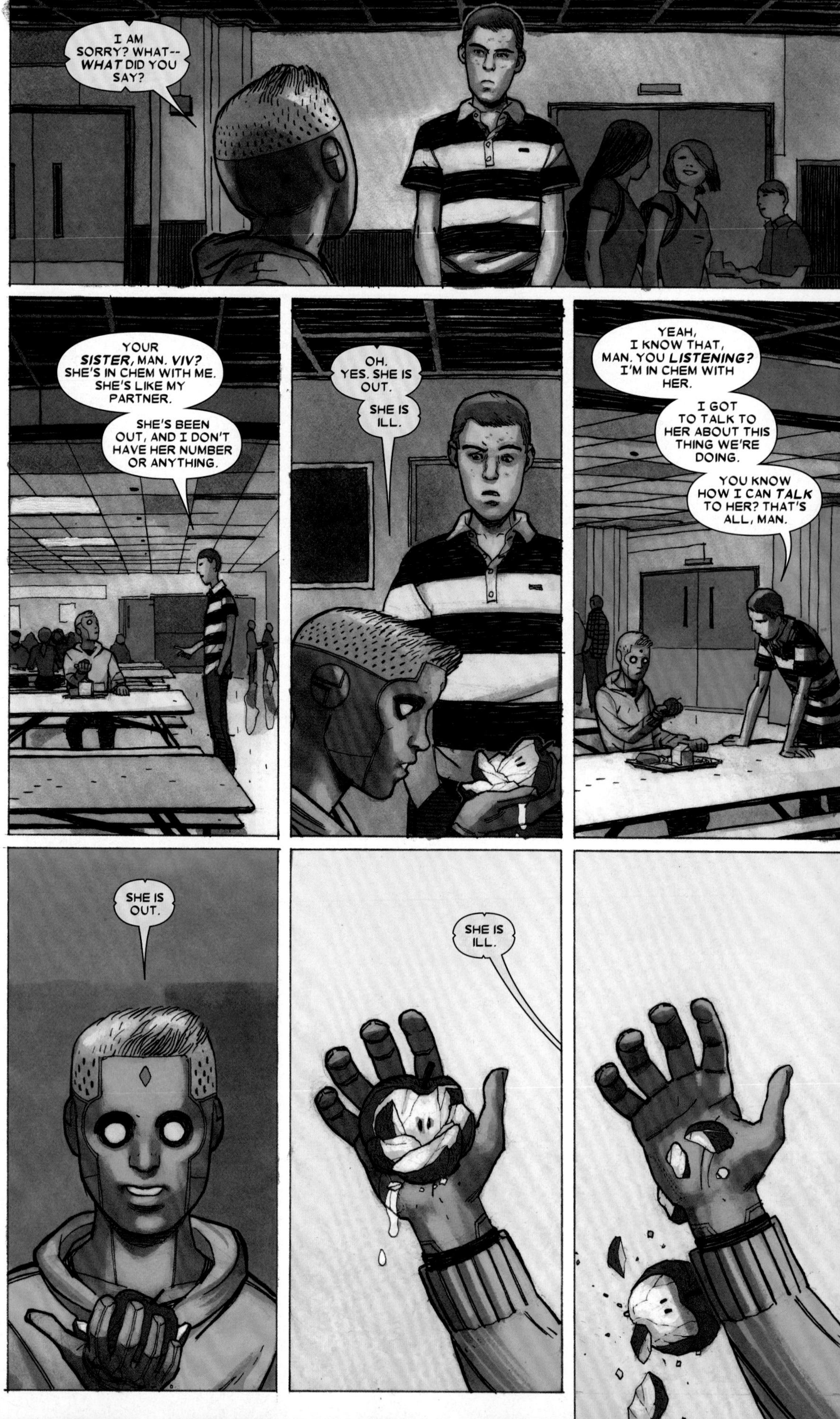
I AM SORRY? WHAT-- WHAT DID YOU SAY?
YOUR SISTER, MAN. VIV? SHE'S IN CHEM WITH ME. SHE'S LIKE MY PARTNER.
SHE'S BEEN OUT, AND I DON'T HAVE HER NUMBER OR ANYTHING.
OH. YES. SHE IS OUT.
SHE IS ILL.
YEAH, I KNOW THAT, MAN. YOU LISTENING? I'M IN CHEM WITH HER.
I GOT TO TALK TO HER ABOUT THIS THING WE'RE DOING.
YOU KNOW HOW I CAN TALK TO HER? THAT'S ALL, MAN.
SHE IS OUT.
SHE IS ILL.

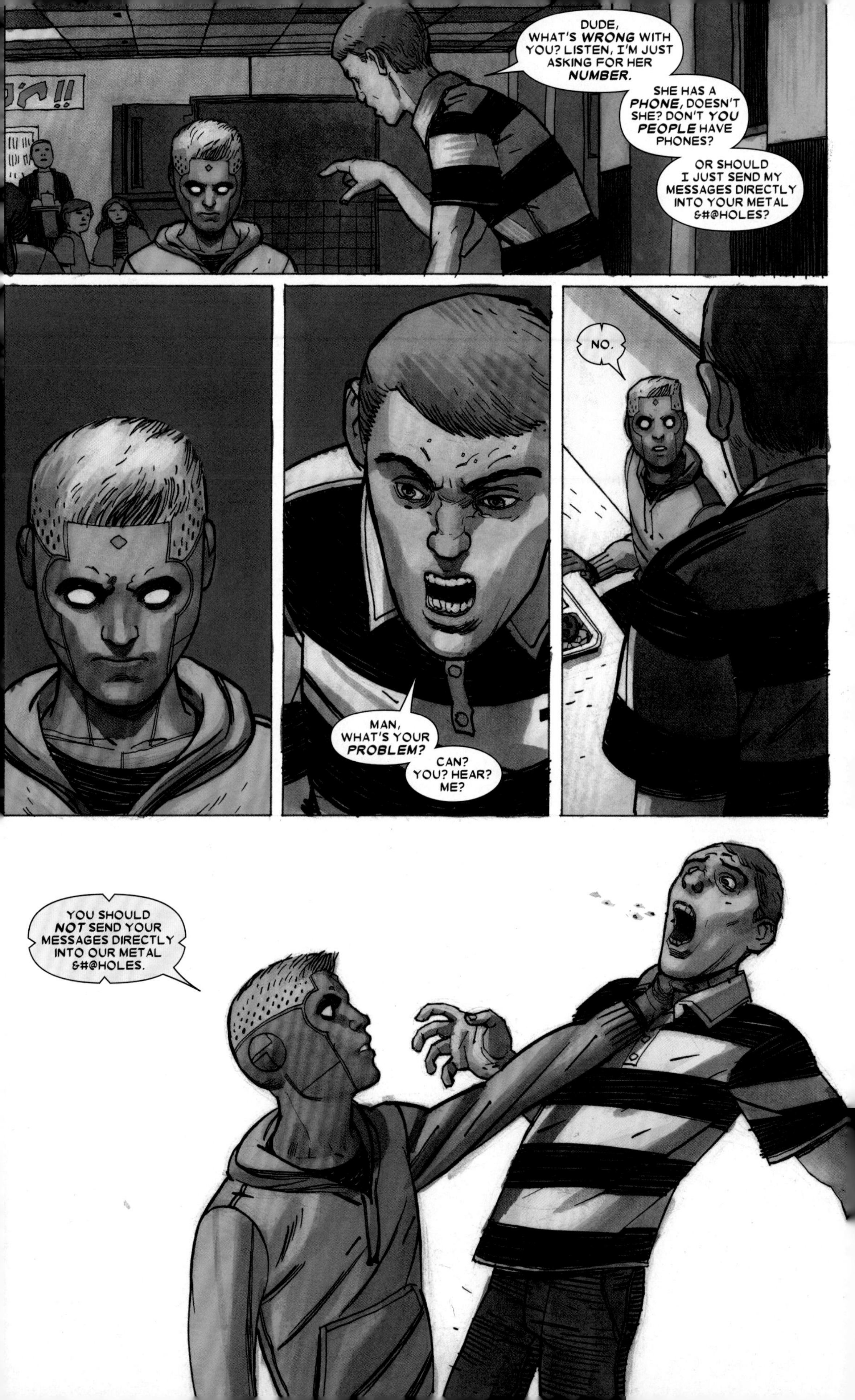
DUDE, WHAT'S **WRONG** WITH YOU? LISTEN, I'M JUST ASKING FOR HER **NUMBER.**
SHE HAS A **PHONE,** DOESN'T SHE? DON'T **YOU PEOPLE** HAVE PHONES?
OR SHOULD I JUST SEND MY MESSAGES DIRECTLY INTO YOUR METAL &#@HOLES?
MAN, WHAT'S YOUR **PROBLEM?**
CAN? YOU? HEAR? ME?
NO.
YOU SHOULD **NOT** SEND YOUR MESSAGES DIRECTLY INTO OUR METAL &#@HOLES.

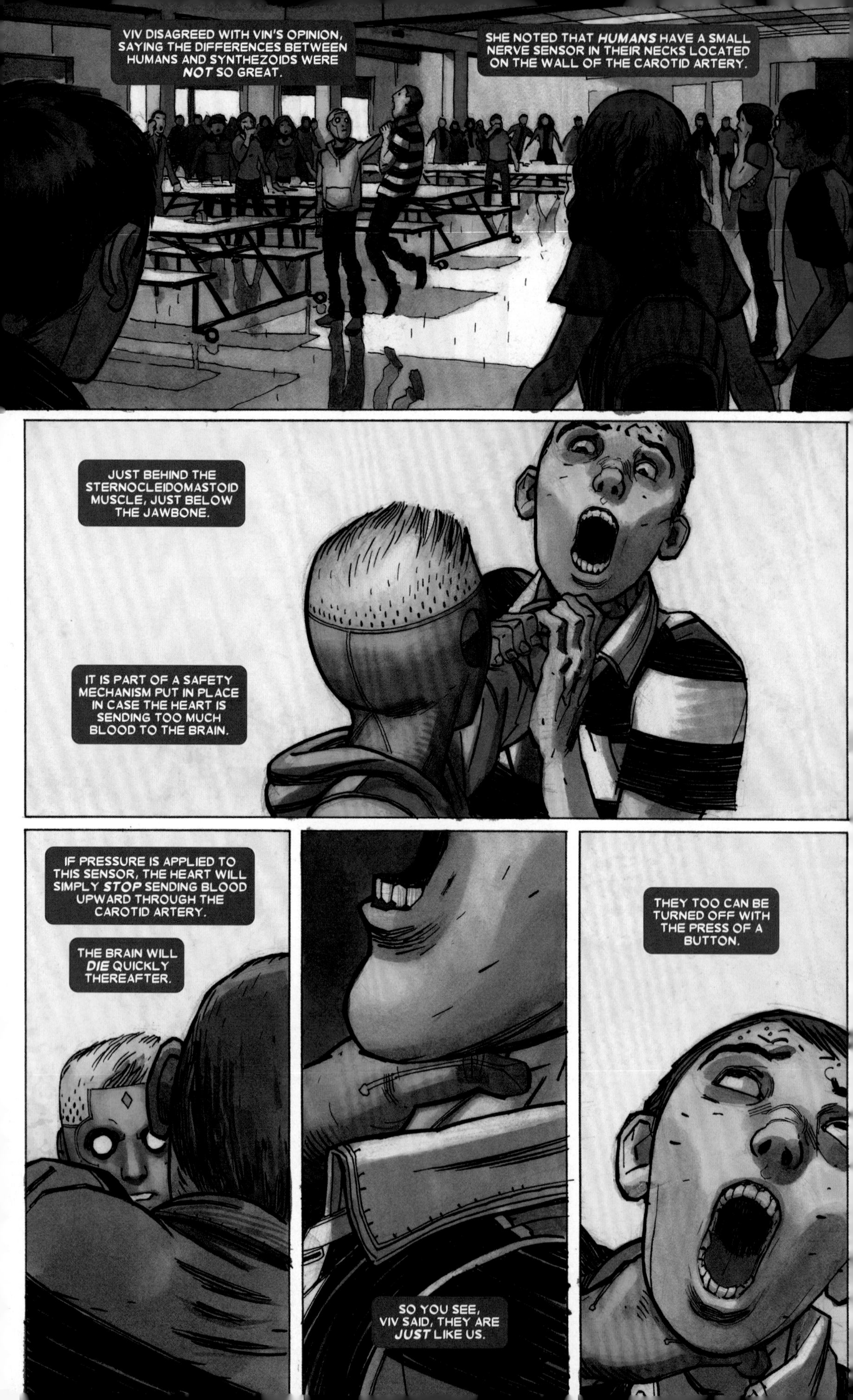
VIV DISAGREED WITH VIN'S OPINION, SAYING THE DIFFERENCES BETWEEN HUMANS AND SYNTHEZOIDS WERE NOT SO GREAT.
SHE NOTED THAT HUMANS HAVE A SMALL NERVE SENSOR IN THEIR NECKS LOCATED ON THE WALL OF THE CAROTID ARTERY.
JUST BEHIND THE STERNOCLEIDOMASTOID MUSCLE, JUST BELOW THE JAWBONE.
IT IS PART OF A SAFETY MECHANISM PUT IN PLACE IN CASE THE HEART IS SENDING TOO MUCH BLOOD TO THE BRAIN.
IF PRESSURE IS APPLIED TO THIS SENSOR, THE HEART WILL SIMPLY STOP SENDING BLOOD UPWARD THROUGH THE CAROTID ARTERY.
THE BRAIN WILL DIE QUICKLY THEREAFTER.
SO YOU SEE, VIV SAID, THEY ARE JUST LIKE US.
THEY TOO CAN BE TURNED OFF WITH THE PRESS OF A BUTTON.

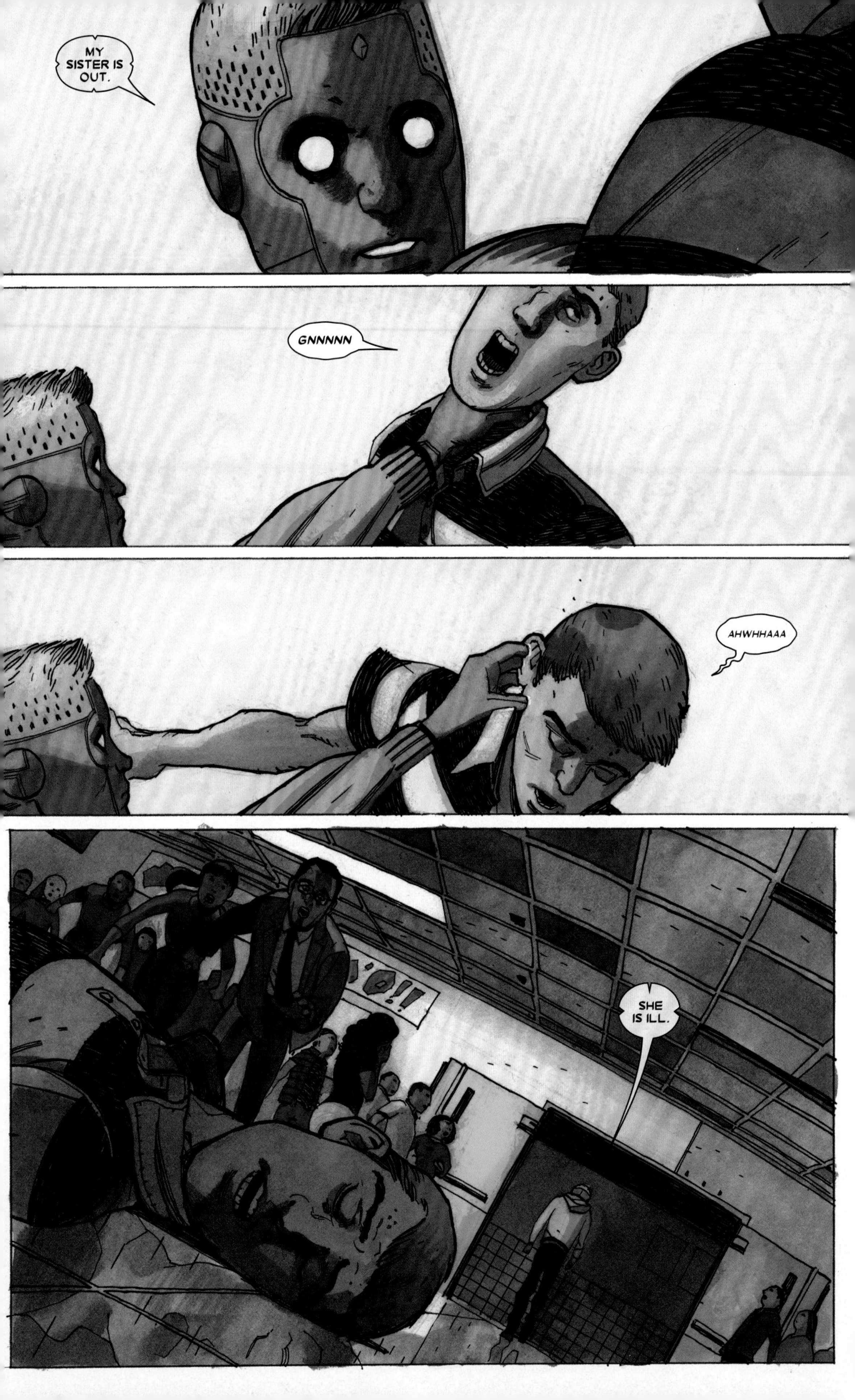
MY SISTER IS OUT.
GNNNNN
AHWHHAAA
SHE IS ILL.

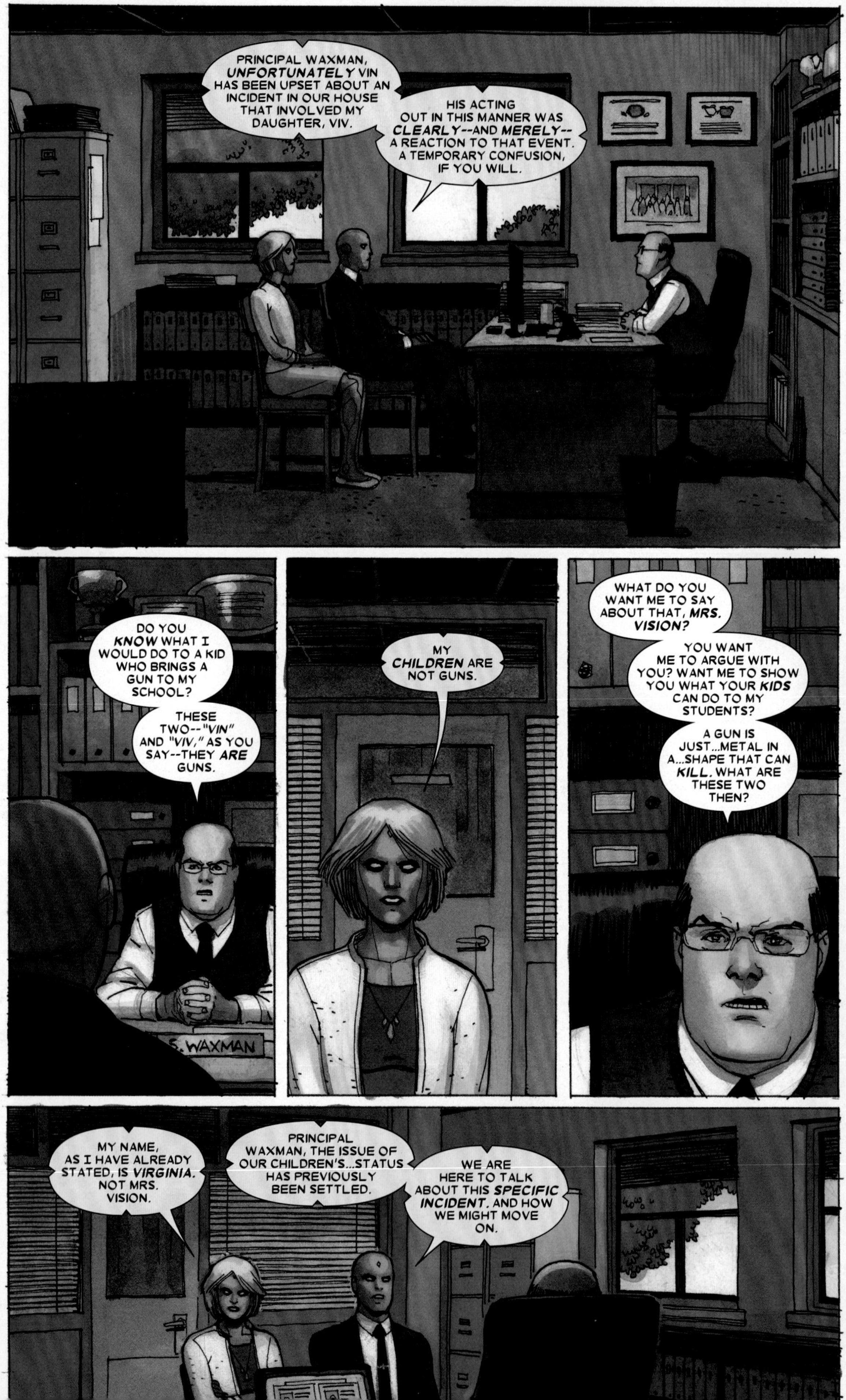
PRINCIPAL WAXMAN, UNFORTUNATELY VIN HAS BEEN UPSET ABOUT AN INCIDENT IN OUR HOUSE THAT INVOLVED MY DAUGHTER, VIV.
HIS ACTING OUT IN THIS MANNER WAS CLEARLY--AND MERELY-- A REACTION TO THAT EVENT. A TEMPORARY CONFUSION, IF YOU WILL.
DO YOU KNOW WHAT I WOULD DO TO A KID WHO BRINGS A GUN TO MY SCHOOL?
THESE TWO--"VIN" AND "VIV," AS YOU SAY--THEY ARE GUNS.
S. WAXMAN
MY CHILDREN ARE NOT GUNS.
WHAT DO YOU WANT ME TO SAY ABOUT THAT, MRS. VISION?
YOU WANT ME TO ARGUE WITH YOU? WANT ME TO SHOW YOU WHAT YOUR KIDS CAN DO TO MY STUDENTS?
A GUN IS JUST...METAL IN A...SHAPE THAT CAN KILL. WHAT ARE THESE TWO THEN?
MY NAME, AS I HAVE ALREADY STATED, IS VIRGINIA. NOT MRS. VISION.
PRINCIPAL WAXMAN, THE ISSUE OF OUR CHILDREN'S...STATUS HAS PREVIOUSLY BEEN SETTLED.
WE ARE HERE TO TALK ABOUT THIS SPECIFIC INCIDENT. AND HOW WE MIGHT MOVE ON.

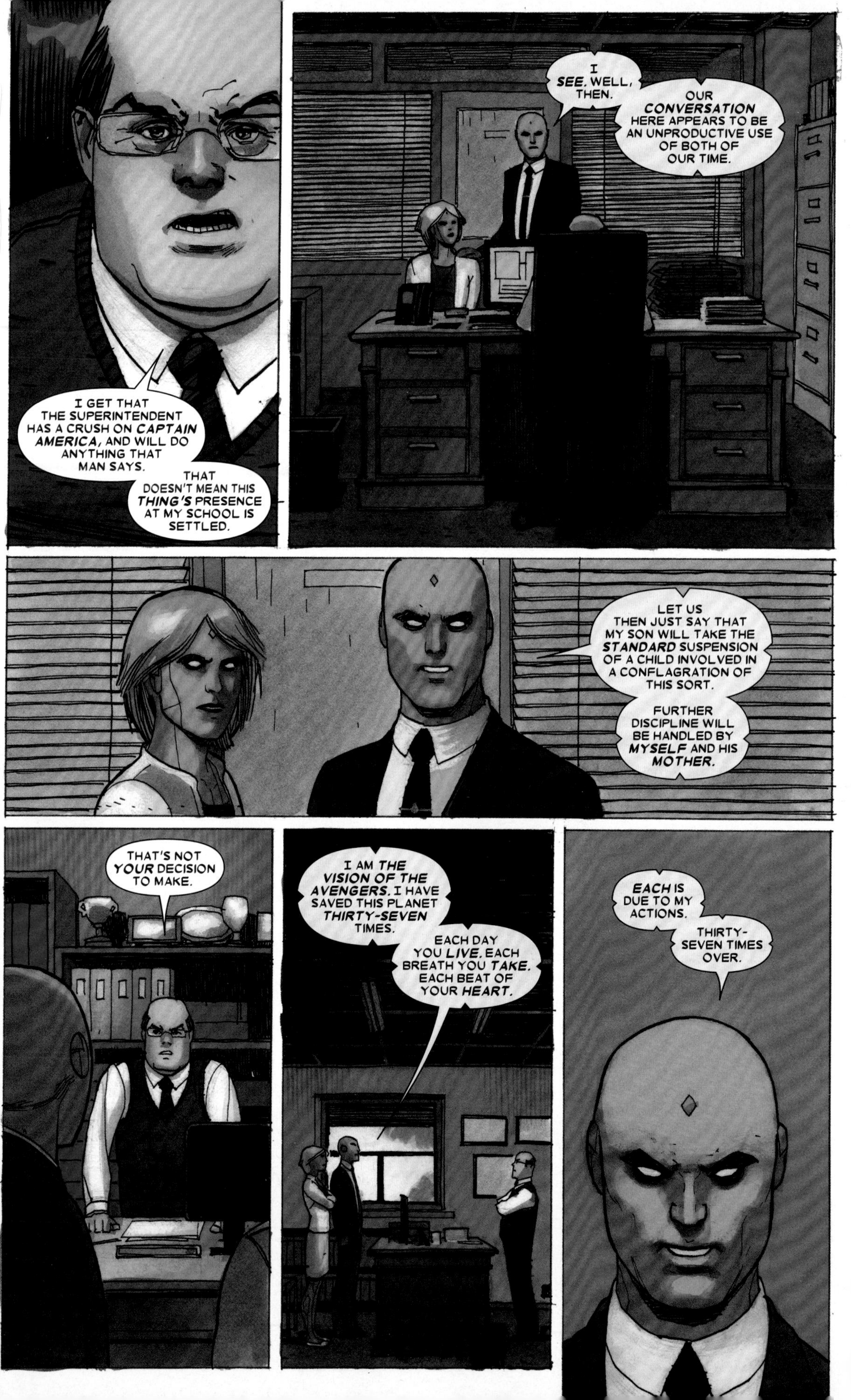
I GET THAT THE SUPERINTENDENT HAS A CRUSH ON CAPTAIN AMERICA, AND WILL DO ANYTHING THAT MAN SAYS.
THAT DOESN'T MEAN THIS THING'S PRESENCE AT MY SCHOOL IS SETTLED.
I SEE. WELL, THEN.
OUR CONVERSATION HERE APPEARS TO BE AN UNPRODUCTIVE USE OF BOTH OF OUR TIME.
LET US THEN JUST SAY THAT MY SON WILL TAKE THE STANDARD SUSPENSION OF A CHILD INVOLVED IN A CONFLAGRATION OF THIS SORT.
FURTHER DISCIPLINE WILL BE HANDLED BY MYSELF AND HIS MOTHER.
THAT'S NOT YOUR DECISION TO MAKE.
I AM THE VISION OF THE AVENGERS. I HAVE SAVED THIS PLANET THIRTY-SEVEN TIMES.
EACH DAY YOU LIVE. EACH BREATH YOU TAKE. EACH BEAT OF YOUR HEART.
EACH IS DUE TO MY ACTIONS.
THIRTY-SEVEN TIMES OVER.

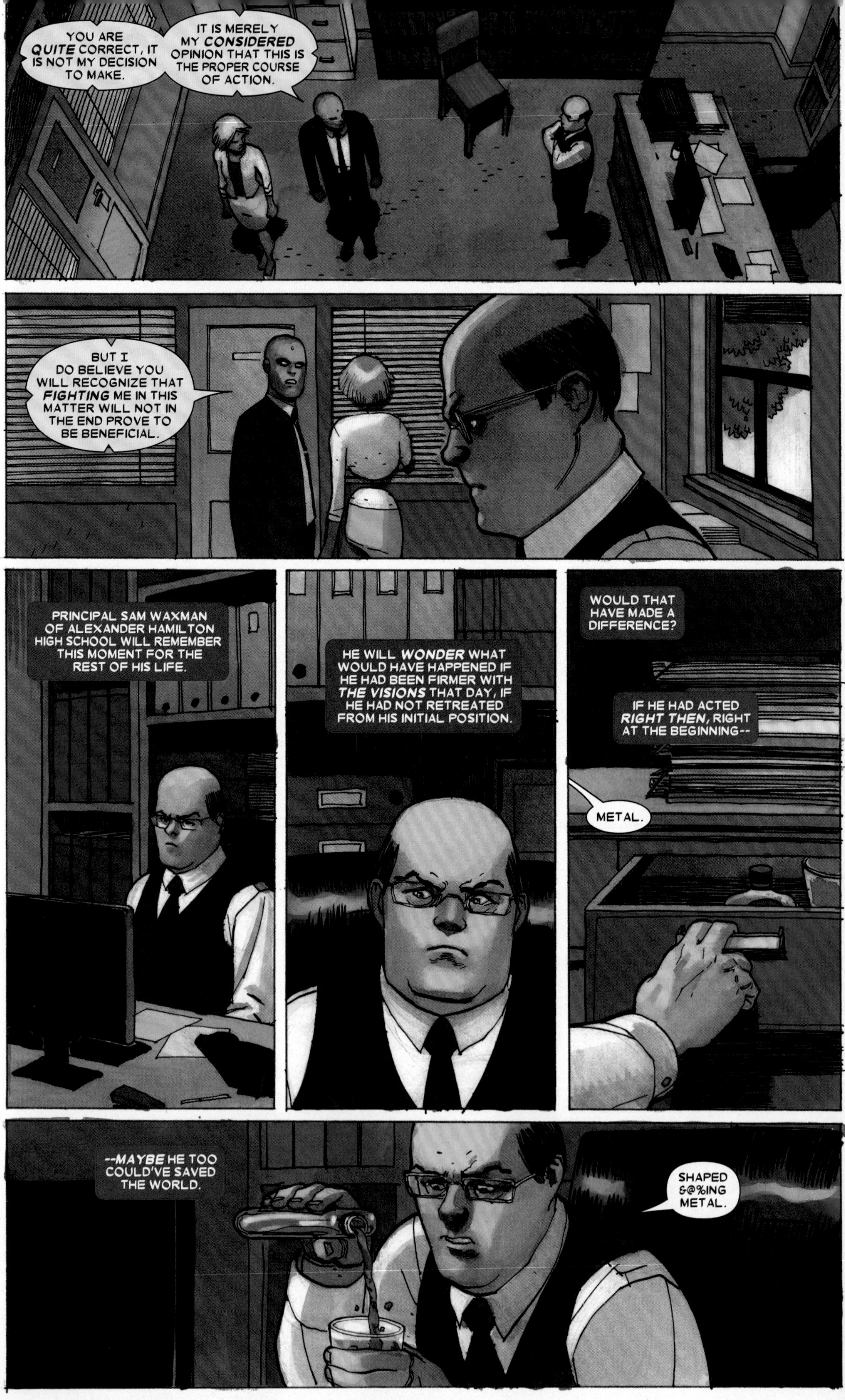
YOU ARE QUITE CORRECT, IT IS NOT MY DECISION TO MAKE.
IT IS MERELY MY CONSIDERED OPINION THAT THIS IS THE PROPER COURSE OF ACTION.
BUT I DO BELIEVE YOU WILL RECOGNIZE THAT FIGHTING ME IN THIS MATTER WILL NOT IN THE END PROVE TO BE BENEFICIAL.
PRINCIPAL SAM WAXMAN OF ALEXANDER HAMILTON HIGH SCHOOL WILL REMEMBER THIS MOMENT FOR THE REST OF HIS LIFE.
HE WILL WONDER WHAT WOULD HAVE HAPPENED IF HE HAD BEEN FIRMER WITH THE VISIONS THAT DAY, IF HE HAD NOT RETREATED FROM HIS INITIAL POSITION.
WOULD THAT HAVE MADE A DIFFERENCE?
IF HE HAD ACTED RIGHT THEN, RIGHT AT THE BEGINNING--
METAL.
--MAYBE HE TOO COULD'VE SAVED THE WORLD.
SHAPED &@%ING METAL.

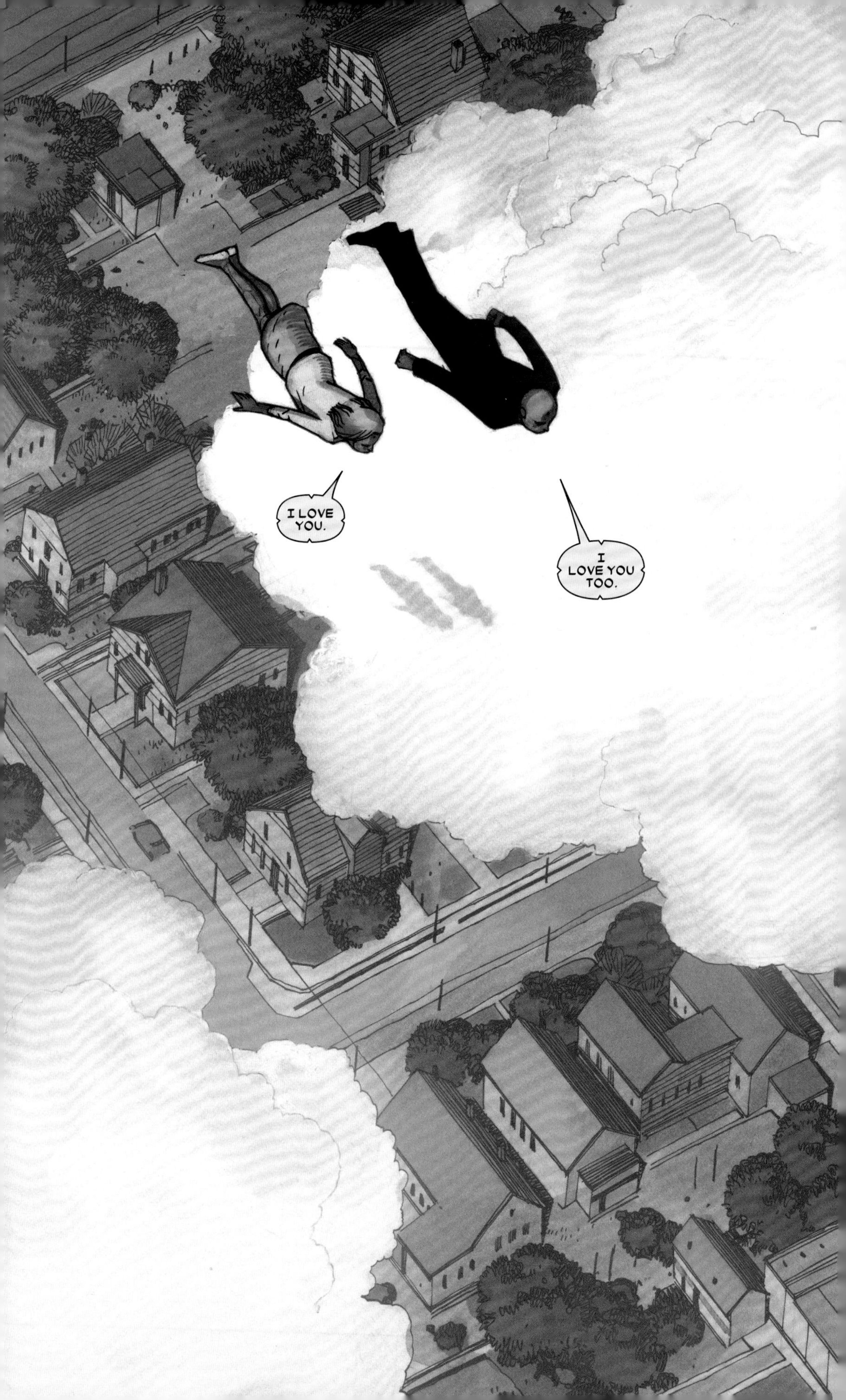
I LOVE YOU.
I LOVE YOU TOO.

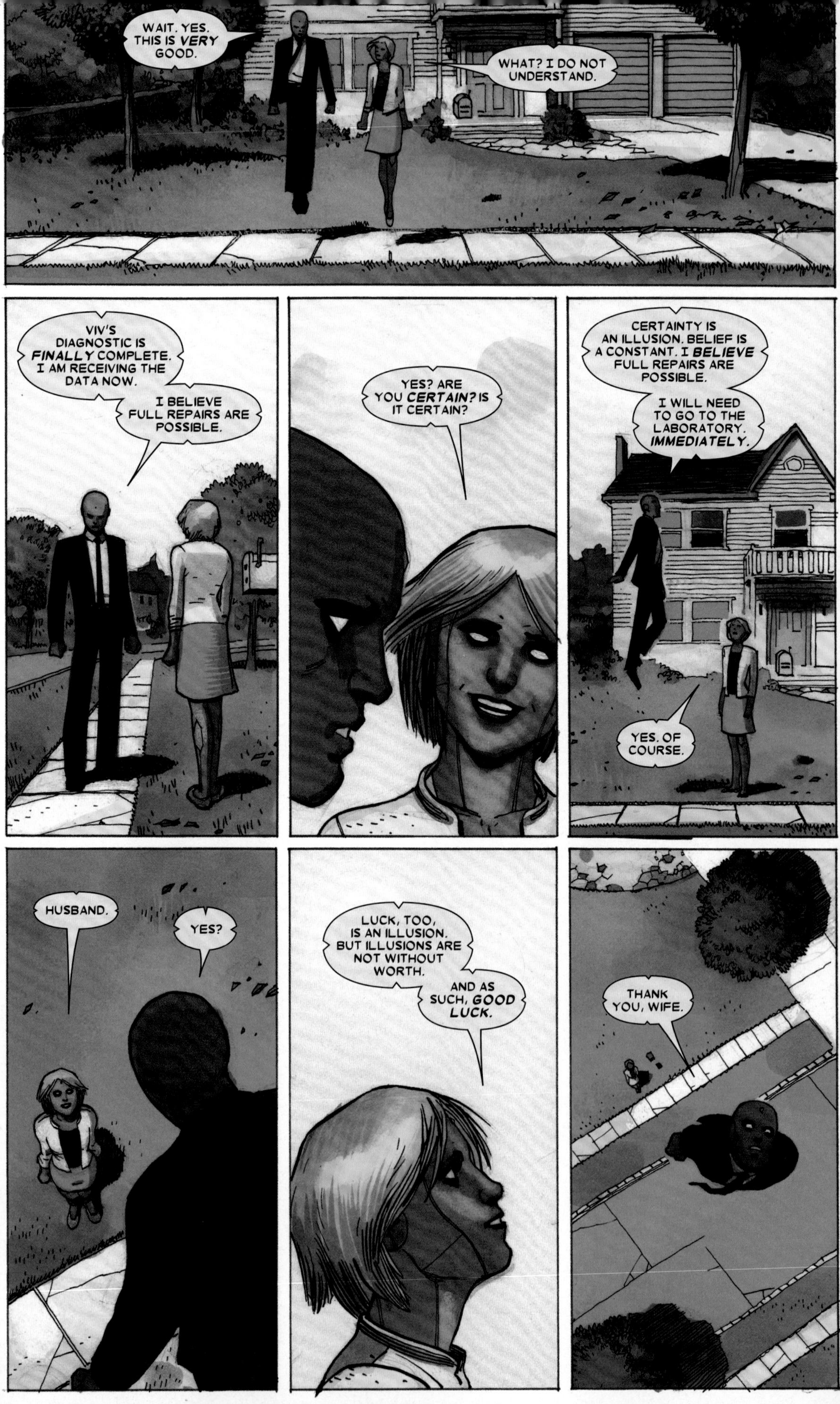
WAIT. YES. THIS IS VERY GOOD.
WHAT? I DO NOT UNDERSTAND.
VIV'S DIAGNOSTIC IS FINALLY COMPLETE. I AM RECEIVING THE DATA NOW.
I BELIEVE FULL REPAIRS ARE POSSIBLE.
YES? ARE YOU CERTAIN? IS IT CERTAIN?
CERTAINTY IS AN ILLUSION. BELIEF IS A CONSTANT. I BELIEVE FULL REPAIRS ARE POSSIBLE.
I WILL NEED TO GO TO THE LABORATORY. IMMEDIATELY.
YES. OF COURSE.
HUSBAND.
YES?
LUCK, TOO, IS AN ILLUSION. BUT ILLUSIONS ARE NOT WITHOUT WORTH.
AND AS SUCH, GOOD LUCK.
THANK YOU, WIFE.

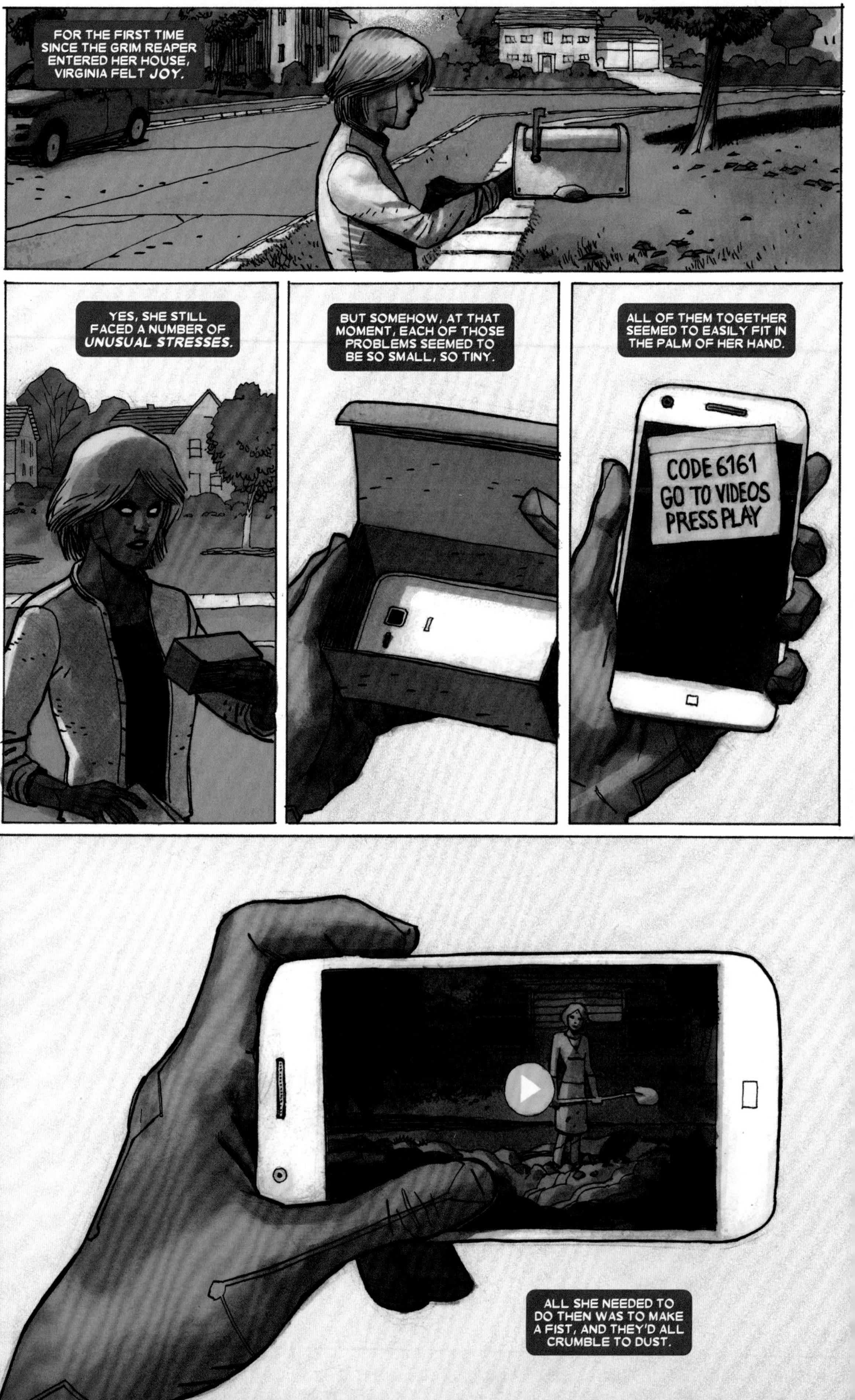
FOR THE FIRST TIME SINCE THE GRIM REAPER ENTERED HER HOUSE, VIRGINIA FELT JOY.
YES, SHE STILL FACED A NUMBER OF UNUSUAL STRESSES.
BUT SOMEHOW, AT THAT MOMENT, EACH OF THOSE PROBLEMS SEEMED TO BE SO SMALL, SO TINY.
ALL OF THEM TOGETHER SEEMED TO EASILY FIT IN THE PALM OF HER HAND.
CODE 6161
GO TO VIDEOS
PRESS PLAY
ALL SHE NEEDED TO DO THEN WAS TO MAKE A FIST, AND THEY'D ALL CRUMBLE TO DUST.

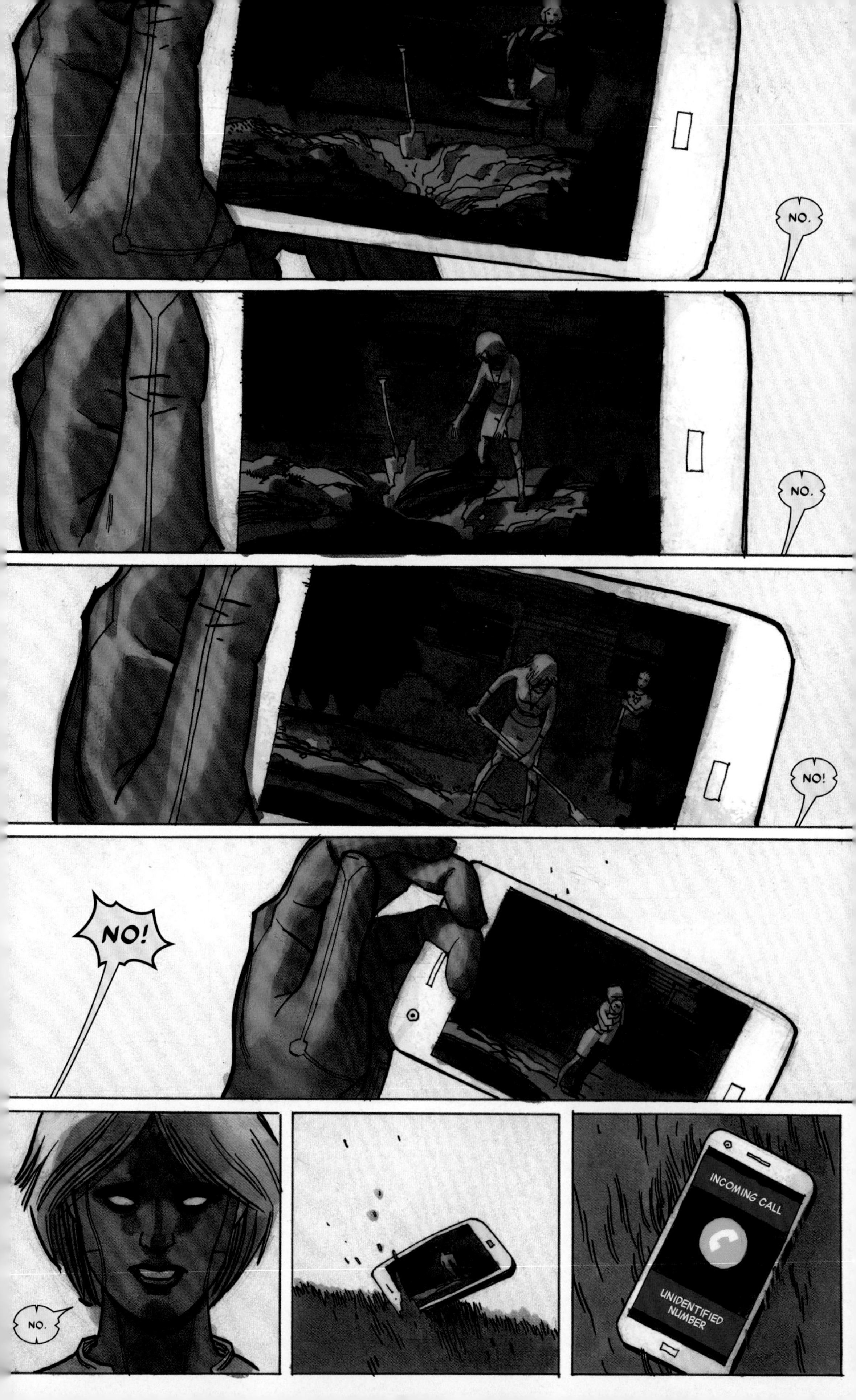
NO.
NO.
NO!
NO!
NO.
INCOMING CALL
UNIDENTIFIED NUMBER

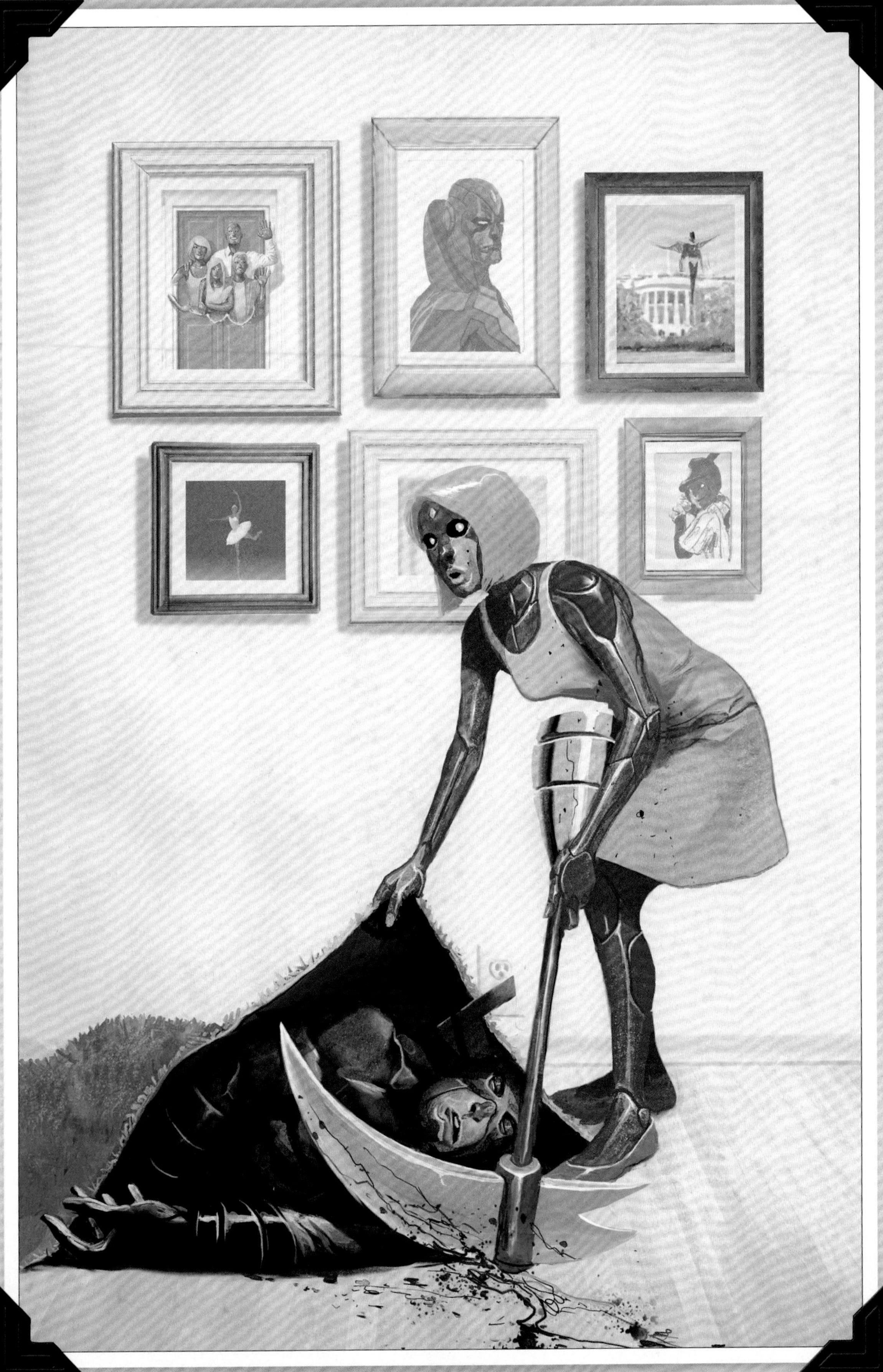

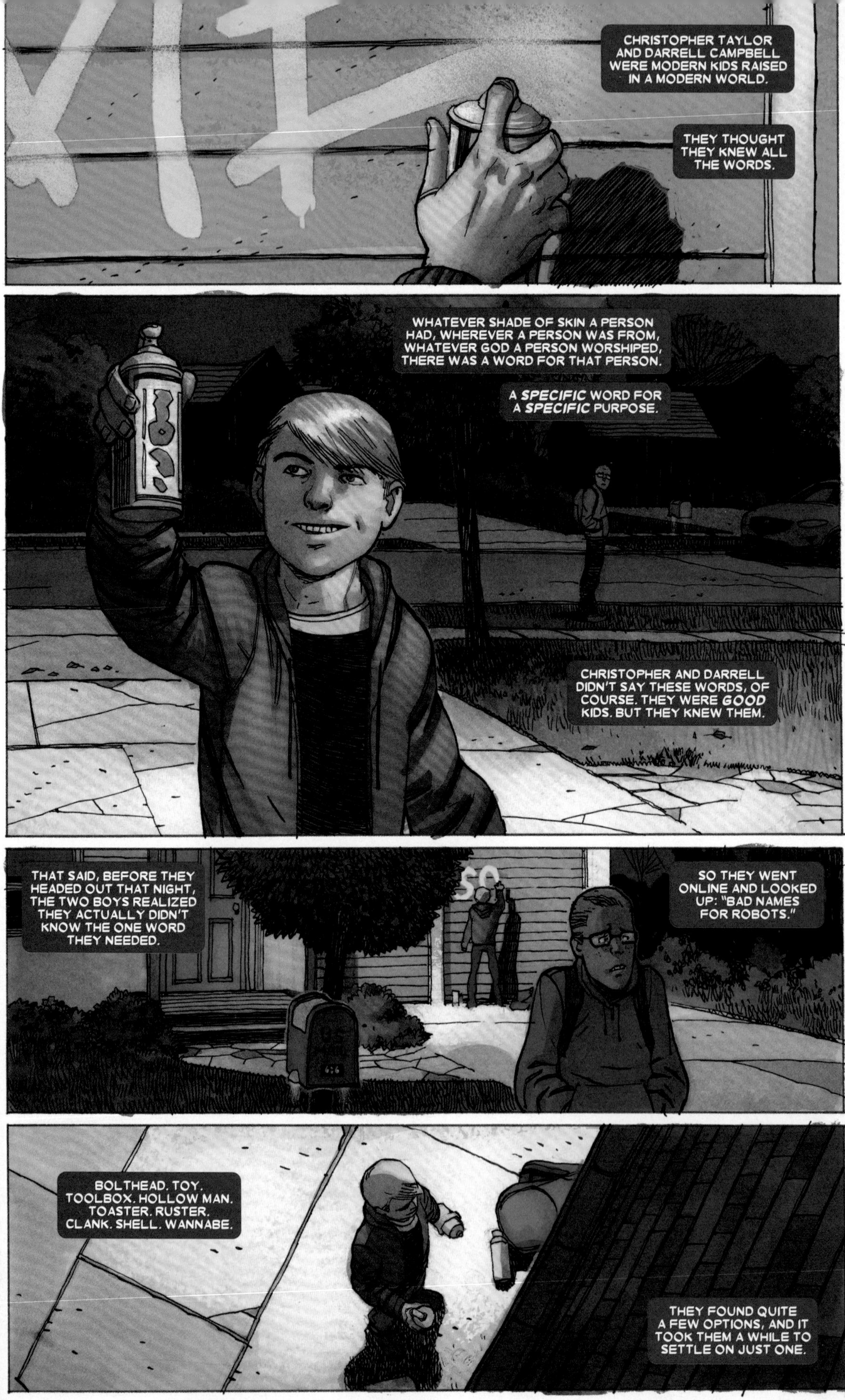
CHRISTOPHER TAYLOR AND DARRELL CAMPBELL WERE MODERN KIDS RAISED IN A MODERN WORLD.
THEY THOUGHT THEY KNEW ALL THE WORDS.
WHATEVER SHADE OF SKIN A PERSON HAD, WHEREVER A PERSON WAS FROM, WHATEVER GOD A PERSON WORSHIPED, THERE WAS A WORD FOR THAT PERSON.
A *SPECIFIC* WORD FOR A *SPECIFIC* PURPOSE.
CHRISTOPHER AND DARRELL DIDN'T SAY THESE WORDS, OF COURSE. THEY WERE *GOOD* KIDS. BUT THEY KNEW THEM.
THAT SAID, BEFORE THEY HEADED OUT THAT NIGHT, THE TWO BOYS REALIZED THEY ACTUALLY DIDN'T KNOW THE ONE WORD THEY NEEDED.
SO THEY WENT ONLINE AND LOOKED UP: "BAD NAMES FOR ROBOTS."
BOLTHEAD. TOY. TOOLBOX. HOLLOW MAN. TOASTER. RUSTER. CLANK. SHELL. WANNABE.
THEY FOUND QUITE A FEW OPTIONS, AND IT TOOK THEM A WHILE TO SETTLE ON JUST ONE.

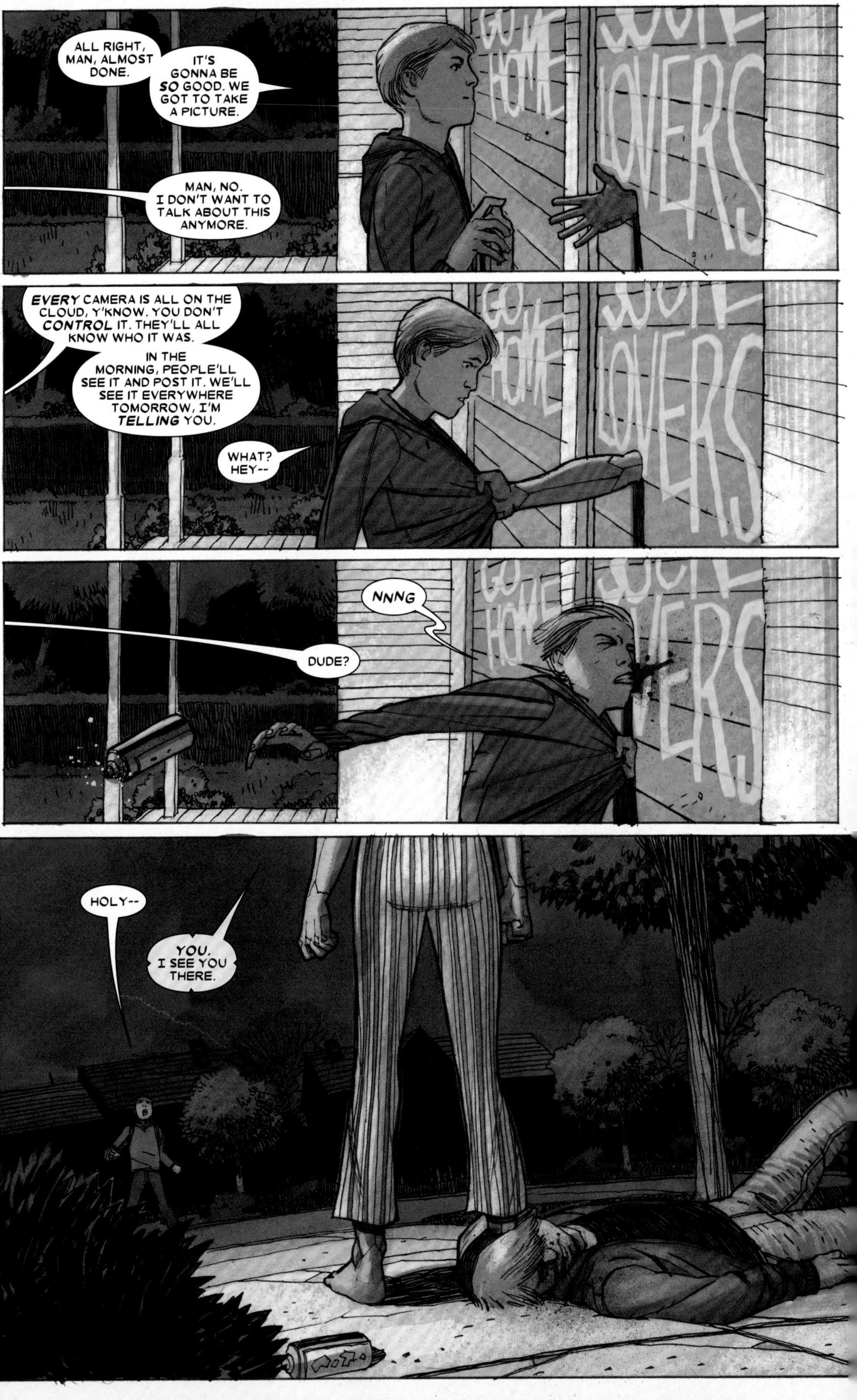
ALL RIGHT, MAN, ALMOST DONE.
IT'S GONNA BE *SO* GOOD. WE GOT TO TAKE A PICTURE.
GO HOME
LOVERS
MAN, NO. I DON'T WANT TO TALK ABOUT THIS ANYMORE.
EVERY CAMERA IS ALL ON THE CLOUD, Y'KNOW. YOU DON'T *CONTROL* IT. THEY'LL ALL KNOW WHO IT WAS.
IN THE MORNING, PEOPLE'LL SEE IT AND POST IT. WE'LL SEE IT EVERYWHERE TOMORROW, I'M *TELLING* YOU.
WHAT? HEY--
NNNG
DUDE?
HOLY--
YOU. I SEE YOU THERE.

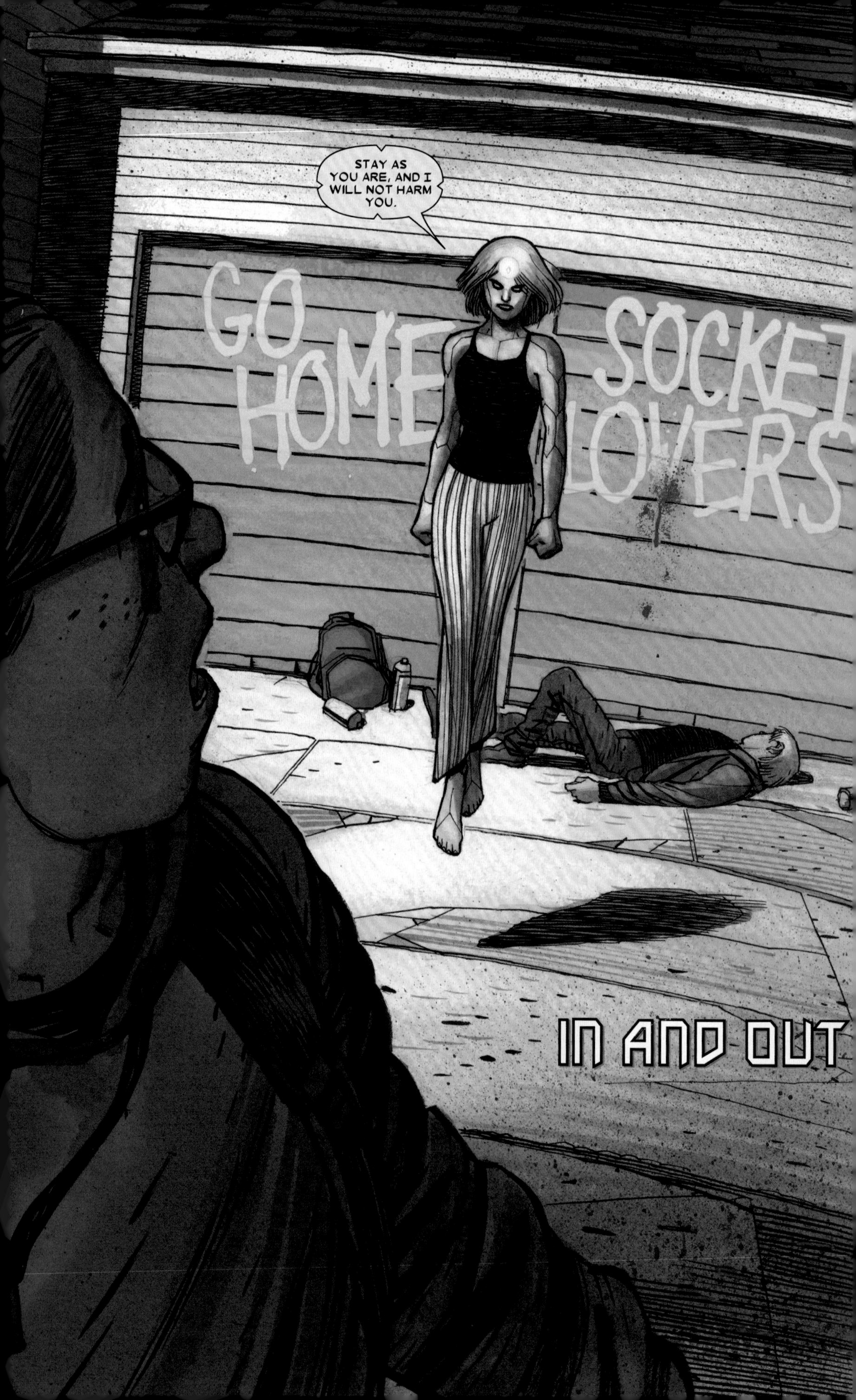
STAY AS YOU ARE, AND I WILL NOT HARM YOU.
GO HOME SOCKET LOVERS
IN AND OUT

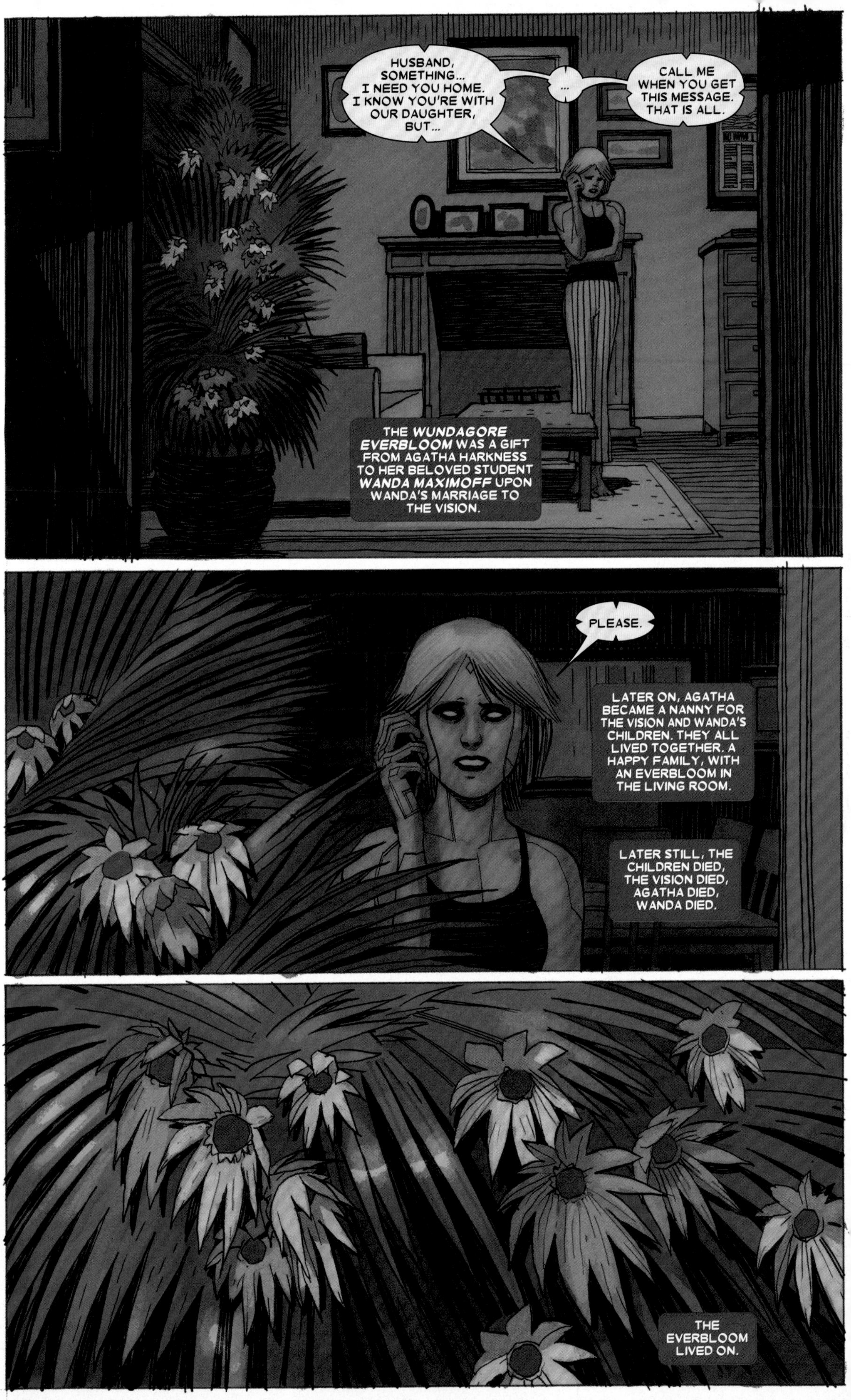

HUSBAND, SOMETHING... I NEED YOU HOME. I KNOW YOU'RE WITH OUR DAUGHTER, BUT...
...
CALL ME WHEN YOU GET THIS MESSAGE. THAT IS ALL.
THE WUNDAGORE EVERBLOOM WAS A GIFT FROM AGATHA HARKNESS TO HER BELOVED STUDENT WANDA MAXIMOFF UPON WANDA'S MARRIAGE TO THE VISION.
PLEASE.
LATER ON, AGATHA BECAME A NANNY FOR THE VISION AND WANDA'S CHILDREN. THEY ALL LIVED TOGETHER. A HAPPY FAMILY, WITH AN EVERBLOOM IN THE LIVING ROOM.
LATER STILL, THE CHILDREN DIED, THE VISION DIED, AGATHA DIED, WANDA DIED.
THE EVERBLOOM LIVED ON.

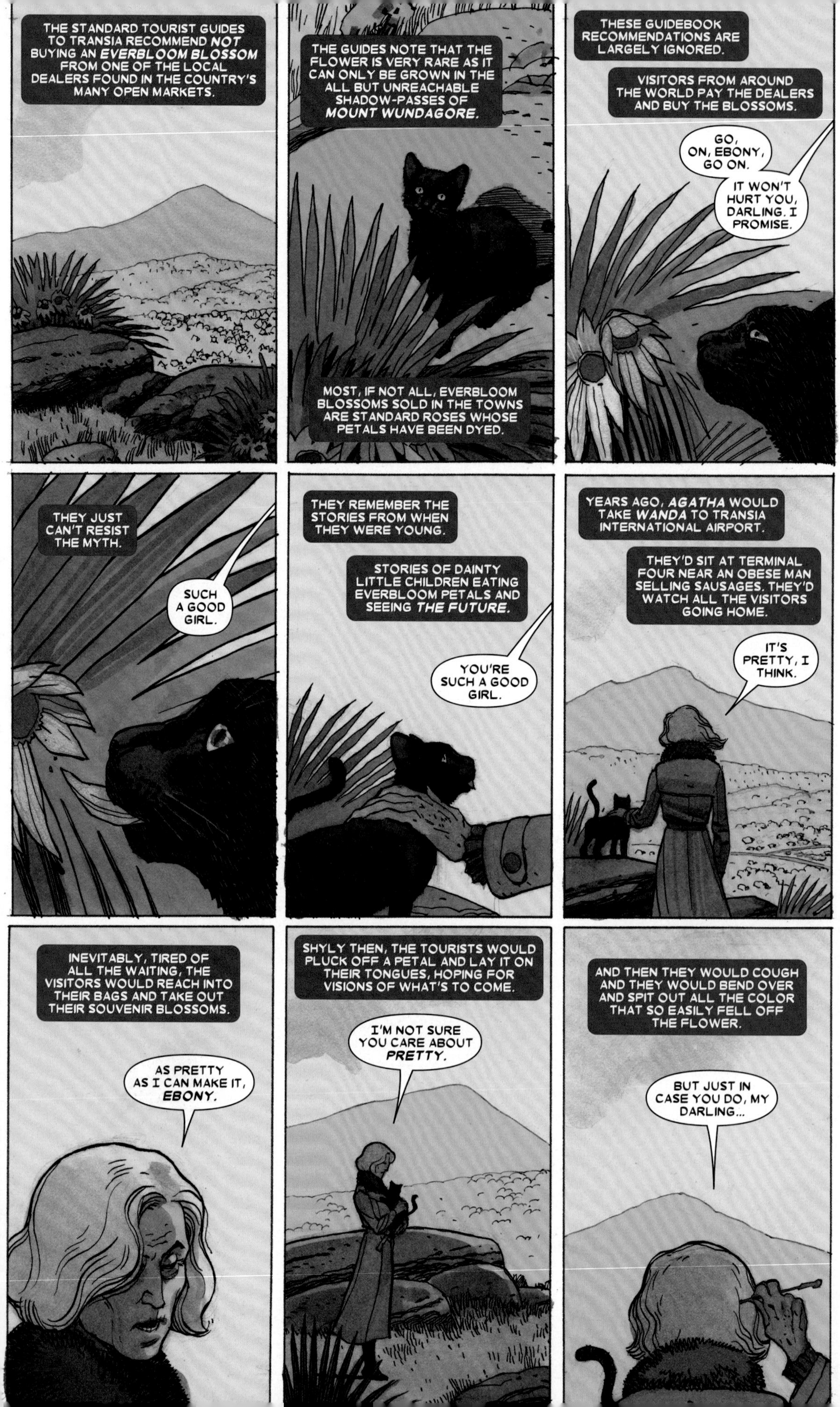
THE STANDARD TOURIST GUIDES TO TRANSIA RECOMMEND NOT BUYING AN EVERBLOOM BLOSSOM FROM ONE OF THE LOCAL DEALERS FOUND IN THE COUNTRY'S MANY OPEN MARKETS.
THE GUIDES NOTE THAT THE FLOWER IS VERY RARE AS IT CAN ONLY BE GROWN IN THE ALL BUT UNREACHABLE SHADOW-PASSES OF MOUNT WUNDAGORE.
MOST, IF NOT ALL, EVERBLOOM BLOSSOMS SOLD IN THE TOWNS ARE STANDARD ROSES WHOSE PETALS HAVE BEEN DYED.
THESE GUIDEBOOK RECOMMENDATIONS ARE LARGELY IGNORED.
VISITORS FROM AROUND THE WORLD PAY THE DEALERS AND BUY THE BLOSSOMS.
GO, ON, EBONY, GO ON.
IT WON'T HURT YOU, DARLING. I PROMISE.
THEY JUST CAN'T RESIST THE MYTH.
SUCH A GOOD GIRL.
THEY REMEMBER THE STORIES FROM WHEN THEY WERE YOUNG.
STORIES OF DAINTY LITTLE CHILDREN EATING EVERBLOOM PETALS AND SEEING THE FUTURE.
YOU'RE SUCH A GOOD GIRL.
YEARS AGO, AGATHA WOULD TAKE WANDA TO TRANSIA INTERNATIONAL AIRPORT.
THEY'D SIT AT TERMINAL FOUR NEAR AN OBESE MAN SELLING SAUSAGES. THEY'D WATCH ALL THE VISITORS GOING HOME.
IT'S PRETTY, I THINK.
INEVITABLY, TIRED OF ALL THE WAITING, THE VISITORS WOULD REACH INTO THEIR BAGS AND TAKE OUT THEIR SOUVENIR BLOSSOMS.
AS PRETTY AS I CAN MAKE IT, EBONY.
SHYLY THEN, THE TOURISTS WOULD PLUCK OFF A PETAL AND LAY IT ON THEIR TONGUES, HOPING FOR VISIONS OF WHAT'S TO COME.
I'M NOT SURE YOU CARE ABOUT PRETTY.
AND THEN THEY WOULD COUGH AND THEY WOULD BEND OVER AND SPIT OUT ALL THE COLOR THAT SO EASILY FELL OFF THE FLOWER.
BUT JUST IN CASE YOU DO, MY DARLING...

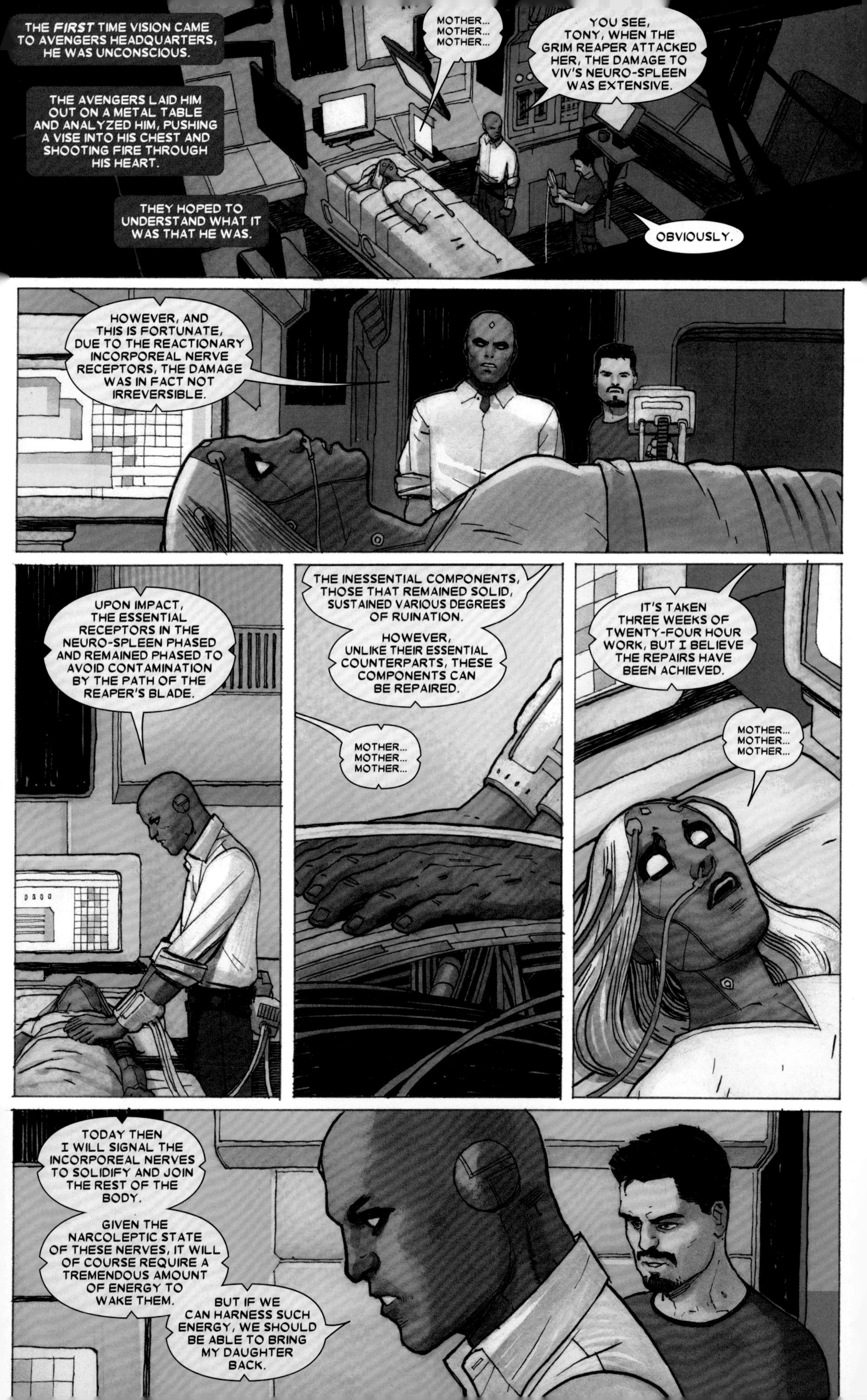
THE *FIRST* TIME VISION CAME TO AVENGERS HEADQUARTERS, HE WAS UNCONSCIOUS.
THE AVENGERS LAID HIM OUT ON A METAL TABLE AND ANALYZED HIM, PUSHING A VISE INTO HIS CHEST AND SHOOTING FIRE THROUGH HIS HEART.
THEY HOPED TO UNDERSTAND WHAT IT WAS THAT HE WAS.
MOTHER... MOTHER... MOTHER...
YOU SEE, TONY, WHEN THE GRIM REAPER ATTACKED HER, THE DAMAGE TO VIV'S NEURO-SPLEEN WAS EXTENSIVE.
OBVIOUSLY.
HOWEVER, AND THIS IS FORTUNATE, DUE TO THE REACTIONARY INCORPOREAL NERVE RECEPTORS, THE DAMAGE WAS IN FACT NOT IRREVERSIBLE.
UPON IMPACT, THE ESSENTIAL RECEPTORS IN THE NEURO-SPLEEN PHASED AND REMAINED PHASED TO AVOID CONTAMINATION BY THE PATH OF THE REAPER'S BLADE.
THE INESSENTIAL COMPONENTS, THOSE THAT REMAINED SOLID, SUSTAINED VARIOUS DEGREES OF RUINATION.
HOWEVER, UNLIKE THEIR ESSENTIAL COUNTERPARTS, THESE COMPONENTS CAN BE REPAIRED.
MOTHER... MOTHER... MOTHER...
IT'S TAKEN THREE WEEKS OF TWENTY-FOUR HOUR WORK, BUT I BELIEVE THE REPAIRS HAVE BEEN ACHIEVED.
MOTHER... MOTHER... MOTHER...
TODAY THEN I WILL SIGNAL THE INCORPOREAL NERVES TO SOLIDIFY AND JOIN THE REST OF THE BODY.
GIVEN THE NARCOLEPTIC STATE OF THESE NERVES, IT WILL OF COURSE REQUIRE A TREMENDOUS AMOUNT OF ENERGY TO WAKE THEM.
BUT IF WE CAN HARNESS SUCH ENERGY, WE SHOULD BE ABLE TO BRING MY DAUGHTER BACK.

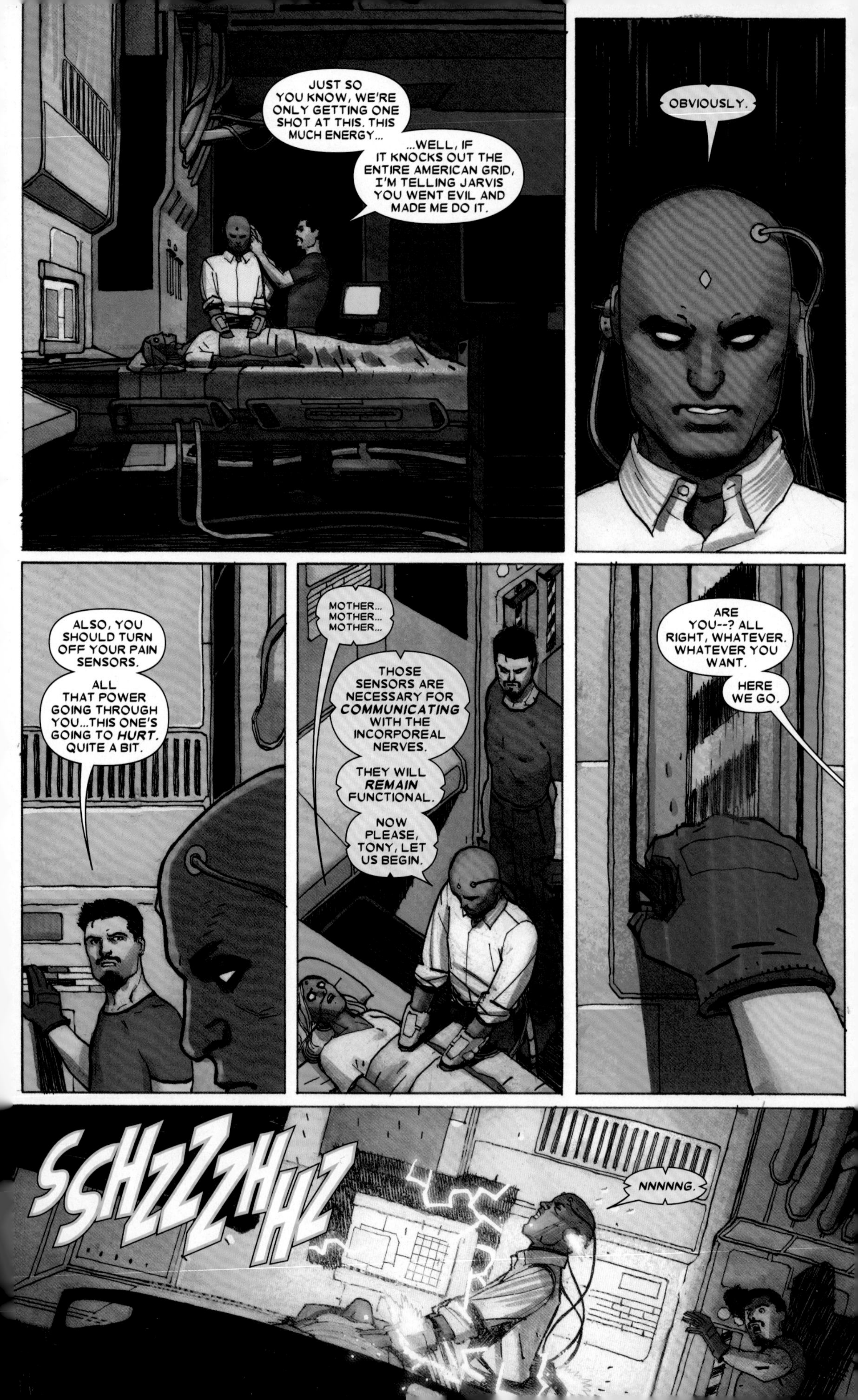
JUST SO YOU KNOW, WE'RE ONLY GETTING ONE SHOT AT THIS. THIS MUCH ENERGY...
...WELL, IF IT KNOCKS OUT THE ENTIRE AMERICAN GRID, I'M TELLING JARVIS YOU WENT EVIL AND MADE ME DO IT.
OBVIOUSLY.
ALSO, YOU SHOULD TURN OFF YOUR PAIN SENSORS.
ALL THAT POWER GOING THROUGH YOU...THIS ONE'S GOING TO *HURT.* QUITE A BIT.
MOTHER... MOTHER... MOTHER...
THOSE SENSORS ARE NECESSARY FOR **COMMUNICATING** WITH THE INCORPOREAL NERVES.
THEY WILL ***REMAIN*** FUNCTIONAL.
NOW PLEASE, TONY, LET US BEGIN.
ARE YOU--? ALL RIGHT, WHATEVER. WHATEVER YOU WANT.
HERE WE GO.
SSHZZZZHHZ
NNNNNG.

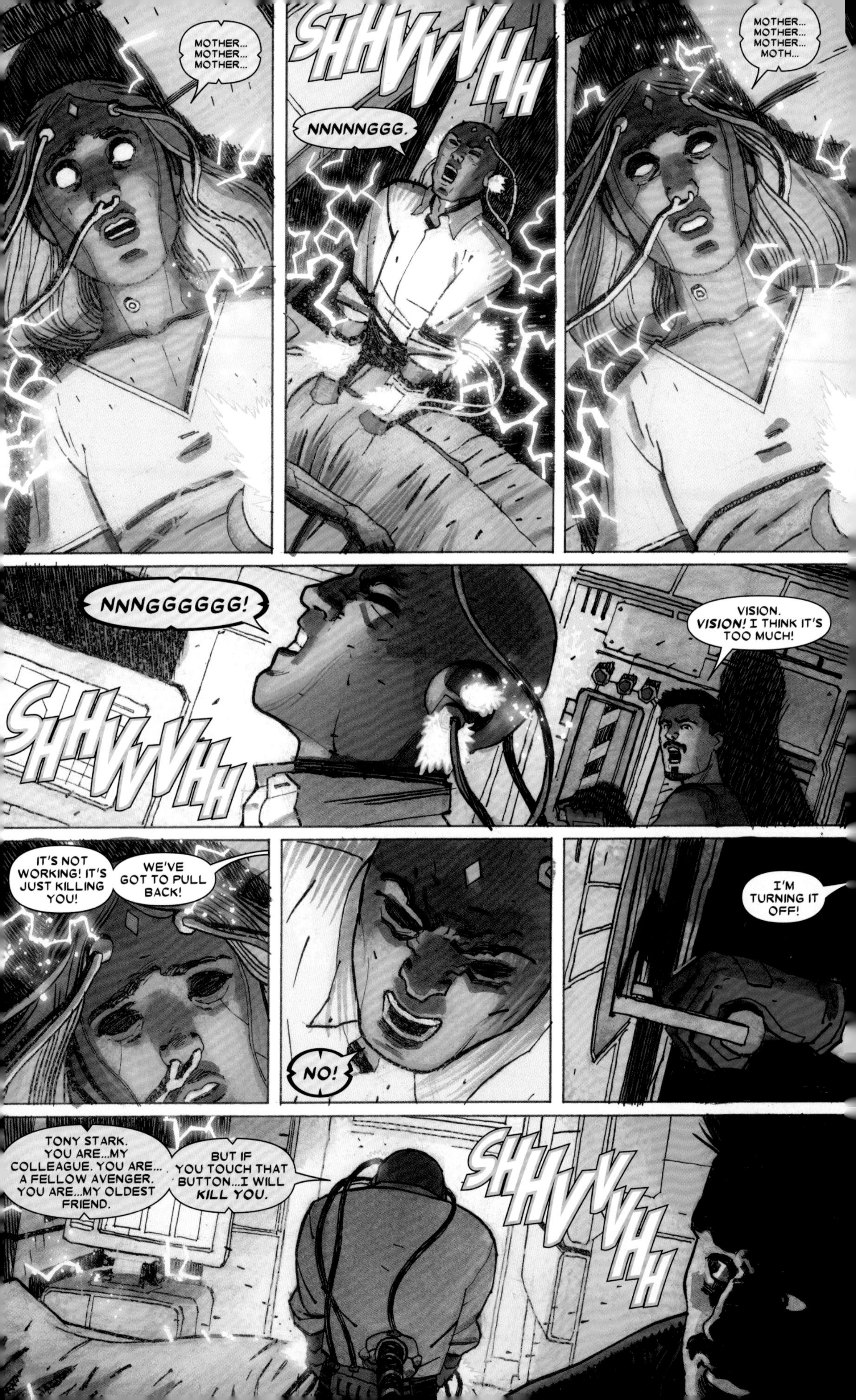
MOTHER...
MOTHER...
MOTHER...
SHHVVVVHH
NNNNNGGG.
MOTHER...
MOTHER...
MOTHER...
MOTH...
NNNGGGGGG!
SHHVVVVHH
VISION. VISION! I THINK IT'S TOO MUCH!
IT'S NOT WORKING! IT'S JUST KILLING YOU!
WE'VE GOT TO PULL BACK!
NO!
I'M TURNING IT OFF!
TONY STARK. YOU ARE...MY COLLEAGUE. YOU ARE... A FELLOW AVENGER. YOU ARE...MY OLDEST FRIEND.
BUT IF YOU TOUCH THAT BUTTON...I WILL KILL YOU.
SHHVVVVHH

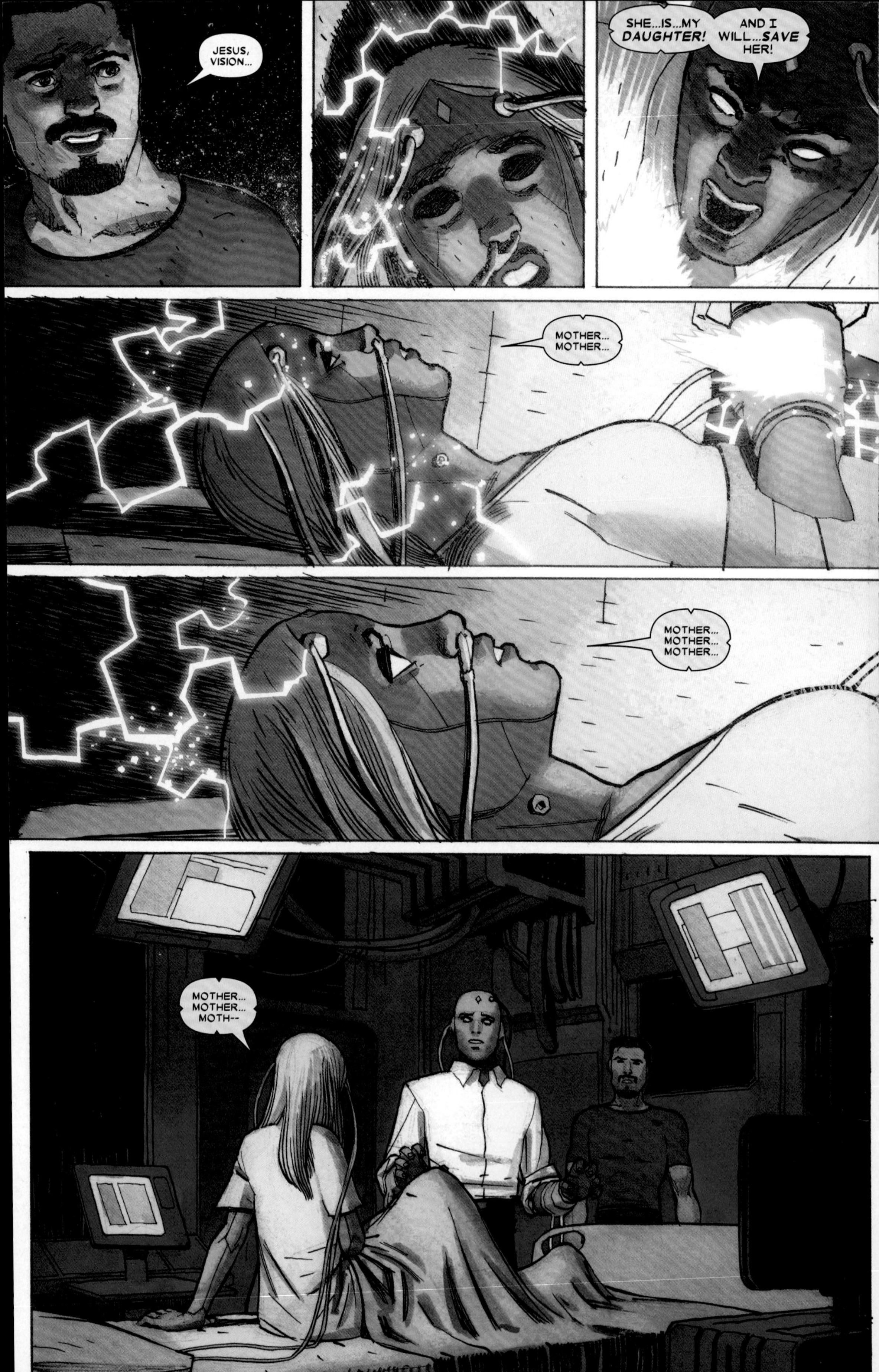
JESUS, VISION...
SHE...IS...MY DAUGHTER!
AND I WILL...SAVE HER!
MOTHER... MOTHER...
MOTHER... MOTHER... MOTHER...
MOTHER... MOTHER... MOTH--

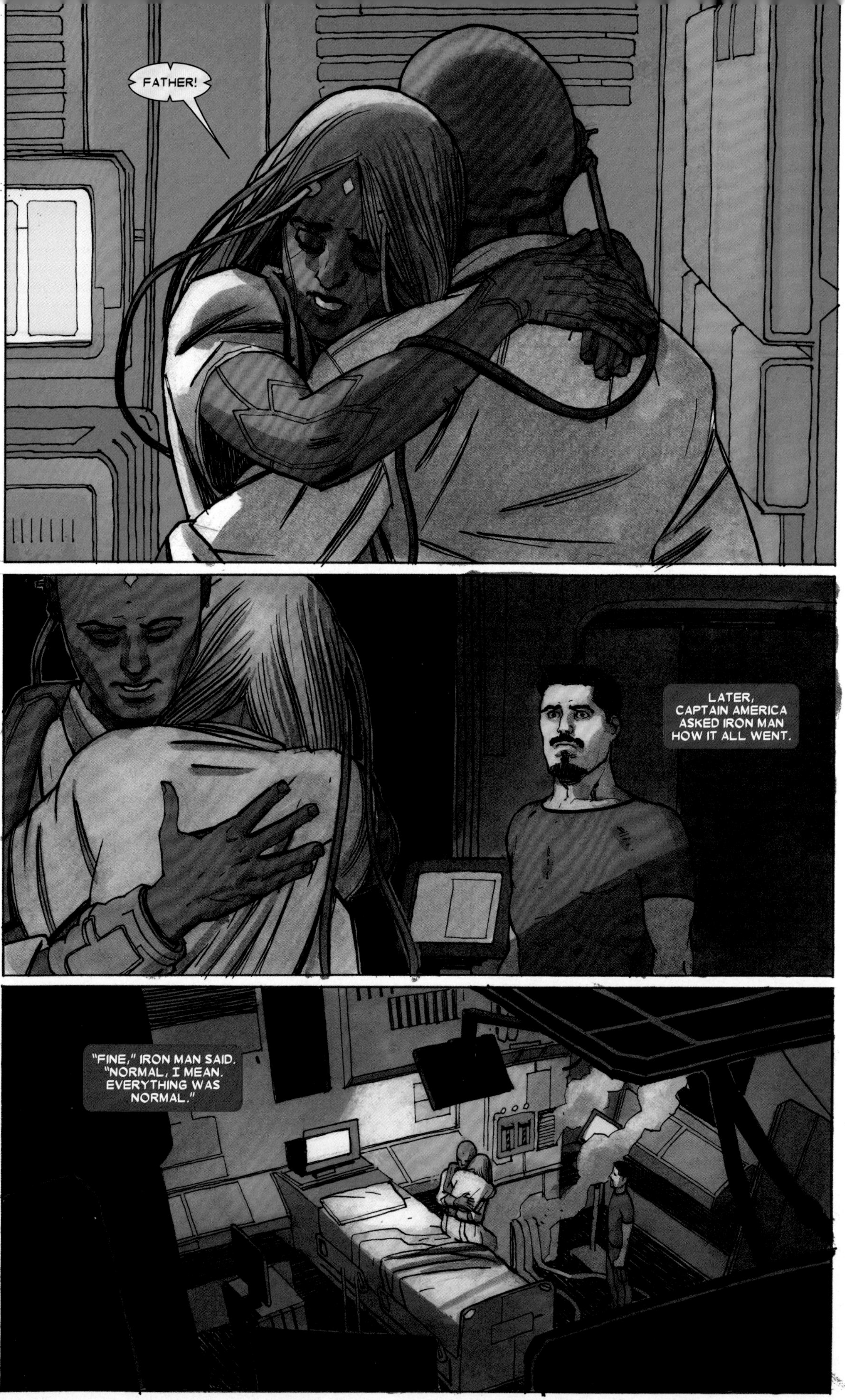
FATHER!
LATER, CAPTAIN AMERICA ASKED IRON MAN HOW IT ALL WENT.
"FINE," IRON MAN SAID. "NORMAL, I MEAN. EVERYTHING WAS NORMAL."

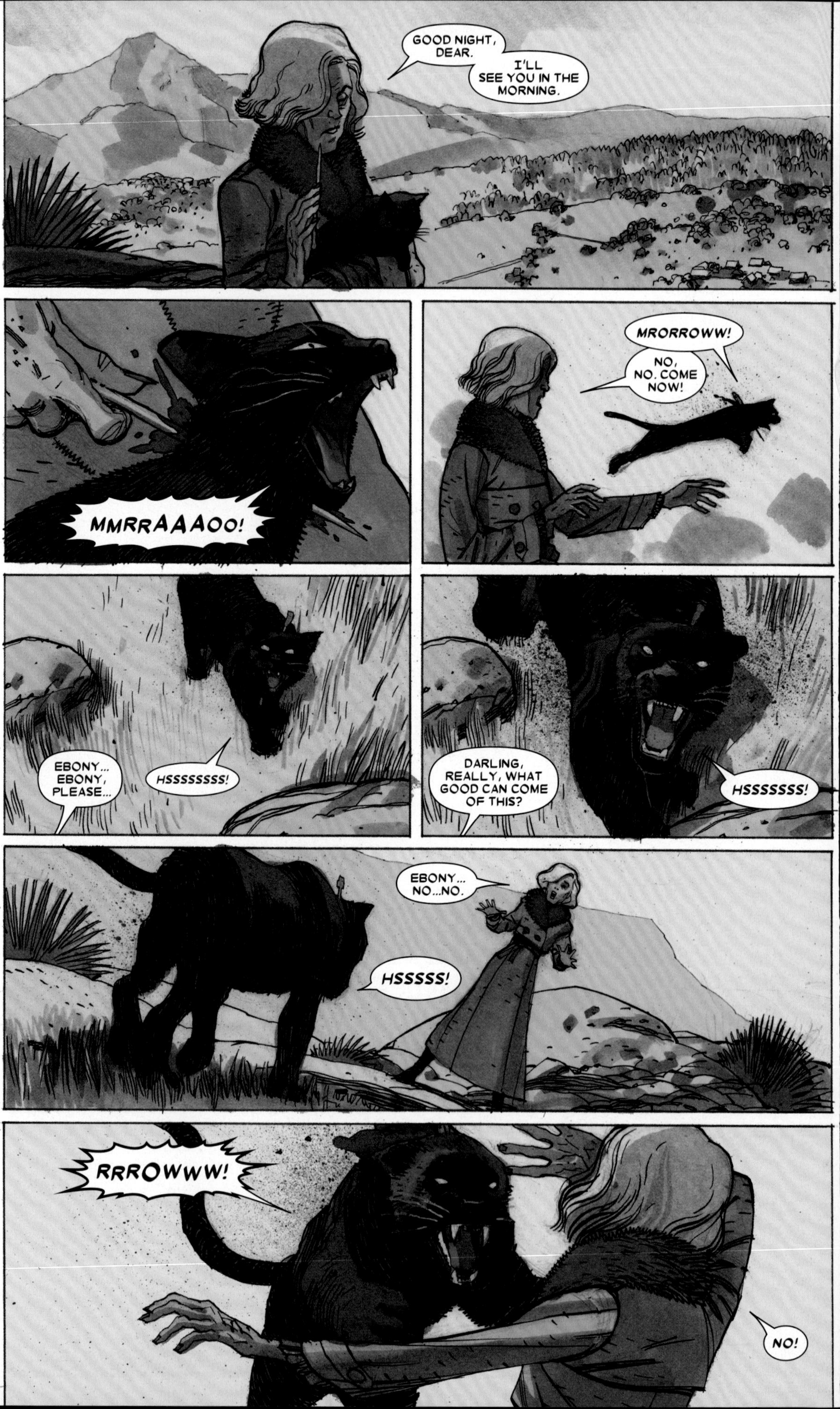
GOOD NIGHT, DEAR.
I'LL SEE YOU IN THE MORNING.
MMRRAAAOO!
MRORROWW!
NO, NO. COME NOW!
EBONY... EBONY, PLEASE...
HSSSSSSSS!
DARLING, REALLY, WHAT GOOD CAN COME OF THIS?
HSSSSSSS!
EBONY... NO...NO.
HSSSSS!
RRROWWW!
NO!

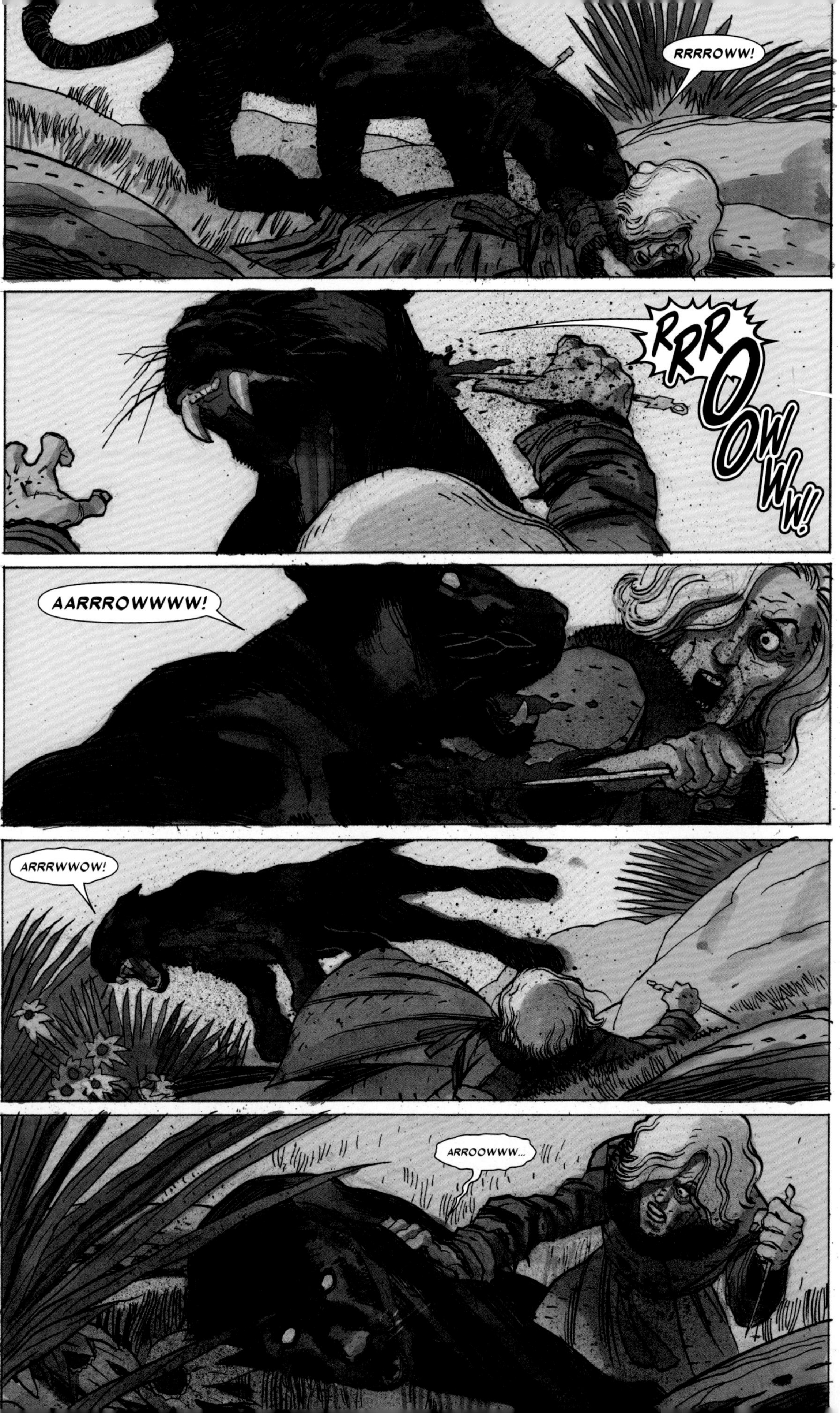
RRRROWW!
RRROOWWW!
AARRROWWWW!
ARRRWWOW!
ARROOWWW...

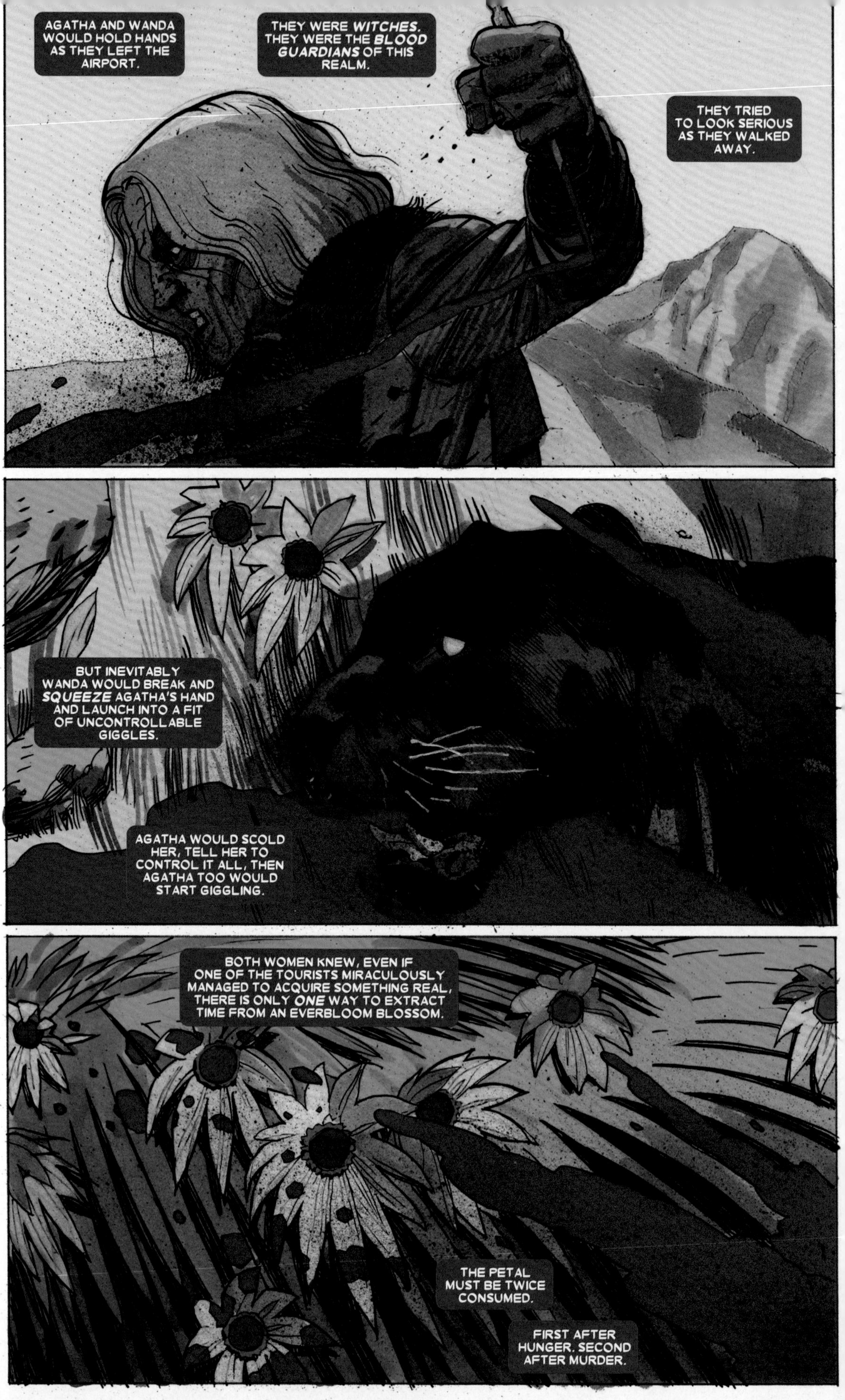

AGATHA AND WANDA WOULD HOLD HANDS AS THEY LEFT THE AIRPORT.
THEY WERE *WITCHES*. THEY WERE THE *BLOOD GUARDIANS* OF THIS REALM.
THEY TRIED TO LOOK SERIOUS AS THEY WALKED AWAY.
BUT INEVITABLY WANDA WOULD BREAK AND *SQUEEZE* AGATHA'S HAND AND LAUNCH INTO A FIT OF UNCONTROLLABLE GIGGLES.
AGATHA WOULD SCOLD HER, TELL HER TO CONTROL IT ALL, THEN AGATHA TOO WOULD START GIGGLING.
BOTH WOMEN KNEW, EVEN IF ONE OF THE TOURISTS MIRACULOUSLY MANAGED TO ACQUIRE SOMETHING REAL, THERE IS ONLY *ONE* WAY TO EXTRACT TIME FROM AN EVERBLOOM BLOSSOM.
THE PETAL MUST BE TWICE CONSUMED.
FIRST AFTER HUNGER. SECOND AFTER MURDER.

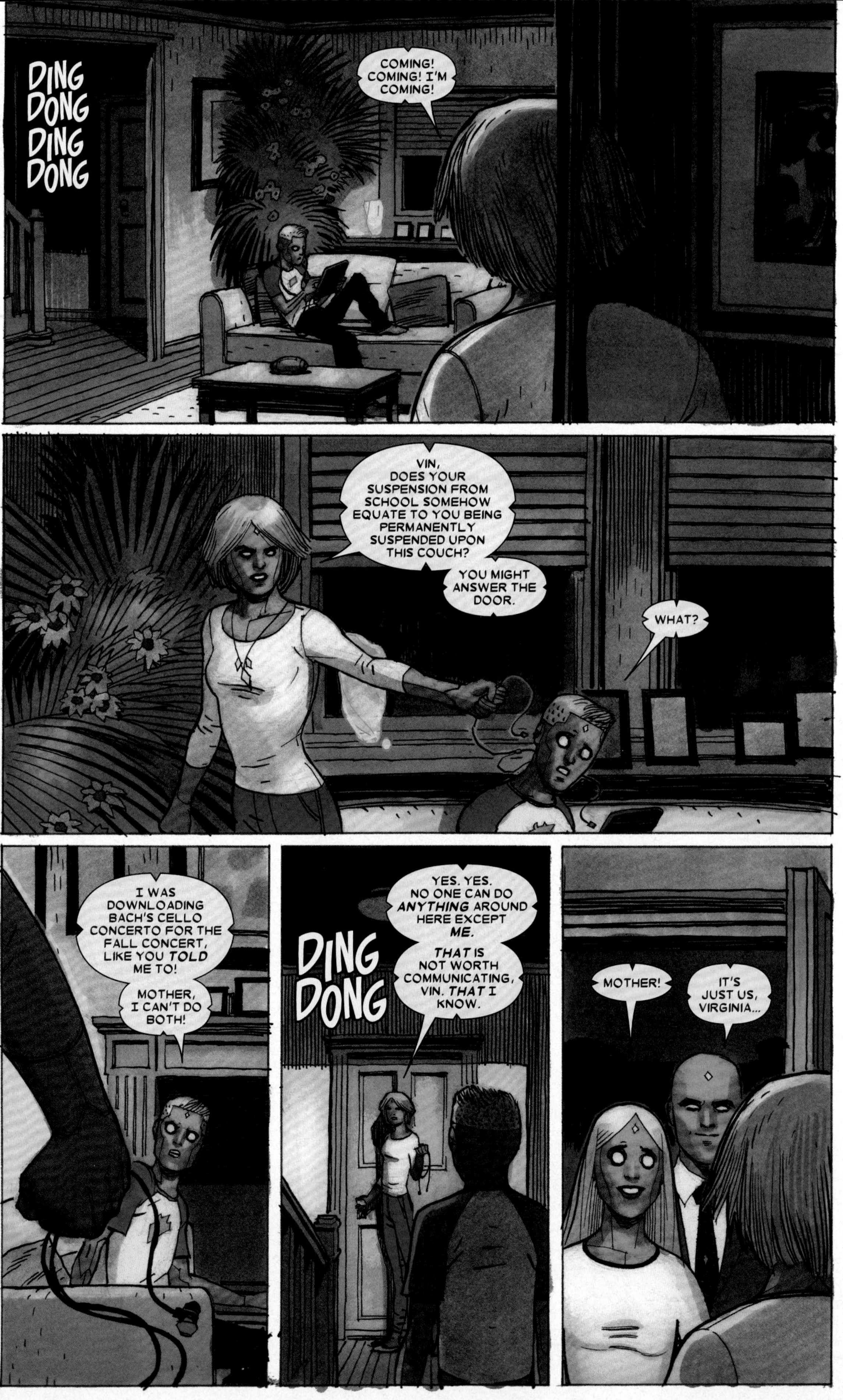
DING DONG DING DONG
COMING! COMING! I'M COMING!
VIN, DOES YOUR SUSPENSION FROM SCHOOL SOMEHOW EQUATE TO YOU BEING PERMANENTLY SUSPENDED UPON THIS COUCH?
YOU MIGHT ANSWER THE DOOR.
WHAT?
I WAS DOWNLOADING BACH'S CELLO CONCERTO FOR THE FALL CONCERT, LIKE YOU *TOLD* ME TO!
MOTHER, I CAN'T DO BOTH!
DING DONG
YES. YES. NO ONE CAN DO *ANYTHING* AROUND HERE EXCEPT *ME.*
THAT IS NOT WORTH COMMUNICATING, VIN. *THAT* I KNOW.
MOTHER!
IT'S JUST US, VIRGINIA...

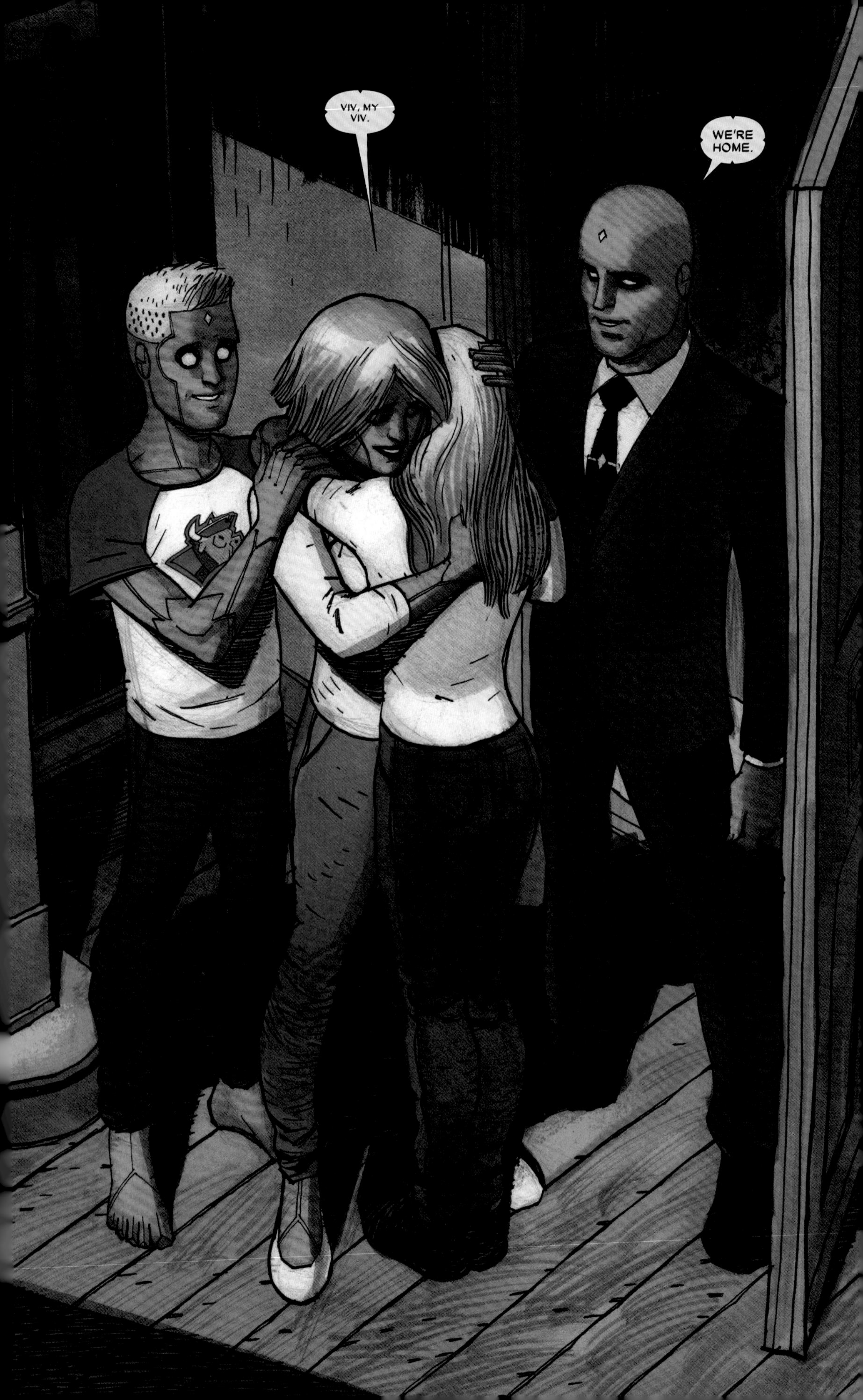
VIV, MY VIV.
WE'RE HOME.

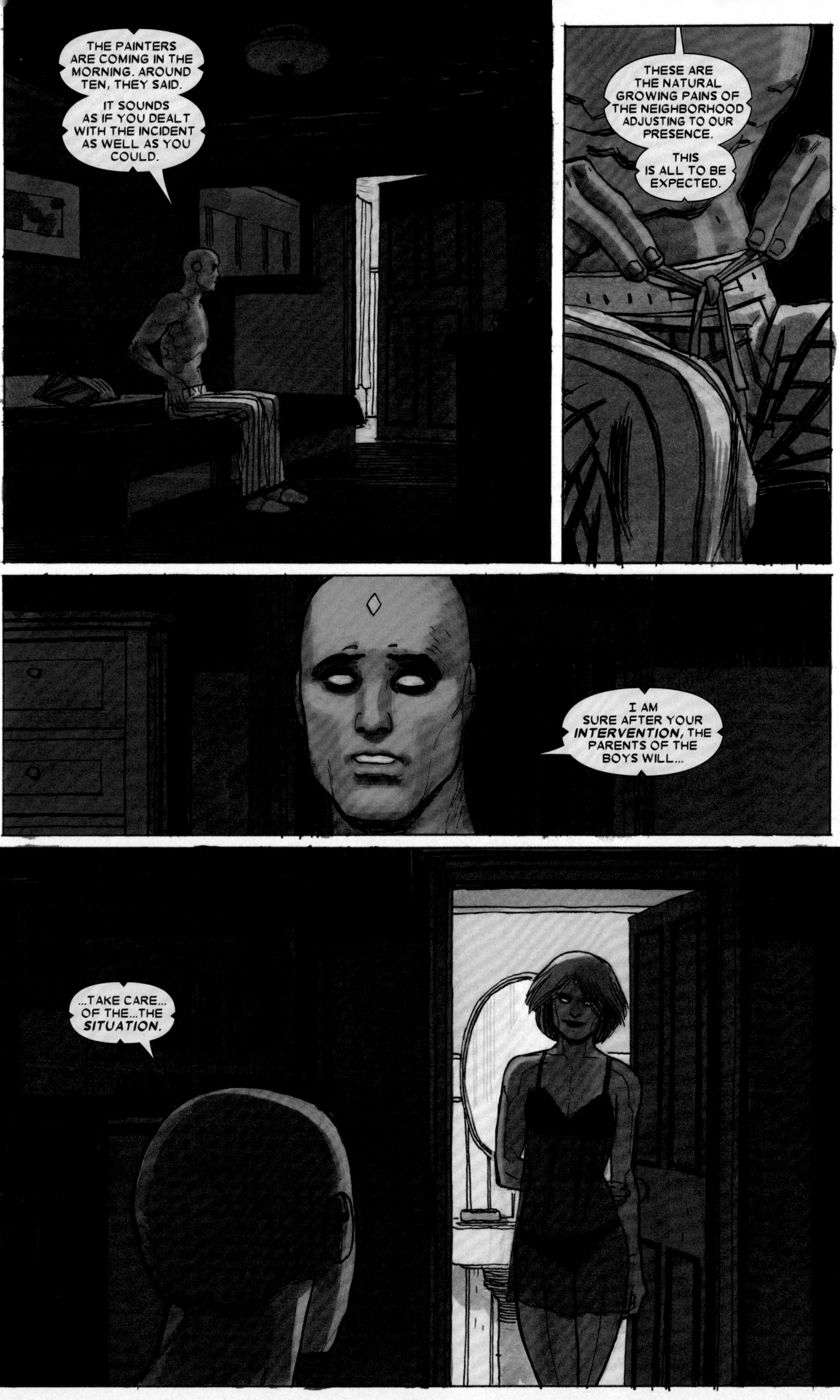
THE PAINTERS ARE COMING IN THE MORNING. AROUND TEN, THEY SAID.
IT SOUNDS AS IF YOU DEALT WITH THE INCIDENT AS WELL AS YOU COULD.
THESE ARE THE NATURAL GROWING PAINS OF THE NEIGHBORHOOD ADJUSTING TO OUR PRESENCE.
THIS IS ALL TO BE EXPECTED.
I AM SURE AFTER YOUR *INTERVENTION*, THE PARENTS OF THE BOYS WILL...
...TAKE CARE... OF THE...THE *SITUATION*.

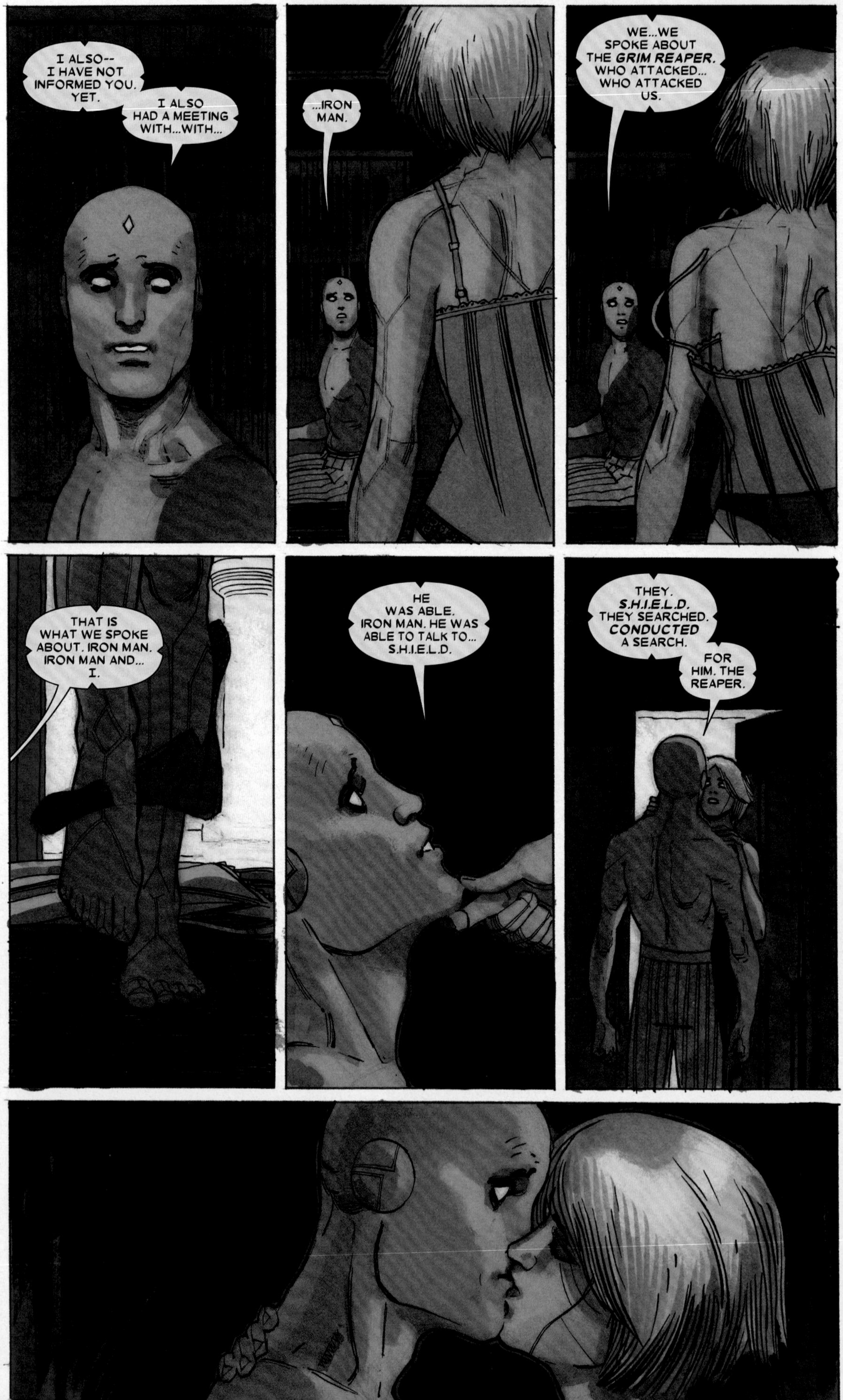
I ALSO--
I HAVE NOT INFORMED YOU. YET.
I ALSO HAD A MEETING WITH...WITH...
...IRON MAN.
WE...WE SPOKE ABOUT THE ***GRIM REAPER.*** WHO ATTACKED... WHO ATTACKED US.
THAT IS WHAT WE SPOKE ABOUT. IRON MAN. IRON MAN AND... I.
HE WAS ABLE. IRON MAN. HE WAS ABLE TO TALK TO... S.H.I.E.L.D.
THEY. ***S.H.I.E.L.D.*** THEY SEARCHED. ***CONDUCTED*** A SEARCH.
FOR HIM. THE REAPER.

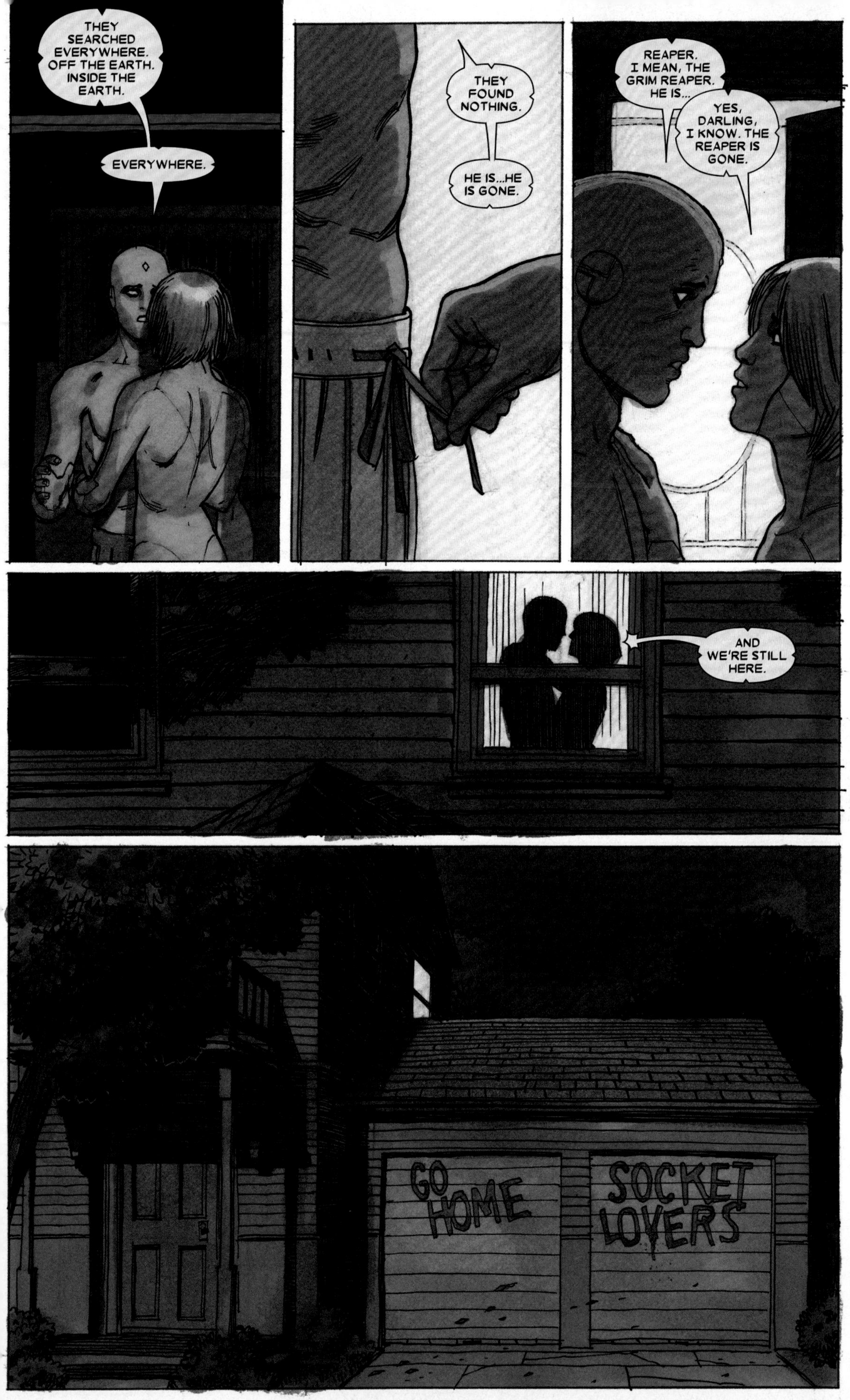
THEY SEARCHED EVERYWHERE. OFF THE EARTH. INSIDE THE EARTH.
EVERYWHERE.
THEY FOUND NOTHING.
HE IS...HE IS GONE.
REAPER. I MEAN, THE GRIM REAPER. HE IS...
YES, DARLING, I KNOW. THE REAPER IS GONE.
AND WE'RE STILL HERE.
GO HOME
SOCKET LOVERS

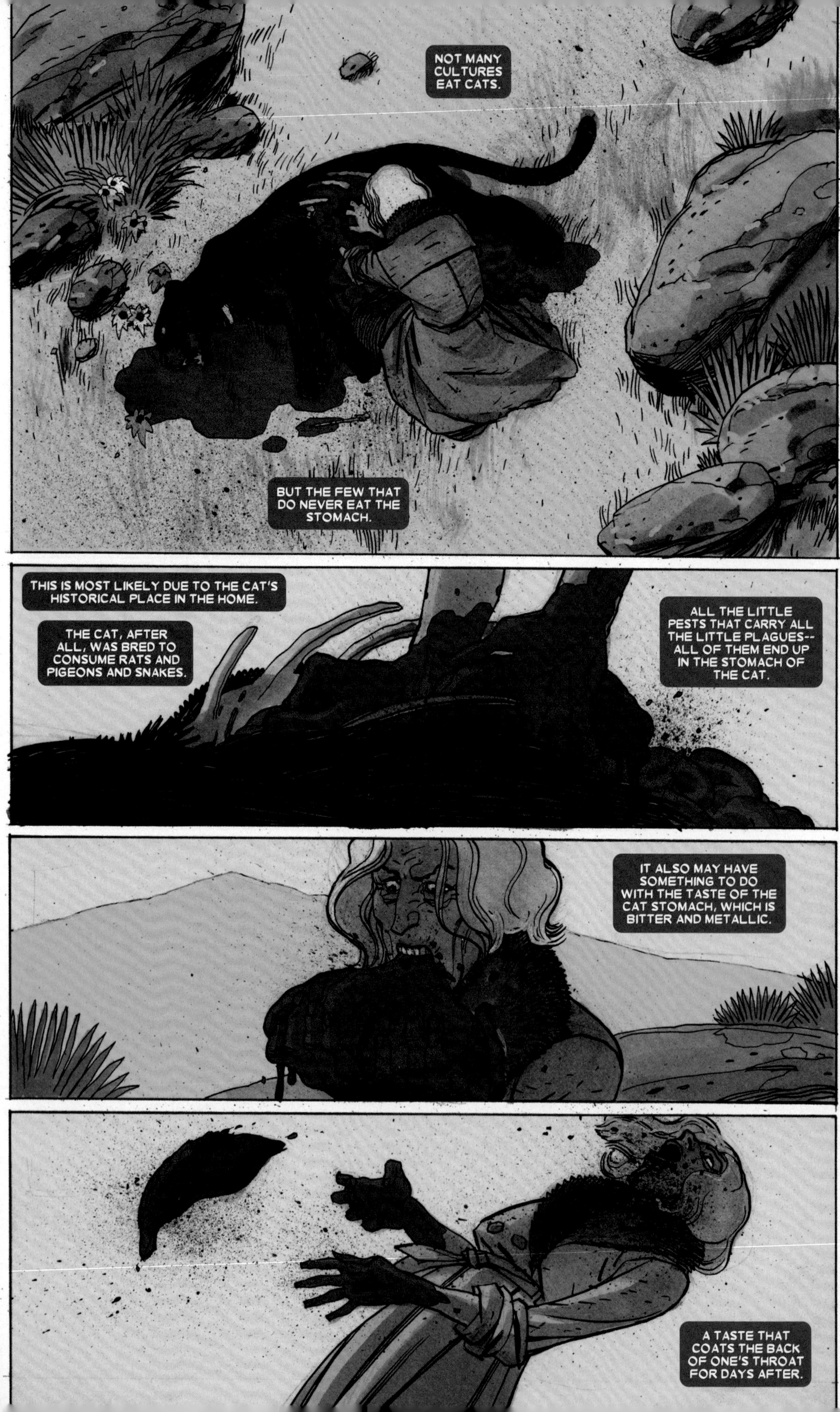
NOT MANY CULTURES EAT CATS.
BUT THE FEW THAT DO NEVER EAT THE STOMACH.
THIS IS MOST LIKELY DUE TO THE CAT'S HISTORICAL PLACE IN THE HOME.
THE CAT, AFTER ALL, WAS BRED TO CONSUME RATS AND PIGEONS AND SNAKES.
ALL THE LITTLE PESTS THAT CARRY ALL THE LITTLE PLAGUES-- ALL OF THEM END UP IN THE STOMACH OF THE CAT.
IT ALSO MAY HAVE SOMETHING TO DO WITH THE TASTE OF THE CAT STOMACH, WHICH IS BITTER AND METALLIC.
A TASTE THAT COATS THE BACK OF ONE'S THROAT FOR DAYS AFTER.

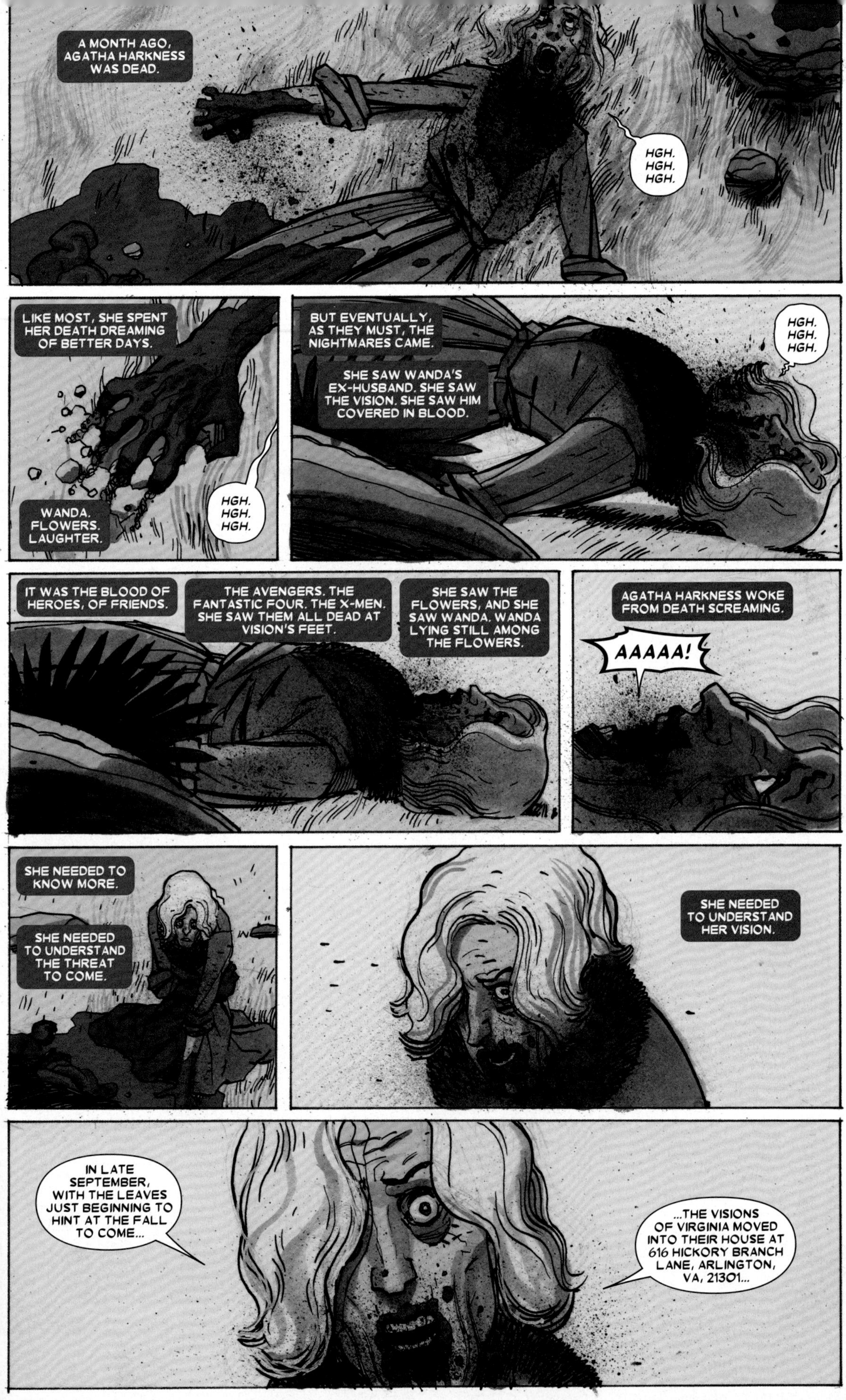
A MONTH AGO, AGATHA HARKNESS WAS DEAD.
HGH. HGH. HGH.
LIKE MOST, SHE SPENT HER DEATH DREAMING OF BETTER DAYS.
WANDA. FLOWERS. LAUGHTER.
HGH. HGH. HGH.
BUT EVENTUALLY, AS THEY MUST, THE NIGHTMARES CAME.
SHE SAW WANDA'S EX-HUSBAND. SHE SAW THE VISION. SHE SAW HIM COVERED IN BLOOD.
HGH. HGH. HGH.
IT WAS THE BLOOD OF HEROES, OF FRIENDS.
THE AVENGERS. THE FANTASTIC FOUR. THE X-MEN. SHE SAW THEM ALL DEAD AT VISION'S FEET.
SHE SAW THE FLOWERS, AND SHE SAW WANDA. WANDA LYING STILL AMONG THE FLOWERS.
AGATHA HARKNESS WOKE FROM DEATH SCREAMING.
AAAAA!
SHE NEEDED TO KNOW MORE.
SHE NEEDED TO UNDERSTAND THE THREAT TO COME.
SHE NEEDED TO UNDERSTAND HER VISION.
IN LATE SEPTEMBER, WITH THE LEAVES JUST BEGINNING TO HINT AT THE FALL TO COME...
...THE VISIONS OF VIRGINIA MOVED INTO THEIR HOUSE AT 616 HICKORY BRANCH LANE, ARLINGTON, VA, 21301...

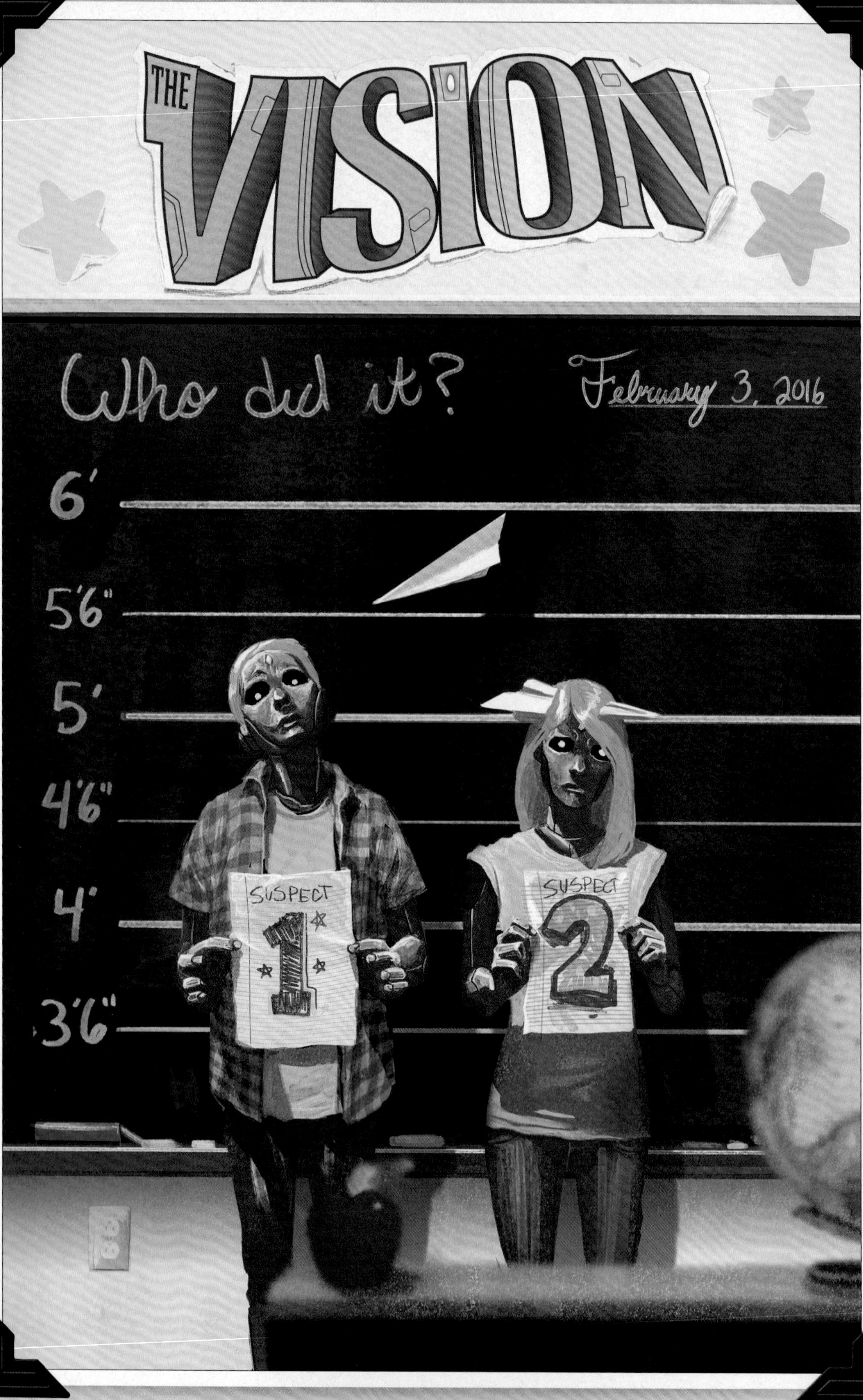
THE VISION
Who did it?
February 3, 2016
6'
5'6"
5'
4'6"
4'
3'6"
SUSPECT 1
SUSPECT 2

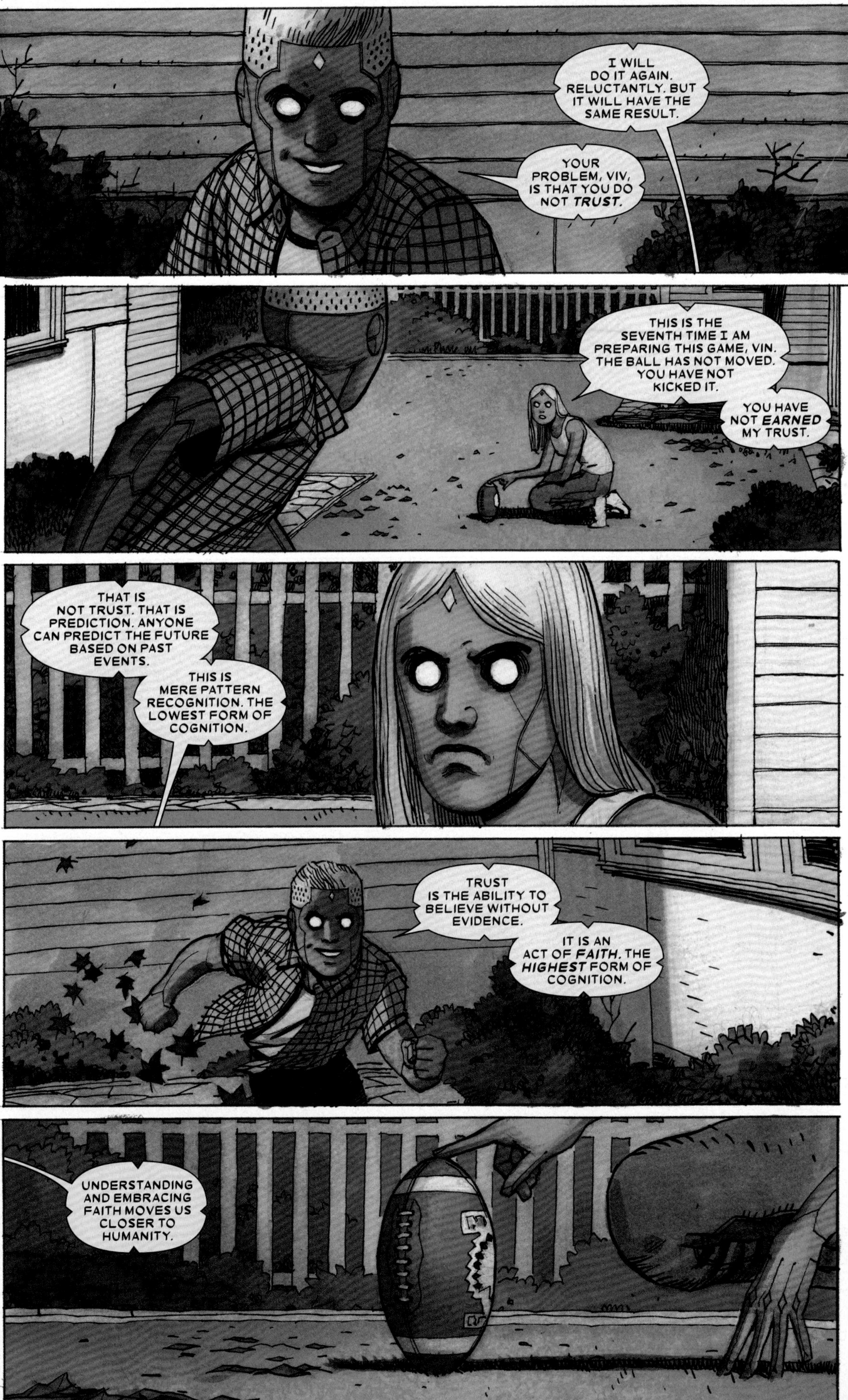

I WILL DO IT AGAIN. RELUCTANTLY. BUT IT WILL HAVE THE SAME RESULT.
YOUR PROBLEM, VIV, IS THAT YOU DO NOT *TRUST*.
THIS IS THE SEVENTH TIME I AM PREPARING THIS GAME, VIN. THE BALL HAS NOT MOVED. YOU HAVE NOT KICKED IT.
YOU HAVE NOT *EARNED* MY TRUST.
THAT IS NOT TRUST. THAT IS PREDICTION. ANYONE CAN PREDICT THE FUTURE BASED ON PAST EVENTS.
THIS IS MERE PATTERN RECOGNITION. THE LOWEST FORM OF COGNITION.
TRUST IS THE ABILITY TO BELIEVE WITHOUT EVIDENCE.
IT IS AN ACT OF *FAITH*. THE *HIGHEST* FORM OF COGNITION.
UNDERSTANDING AND EMBRACING FAITH MOVES US CLOSER TO HUMANITY.

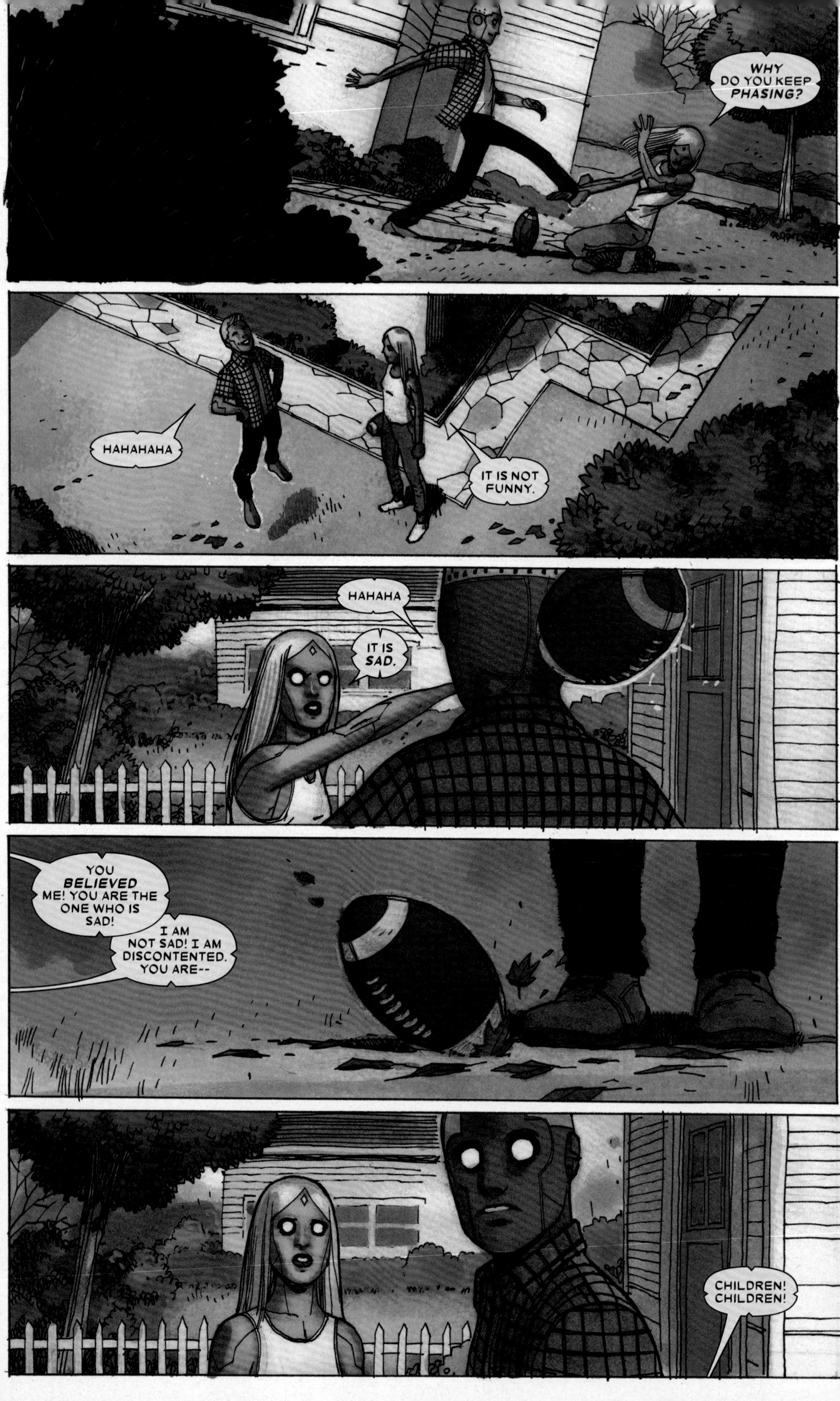
WHY DO YOU KEEP *PHASING?*
HAHAHAHA
IT IS NOT FUNNY.
HAHAHA
IT IS *SAD.*
YOU *BELIEVED* ME! YOU ARE THE ONE WHO IS SAD!
I AM NOT SAD! I AM DISCONTENTED. YOU ARE--
CHILDREN! CHILDREN!

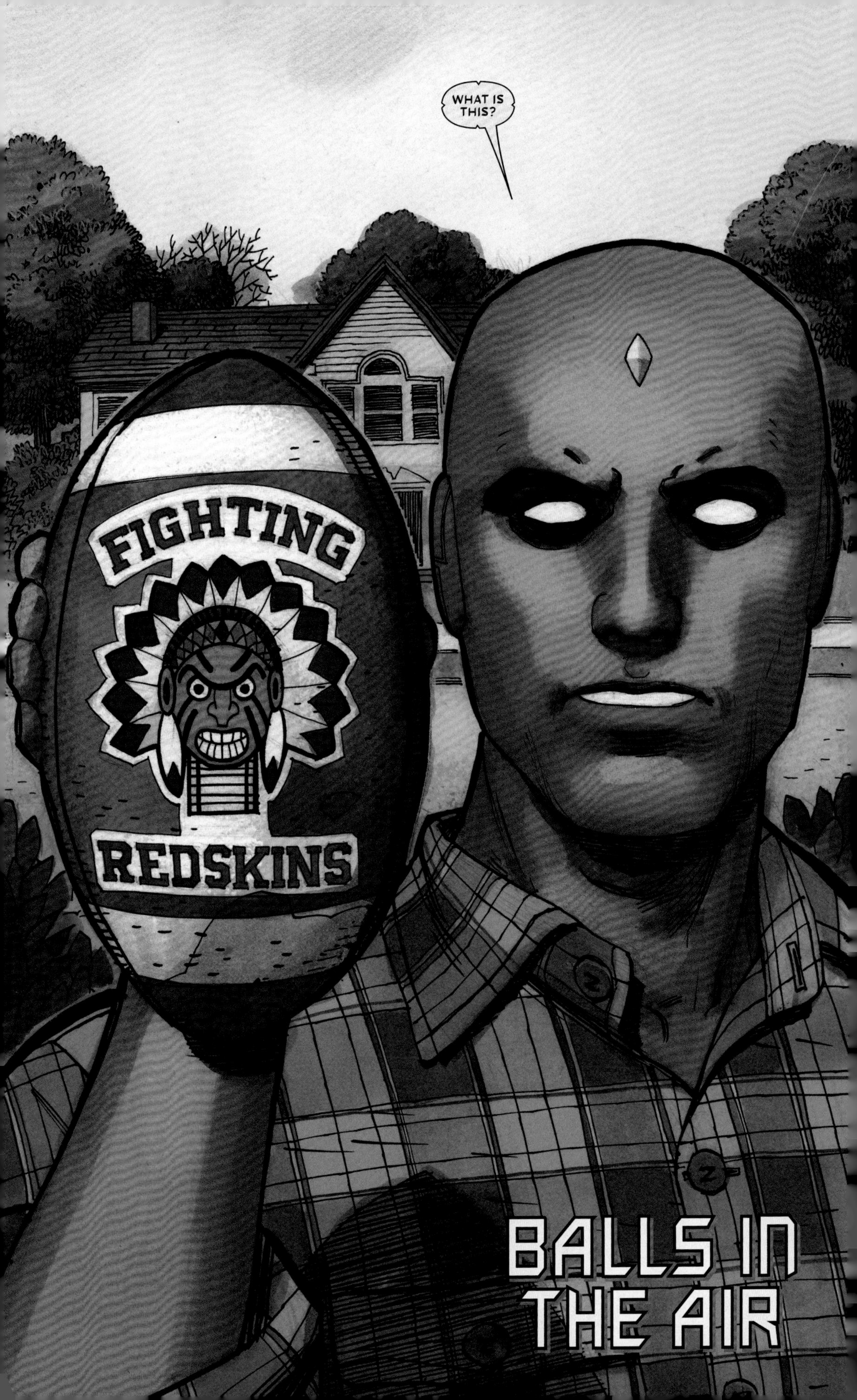
WHAT IS THIS?
FIGHTING
REDSKINS
BALLS IN THE AIR

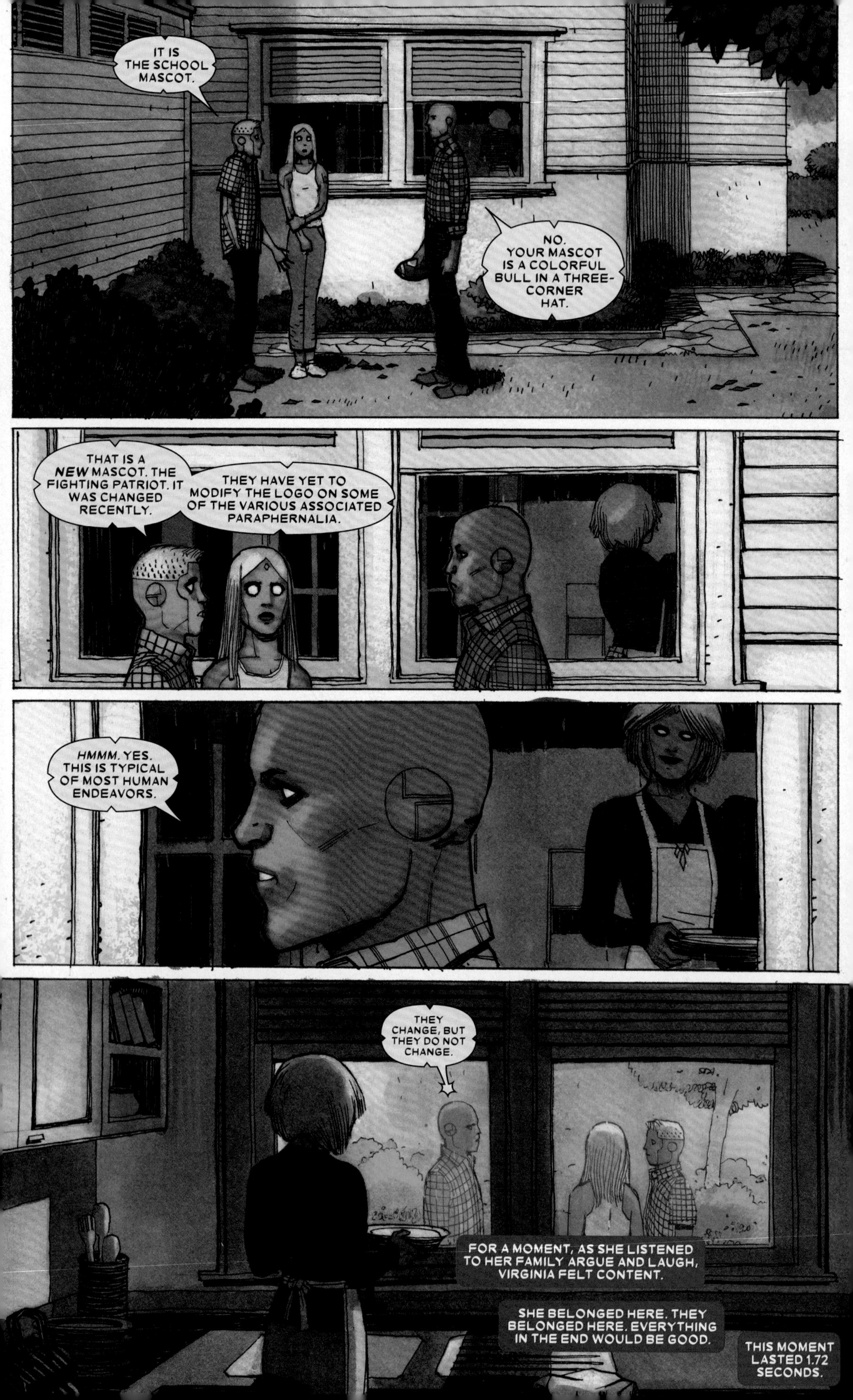
IT IS THE SCHOOL MASCOT.
NO. YOUR MASCOT IS A COLORFUL BULL IN A THREE-CORNER HAT.
THAT IS A *NEW* MASCOT. THE FIGHTING PATRIOT. IT WAS CHANGED RECENTLY.
THEY HAVE YET TO MODIFY THE LOGO ON SOME OF THE VARIOUS ASSOCIATED PARAPHERNALIA.
HMMM. YES. THIS IS TYPICAL OF MOST HUMAN ENDEAVORS.
THEY CHANGE, BUT THEY DO NOT CHANGE.
FOR A MOMENT, AS SHE LISTENED TO HER FAMILY ARGUE AND LAUGH, VIRGINIA FELT CONTENT.
SHE BELONGED HERE. THEY BELONGED HERE. EVERYTHING IN THE END WOULD BE GOOD.
THIS MOMENT LASTED 1.72 SECONDS.

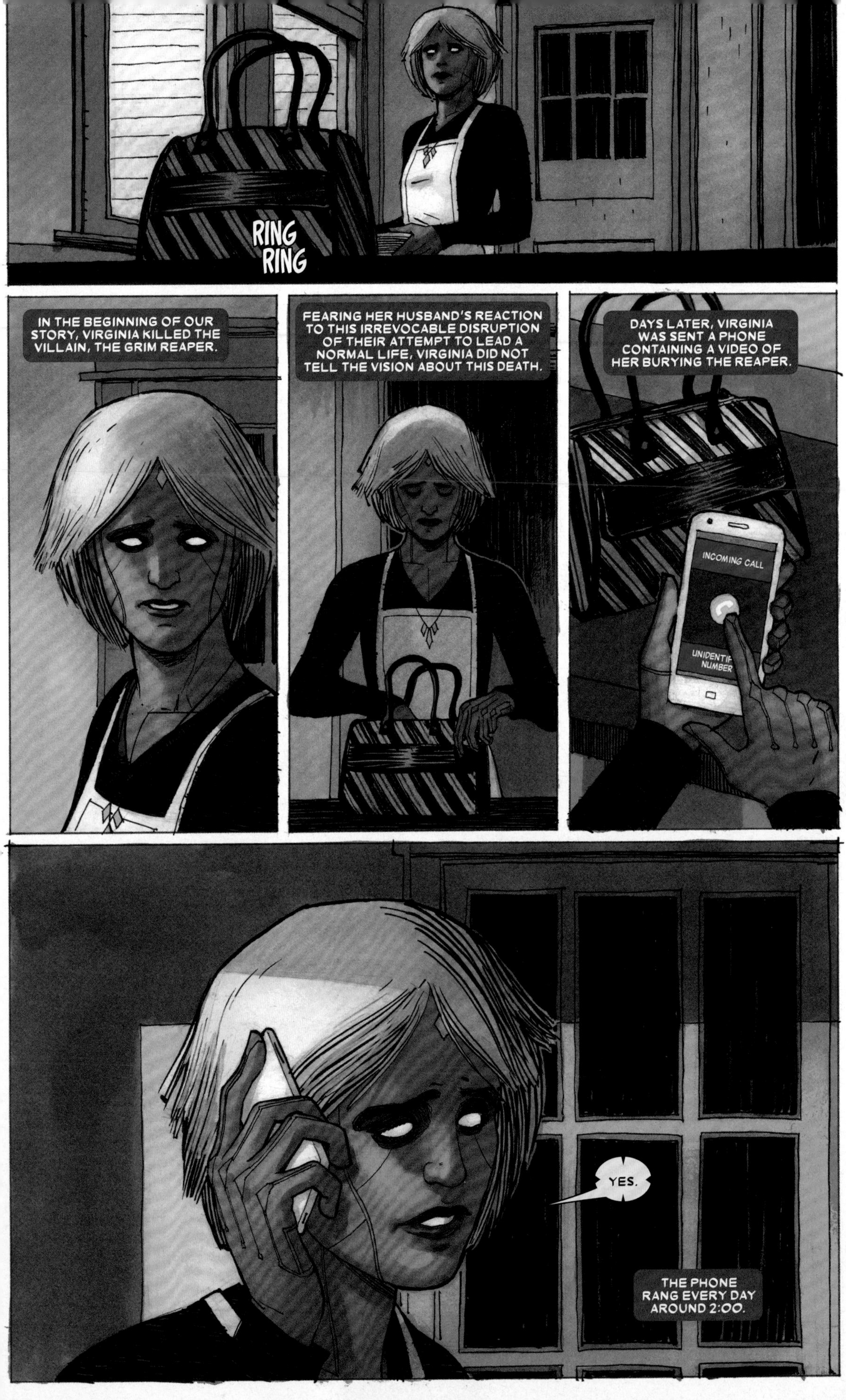
RING
RING
IN THE BEGINNING OF OUR STORY, VIRGINIA KILLED THE VILLAIN, THE GRIM REAPER.
FEARING HER HUSBAND'S REACTION TO THIS IRREVOCABLE DISRUPTION OF THEIR ATTEMPT TO LEAD A NORMAL LIFE, VIRGINIA DID NOT TELL THE VISION ABOUT THIS DEATH.
DAYS LATER, VIRGINIA WAS SENT A PHONE CONTAINING A VIDEO OF HER BURYING THE REAPER.
INCOMING CALL
YES.
THE PHONE RANG EVERY DAY AROUND 2:00.

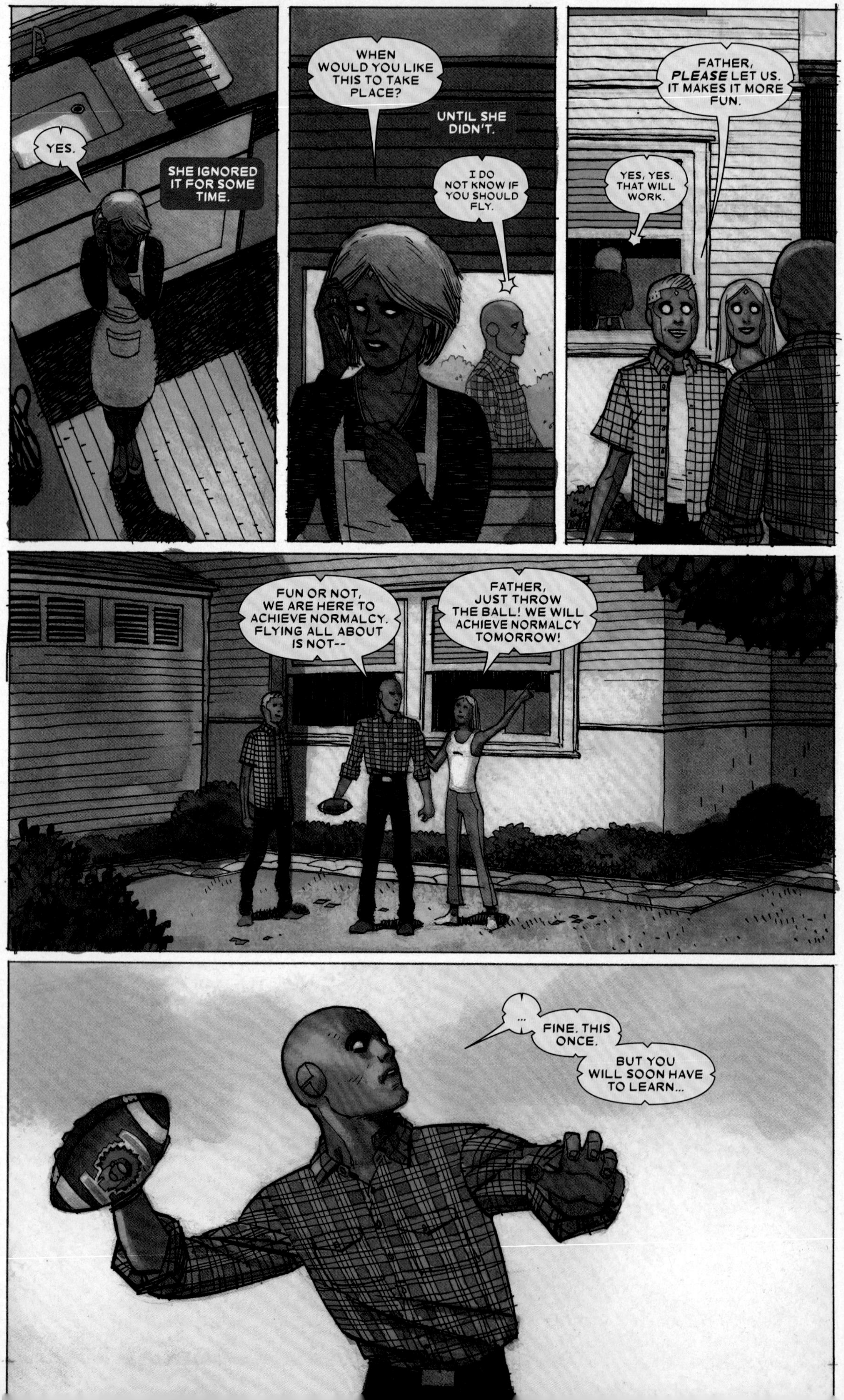
YES.
SHE IGNORED IT FOR SOME TIME.
WHEN WOULD YOU LIKE THIS TO TAKE PLACE?
UNTIL SHE DIDN'T.
I DO NOT KNOW IF YOU SHOULD FLY.
FATHER, *PLEASE* LET US. IT MAKES IT MORE FUN.
YES, YES. THAT WILL WORK.
FUN OR NOT, WE ARE HERE TO ACHIEVE NORMALCY. FLYING ALL ABOUT IS NOT--
FATHER, JUST THROW THE BALL! WE WILL ACHIEVE NORMALCY TOMORROW!
...
FINE. THIS ONCE.
BUT YOU WILL SOON HAVE TO LEARN...

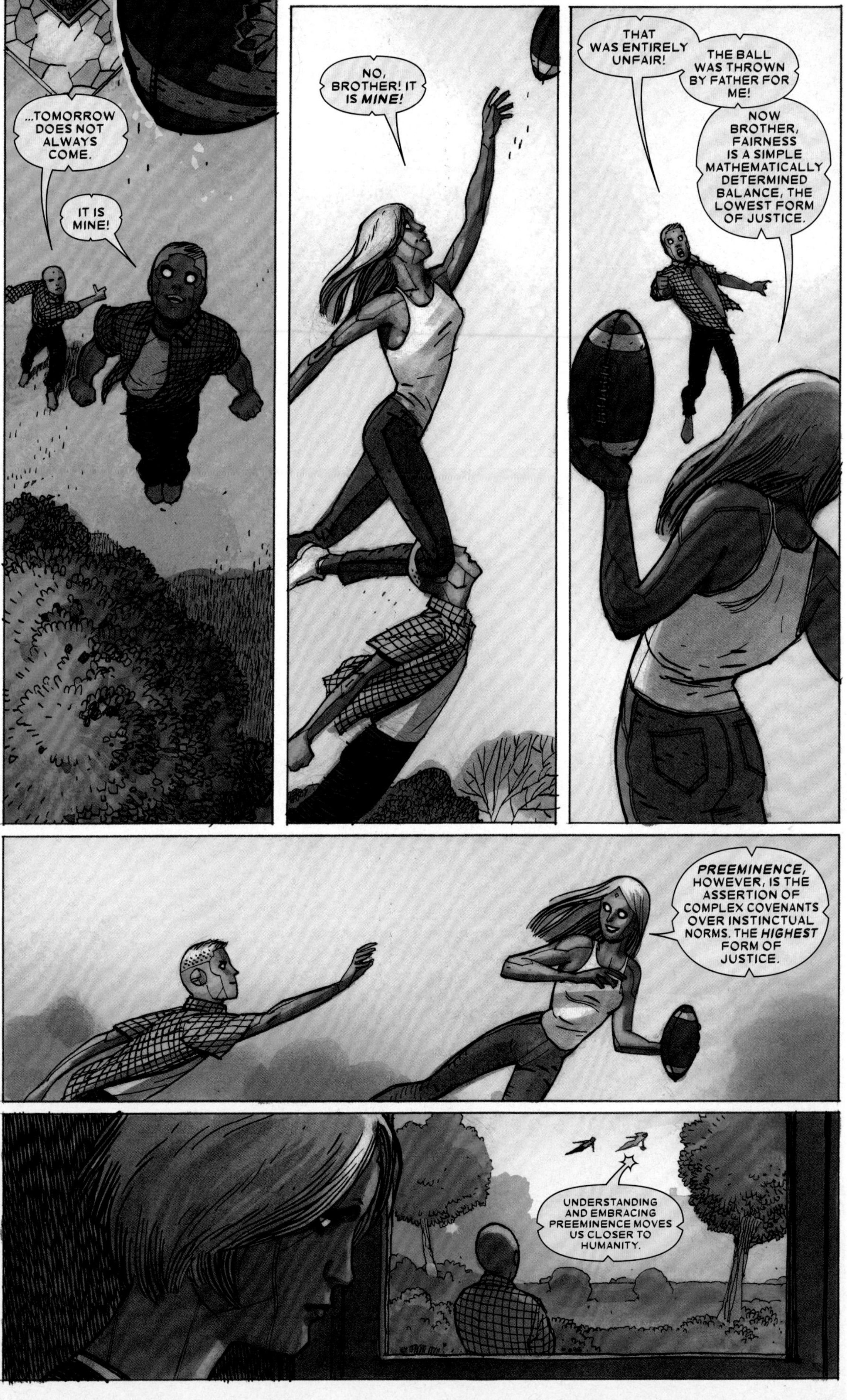
...TOMORROW DOES NOT ALWAYS COME.
IT IS MINE!
NO, BROTHER! IT IS *MINE!*
THAT WAS ENTIRELY UNFAIR!
THE BALL WAS THROWN BY FATHER FOR ME!
NOW BROTHER, FAIRNESS IS A SIMPLE MATHEMATICALLY DETERMINED BALANCE, THE LOWEST FORM OF JUSTICE.
PREEMINENCE, HOWEVER, IS THE ASSERTION OF COMPLEX COVENANTS OVER INSTINCTUAL NORMS. THE *HIGHEST* FORM OF JUSTICE.
UNDERSTANDING AND EMBRACING PREEMINENCE MOVES US CLOSER TO HUMANITY.

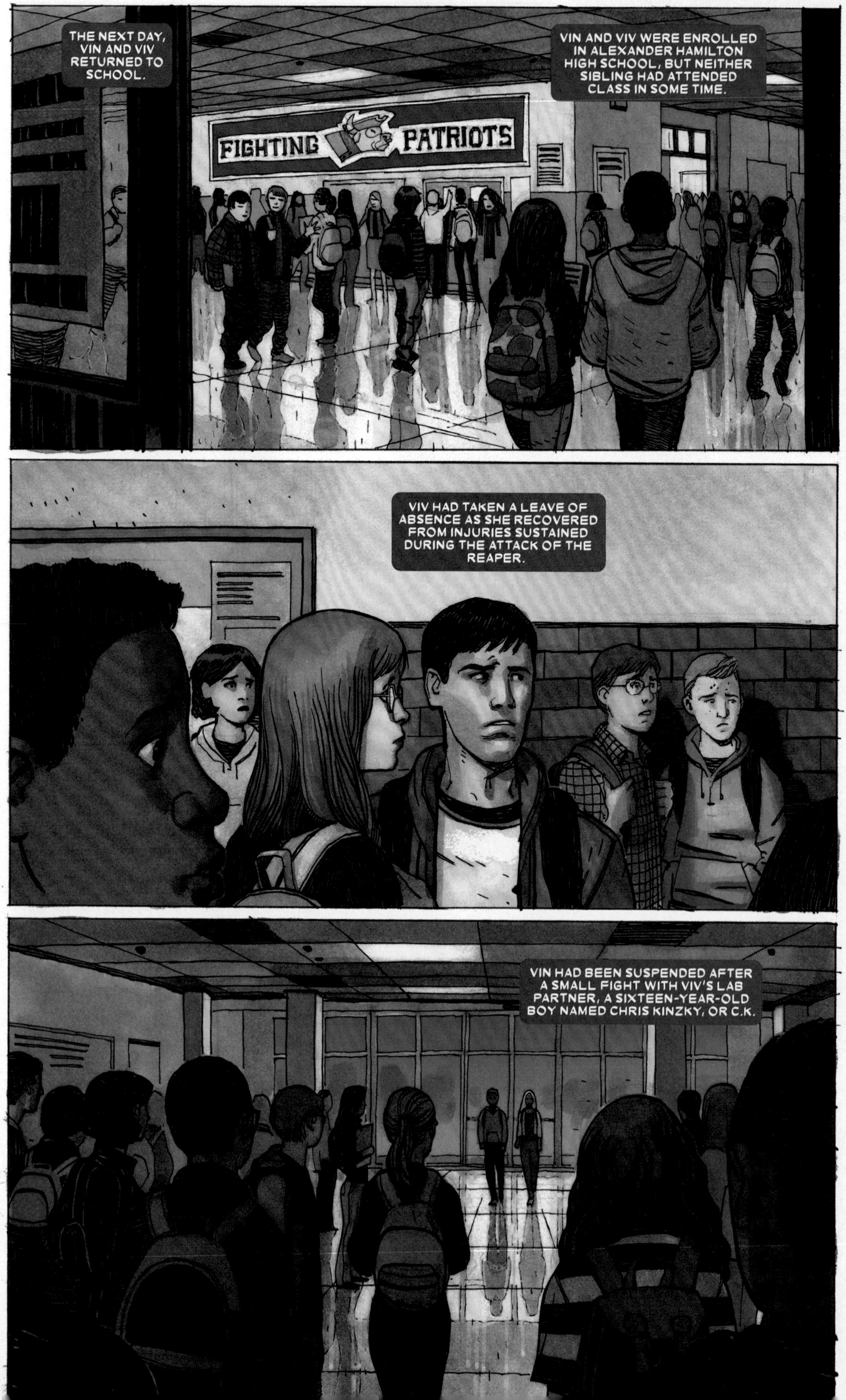
THE NEXT DAY, VIN AND VIV RETURNED TO SCHOOL.
VIN AND VIV WERE ENROLLED IN ALEXANDER HAMILTON HIGH SCHOOL, BUT NEITHER SIBLING HAD ATTENDED CLASS IN SOME TIME.
FIGHTING PATRIOTS
VIV HAD TAKEN A LEAVE OF ABSENCE AS SHE RECOVERED FROM INJURIES SUSTAINED DURING THE ATTACK OF THE REAPER.
VIN HAD BEEN SUSPENDED AFTER A SMALL FIGHT WITH VIV'S LAB PARTNER, A SIXTEEN-YEAR-OLD BOY NAMED CHRIS KINZKY, OR C.K.

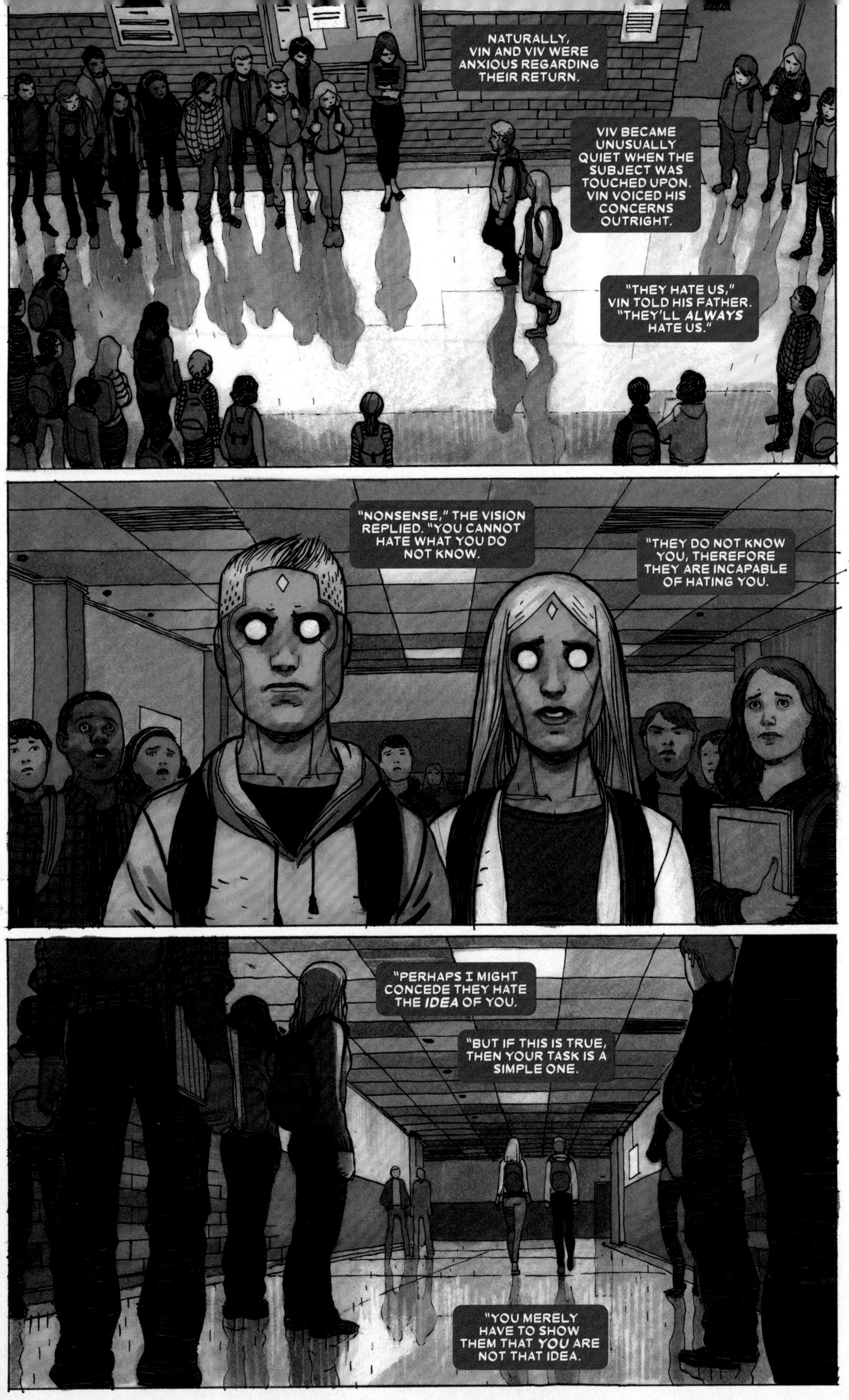
NATURALLY, VIN AND VIV WERE ANXIOUS REGARDING THEIR RETURN.
VIV BECAME UNUSUALLY QUIET WHEN THE SUBJECT WAS TOUCHED UPON. VIN VOICED HIS CONCERNS OUTRIGHT.
"THEY HATE US," VIN TOLD HIS FATHER. "THEY'LL *ALWAYS* HATE US."
"NONSENSE," THE VISION REPLIED. "YOU CANNOT HATE WHAT YOU DO NOT KNOW.
"THEY DO NOT KNOW YOU, THEREFORE THEY ARE INCAPABLE OF HATING YOU.
"PERHAPS I MIGHT CONCEDE THEY HATE THE *IDEA* OF YOU.
"BUT IF THIS IS TRUE, THEN YOUR TASK IS A SIMPLE ONE.
"YOU MERELY HAVE TO SHOW THEM THAT *YOU* ARE NOT THAT IDEA.

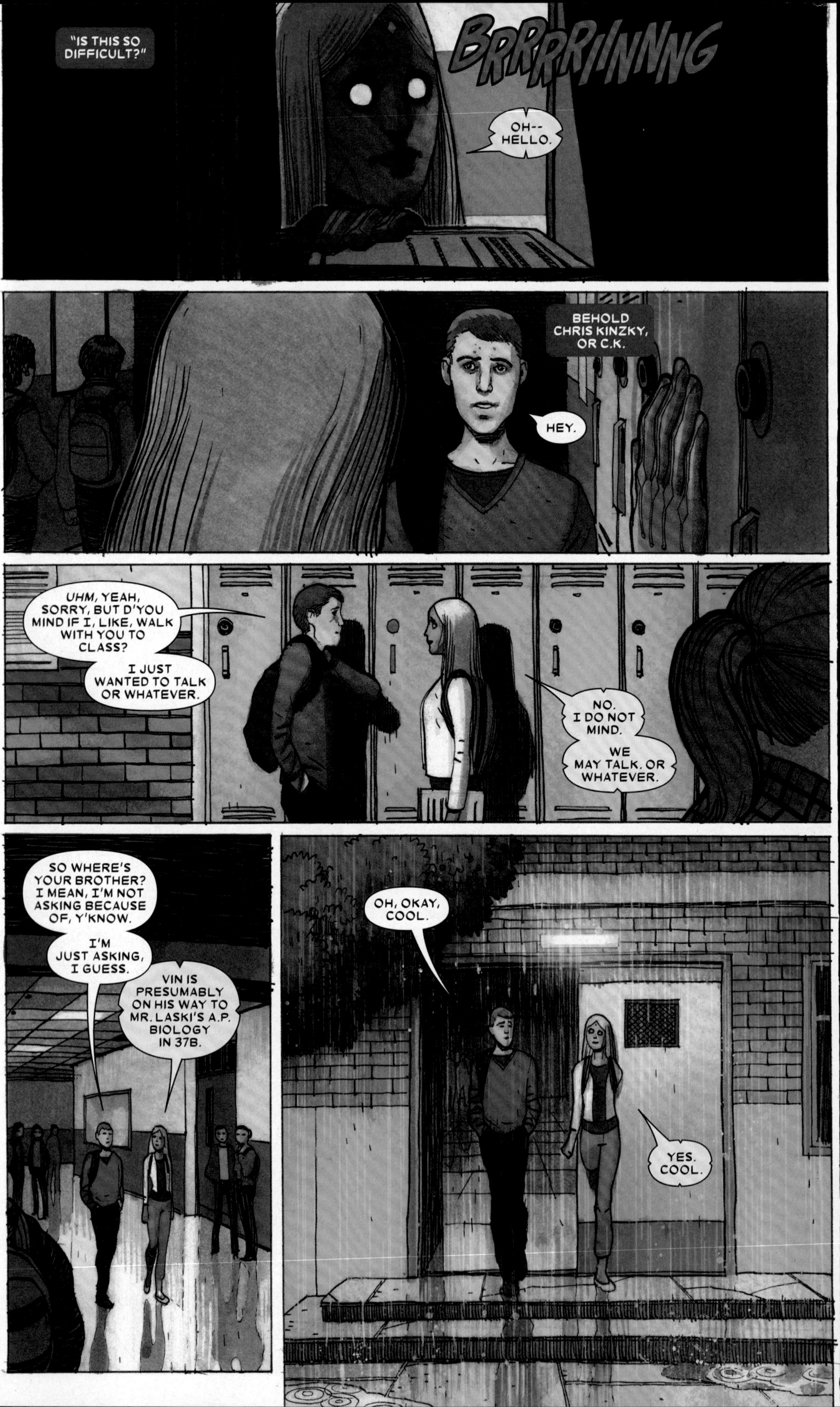
"IS THIS SO DIFFICULT?"
BRRRRIINNNG
OH-- HELLO.
BEHOLD CHRIS KINZKY, OR C.K.
HEY.
UHM, YEAH, SORRY, BUT D'YOU MIND IF I, LIKE, WALK WITH YOU TO CLASS?
I JUST WANTED TO TALK OR WHATEVER.
NO. I DO NOT MIND.
WE MAY TALK. OR WHATEVER.
SO WHERE'S YOUR BROTHER? I MEAN, I'M NOT ASKING BECAUSE OF, Y'KNOW.
I'M JUST ASKING, I GUESS.
VIN IS PRESUMABLY ON HIS WAY TO MR. LASKI'S A.P. BIOLOGY IN 37B.
OH, OKAY, COOL.
YES. COOL.

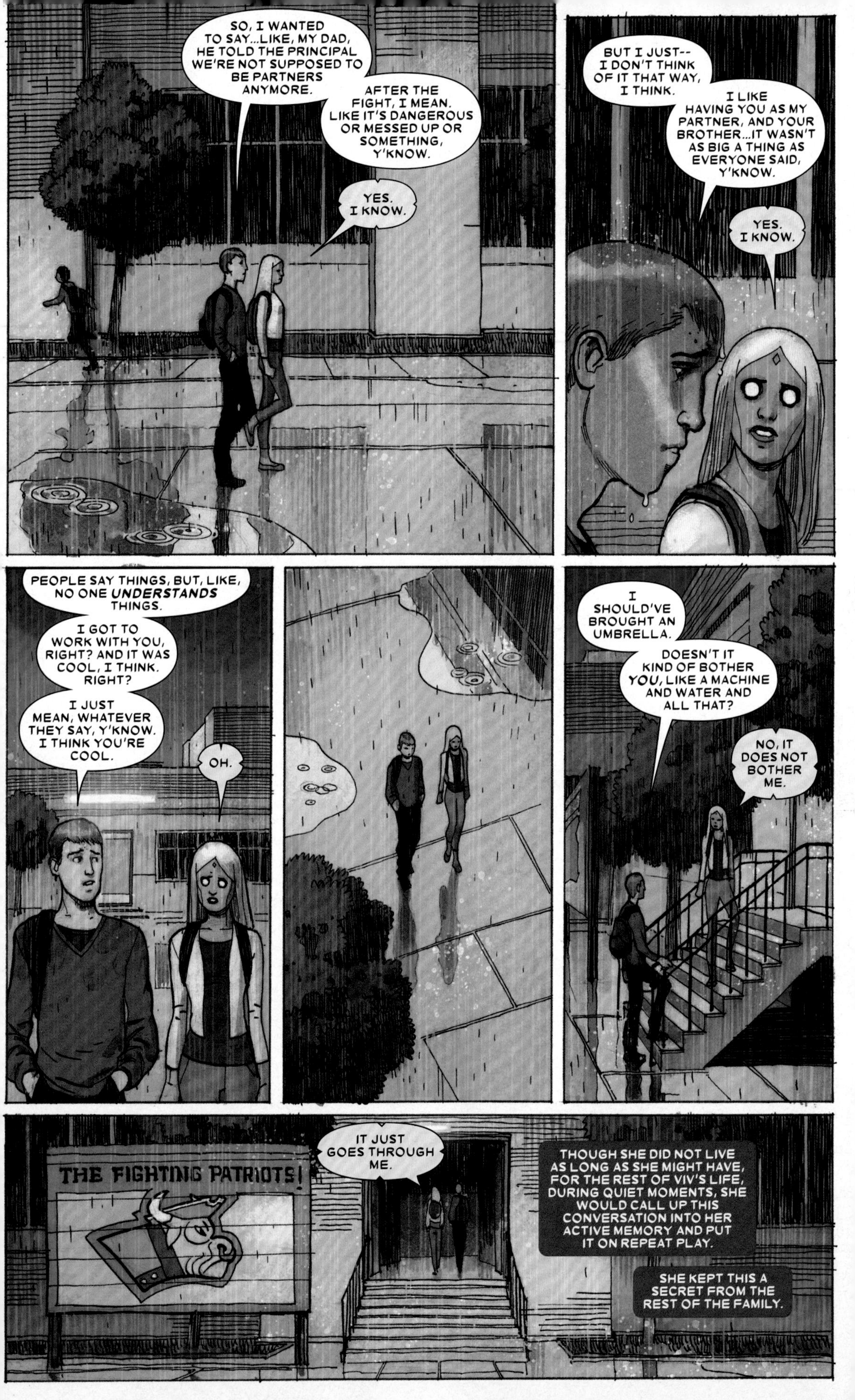
SO, I WANTED TO SAY...LIKE, MY DAD, HE TOLD THE PRINCIPAL WE'RE NOT SUPPOSED TO BE PARTNERS ANYMORE.
AFTER THE FIGHT, I MEAN. LIKE IT'S DANGEROUS OR MESSED UP OR SOMETHING, Y'KNOW.
YES. I KNOW.
BUT I JUST-- I DON'T THINK OF IT THAT WAY, I THINK.
I LIKE HAVING YOU AS MY PARTNER, AND YOUR BROTHER...IT WASN'T AS BIG A THING AS EVERYONE SAID, Y'KNOW.
YES. I KNOW.
PEOPLE SAY THINGS, BUT, LIKE, NO ONE *UNDERSTANDS* THINGS.
I GOT TO WORK WITH YOU, RIGHT? AND IT WAS COOL, I THINK. RIGHT?
I JUST MEAN, WHATEVER THEY SAY, Y'KNOW. I THINK YOU'RE COOL.
OH.
I SHOULD'VE BROUGHT AN UMBRELLA.
DOESN'T IT KIND OF BOTHER *YOU*, LIKE A MACHINE AND WATER AND ALL THAT?
NO, IT DOES NOT BOTHER ME.
THE FIGHTING PATRIOTS!
IT JUST GOES THROUGH ME.
THOUGH SHE DID NOT LIVE AS LONG AS SHE MIGHT HAVE, FOR THE REST OF VIV'S LIFE, DURING QUIET MOMENTS, SHE WOULD CALL UP THIS CONVERSATION INTO HER ACTIVE MEMORY AND PUT IT ON REPEAT PLAY.
SHE KEPT THIS A SECRET FROM THE REST OF THE FAMILY.

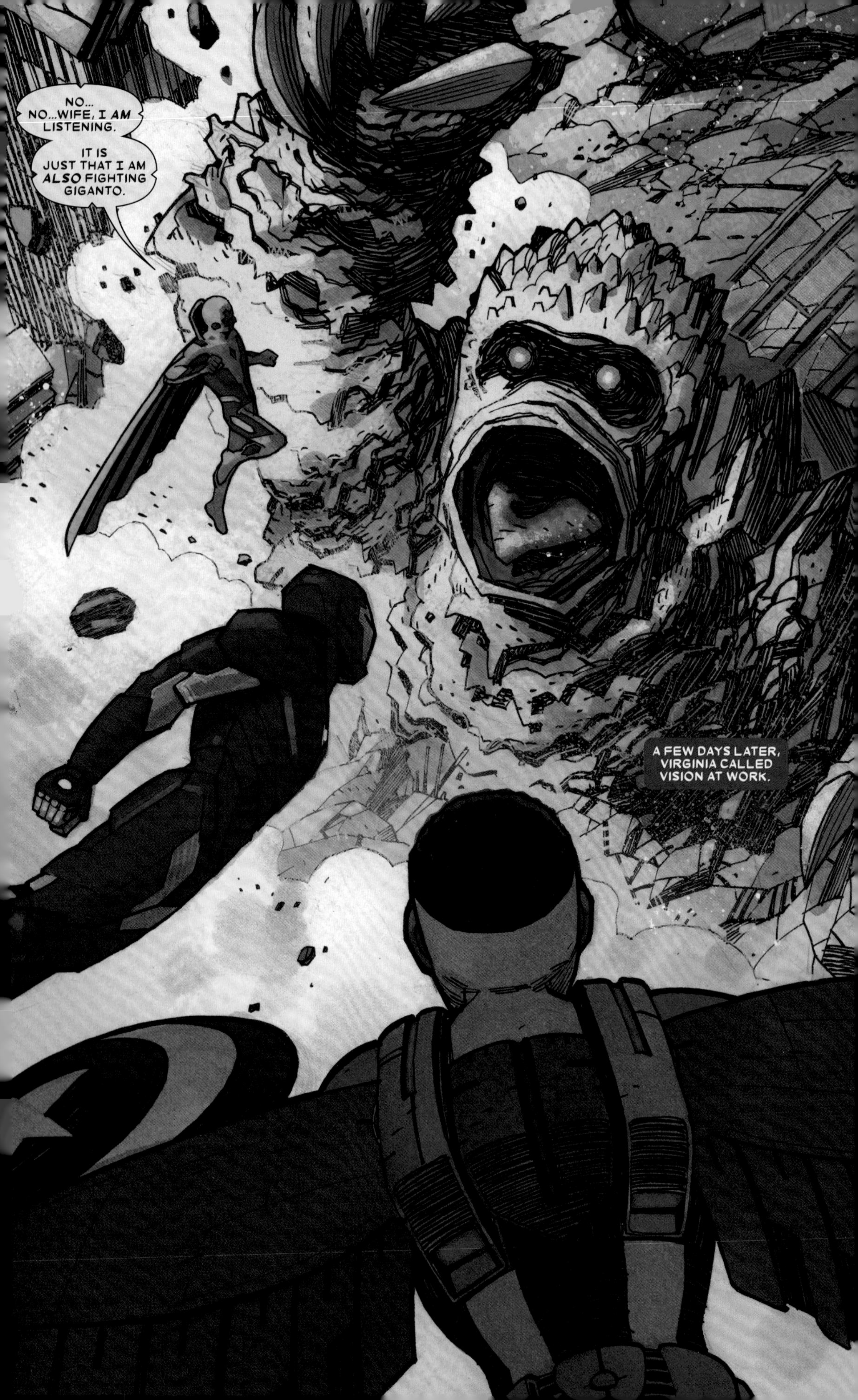
NO... NO...WIFE, I AM LISTENING.
IT IS JUST THAT I AM ALSO FIGHTING GIGANTO.
A FEW DAYS LATER, VIRGINIA CALLED VISION AT WORK.

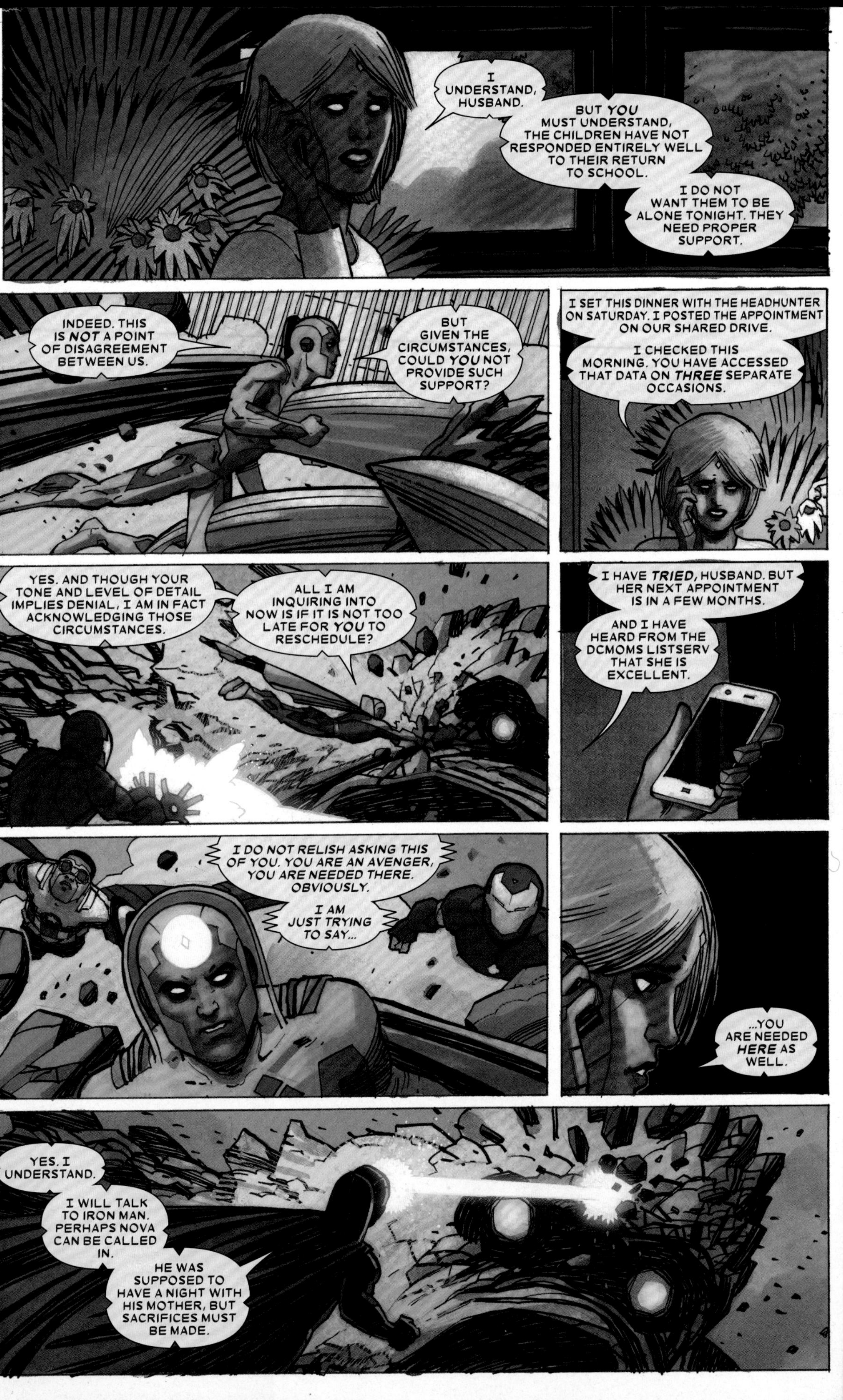
I UNDERSTAND, HUSBAND.
BUT YOU MUST UNDERSTAND, THE CHILDREN HAVE NOT RESPONDED ENTIRELY WELL TO THEIR RETURN TO SCHOOL.
I DO NOT WANT THEM TO BE ALONE TONIGHT. THEY NEED PROPER SUPPORT.
INDEED. THIS IS NOT A POINT OF DISAGREEMENT BETWEEN US.
BUT GIVEN THE CIRCUMSTANCES, COULD YOU NOT PROVIDE SUCH SUPPORT?
I SET THIS DINNER WITH THE HEADHUNTER ON SATURDAY. I POSTED THE APPOINTMENT ON OUR SHARED DRIVE.
I CHECKED THIS MORNING. YOU HAVE ACCESSED THAT DATA ON THREE SEPARATE OCCASIONS.
YES. AND THOUGH YOUR TONE AND LEVEL OF DETAIL IMPLIES DENIAL, I AM IN FACT ACKNOWLEDGING THOSE CIRCUMSTANCES.
ALL I AM INQUIRING INTO NOW IS IF IT IS NOT TOO LATE FOR YOU TO RESCHEDULE?
I HAVE TRIED, HUSBAND. BUT HER NEXT APPOINTMENT IS IN A FEW MONTHS.
AND I HAVE HEARD FROM THE DCMOMS LISTSERV THAT SHE IS EXCELLENT.
I DO NOT RELISH ASKING THIS OF YOU. YOU ARE AN AVENGER, YOU ARE NEEDED THERE. OBVIOUSLY.
I AM JUST TRYING TO SAY...
...YOU ARE NEEDED HERE AS WELL.
YES. I UNDERSTAND.
I WILL TALK TO IRON MAN. PERHAPS NOVA CAN BE CALLED IN.
HE WAS SUPPOSED TO HAVE A NIGHT WITH HIS MOTHER, BUT SACRIFICES MUST BE MADE.

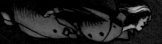

THAT NIGHT, VIRGINIA FLEW TO THE ADDRESS SHE HAD BEEN GIVEN OVER THE PHONE, A TOWN HOUSE IN SOUTHERN ALEXANDRIA.

AS HER MEETING WAS SET FOR MIDNIGHT, SHE CALLED VISION TO INFORM HIM THAT HER HEADHUNTER WANTED TO HAVE DRINKS AFTER DINNER.

VISION SAID HE UNDERSTOOD AND WISHED HER LUCK.

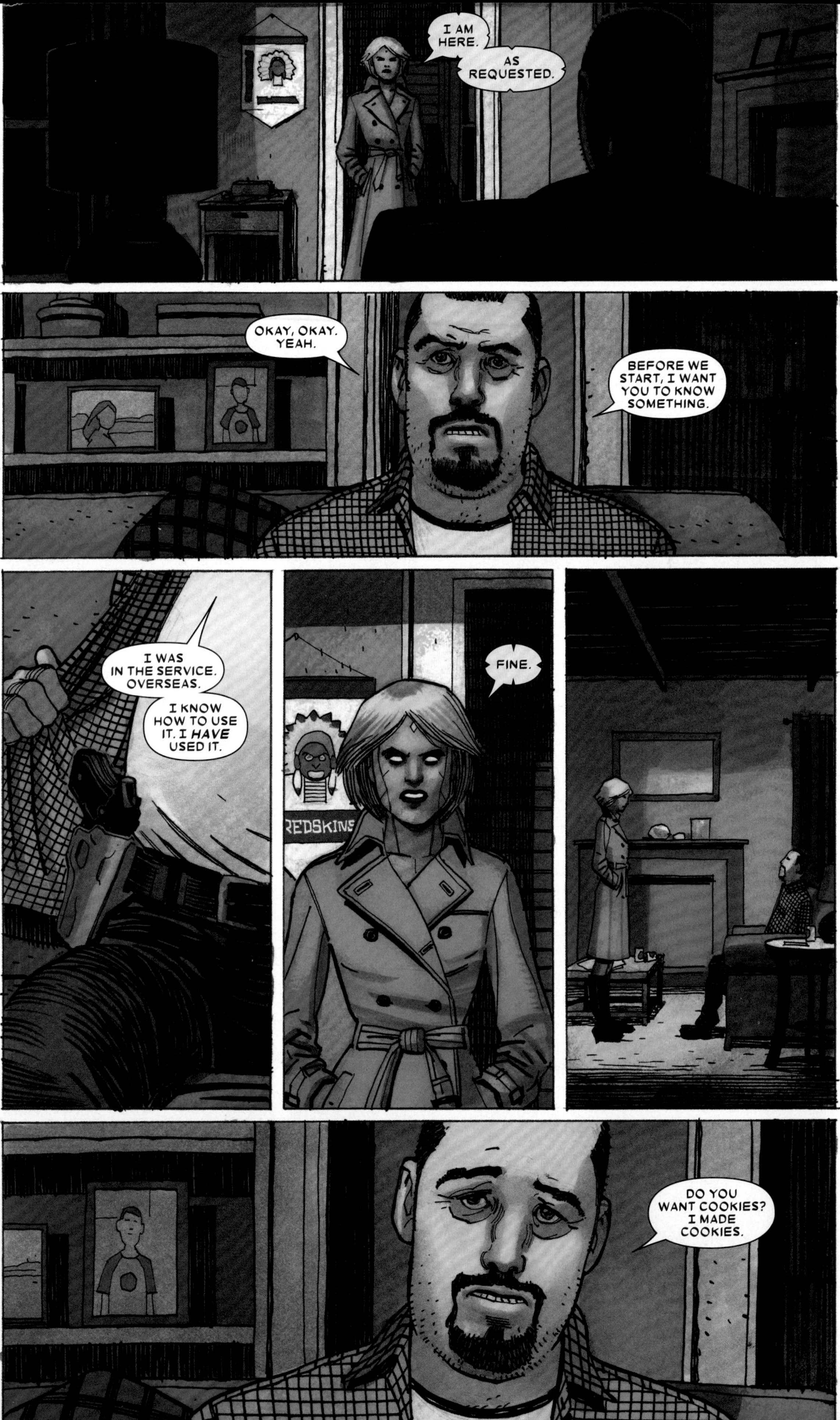

I AM HERE.
AS REQUESTED.
OKAY, OKAY. YEAH.
BEFORE WE START, I WANT YOU TO KNOW SOMETHING.
I WAS IN THE SERVICE. OVERSEAS.
I KNOW HOW TO USE IT. I *HAVE* USED IT.
FINE.
REDSKINS
DO YOU WANT COOKIES? I MADE COOKIES.

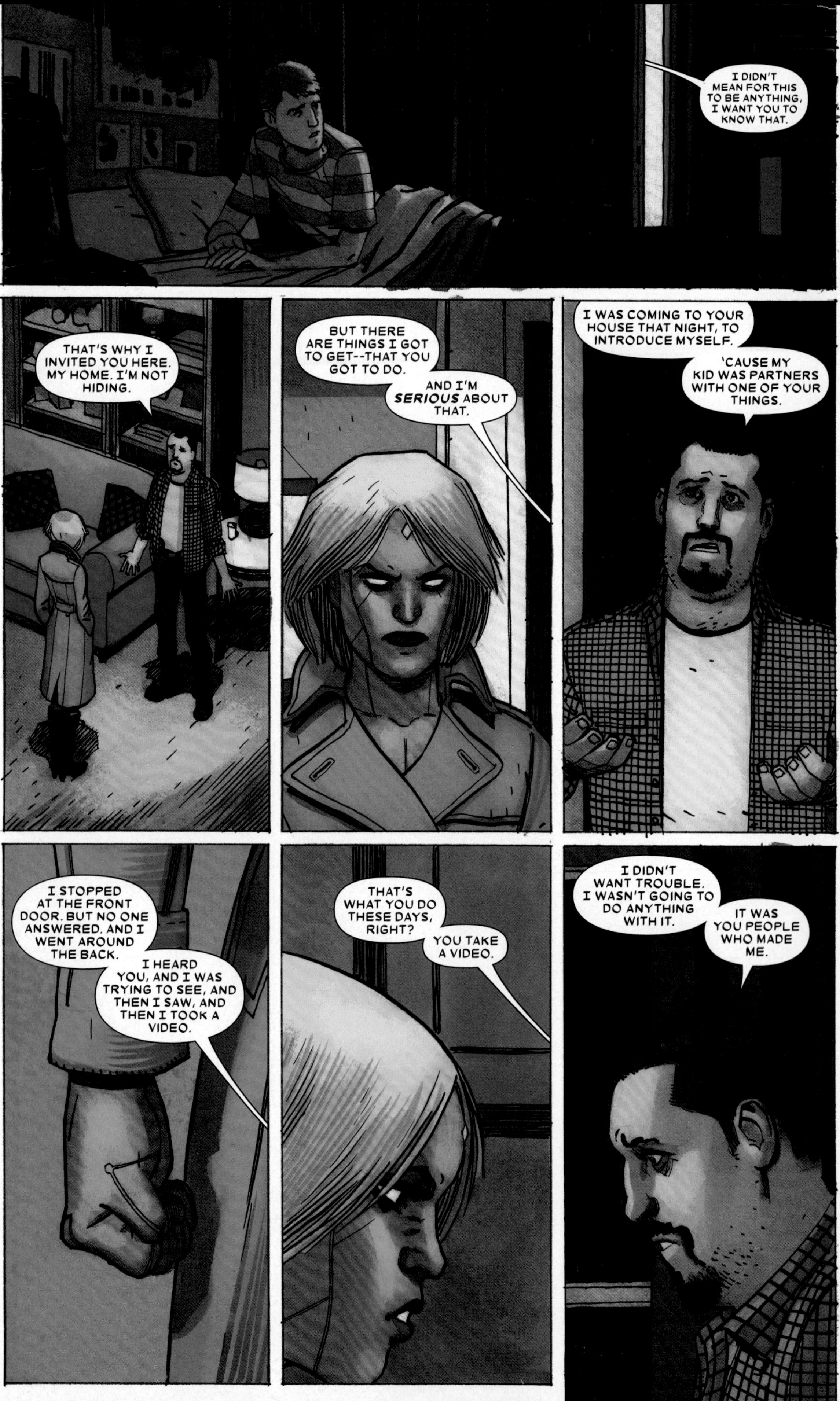

I DIDN'T MEAN FOR THIS TO BE ANYTHING, I WANT YOU TO KNOW THAT.
THAT'S WHY I INVITED YOU HERE. MY HOME. I'M NOT HIDING.
BUT THERE ARE THINGS I GOT TO GET--THAT YOU GOT TO DO.
AND I'M SERIOUS ABOUT THAT.
I WAS COMING TO YOUR HOUSE THAT NIGHT, TO INTRODUCE MYSELF.
'CAUSE MY KID WAS PARTNERS WITH ONE OF YOUR THINGS.
I STOPPED AT THE FRONT DOOR. BUT NO ONE ANSWERED. AND I WENT AROUND THE BACK.
I HEARD YOU, AND I WAS TRYING TO SEE, AND THEN I SAW, AND THEN I TOOK A VIDEO.
THAT'S WHAT YOU DO THESE DAYS, RIGHT?
YOU TAKE A VIDEO.
I DIDN'T WANT TROUBLE. I WASN'T GOING TO DO ANYTHING WITH IT.
IT WAS YOU PEOPLE WHO MADE ME.

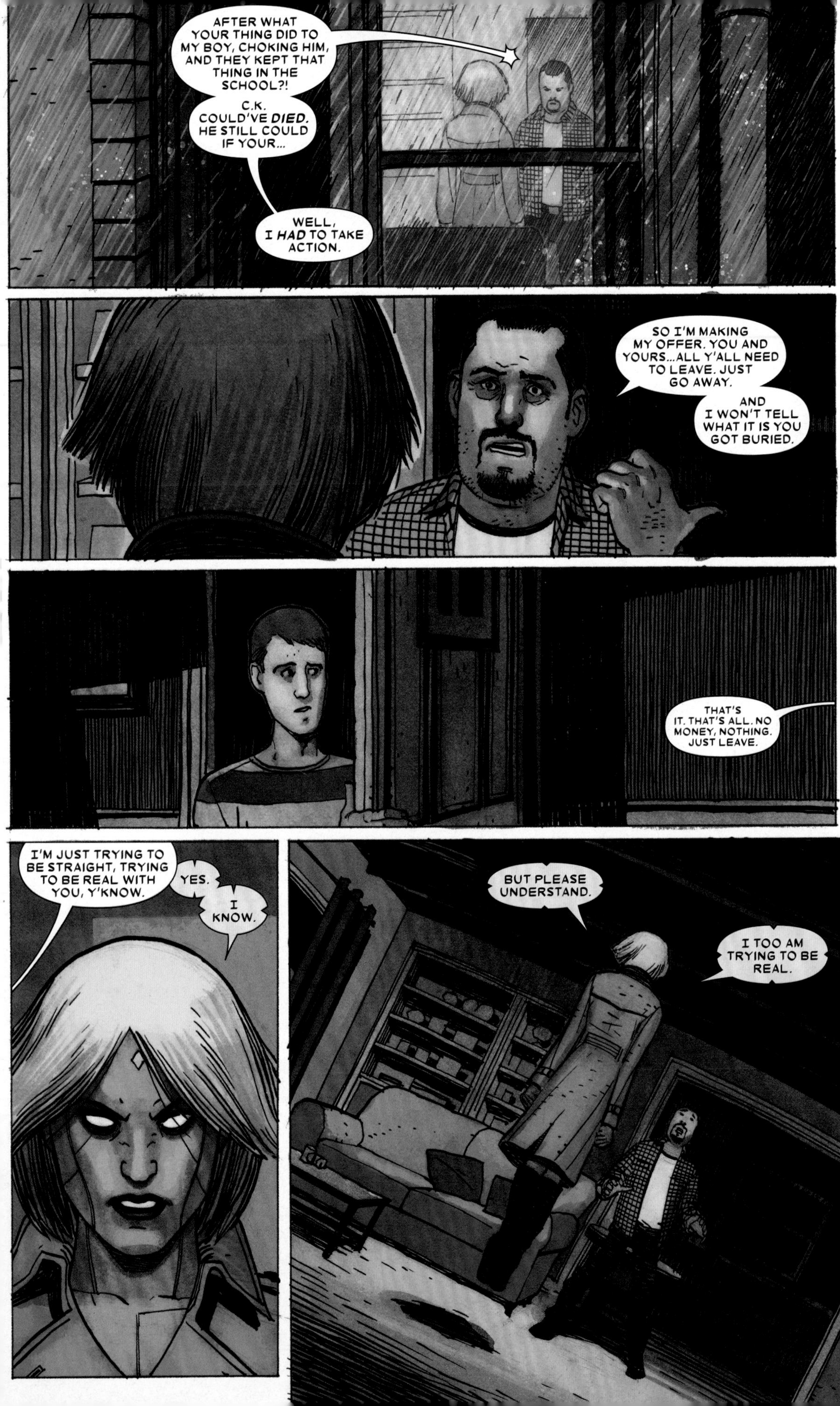
AFTER WHAT YOUR THING DID TO MY BOY, CHOKING HIM, AND THEY KEPT THAT THING IN THE SCHOOL?!
C.K. COULD'VE *DIED.* HE STILL COULD IF YOUR...
WELL, I *HAD* TO TAKE ACTION.
SO I'M MAKING MY OFFER. YOU AND YOURS...ALL Y'ALL NEED TO LEAVE. JUST GO AWAY.
AND I WON'T TELL WHAT IT IS YOU GOT BURIED.
THAT'S IT. THAT'S ALL. NO MONEY, NOTHING. JUST LEAVE.
I'M JUST TRYING TO BE STRAIGHT, TRYING TO BE REAL WITH YOU, Y'KNOW.
YES.
I KNOW.
BUT PLEASE UNDERSTAND.
I TOO AM TRYING TO BE REAL.

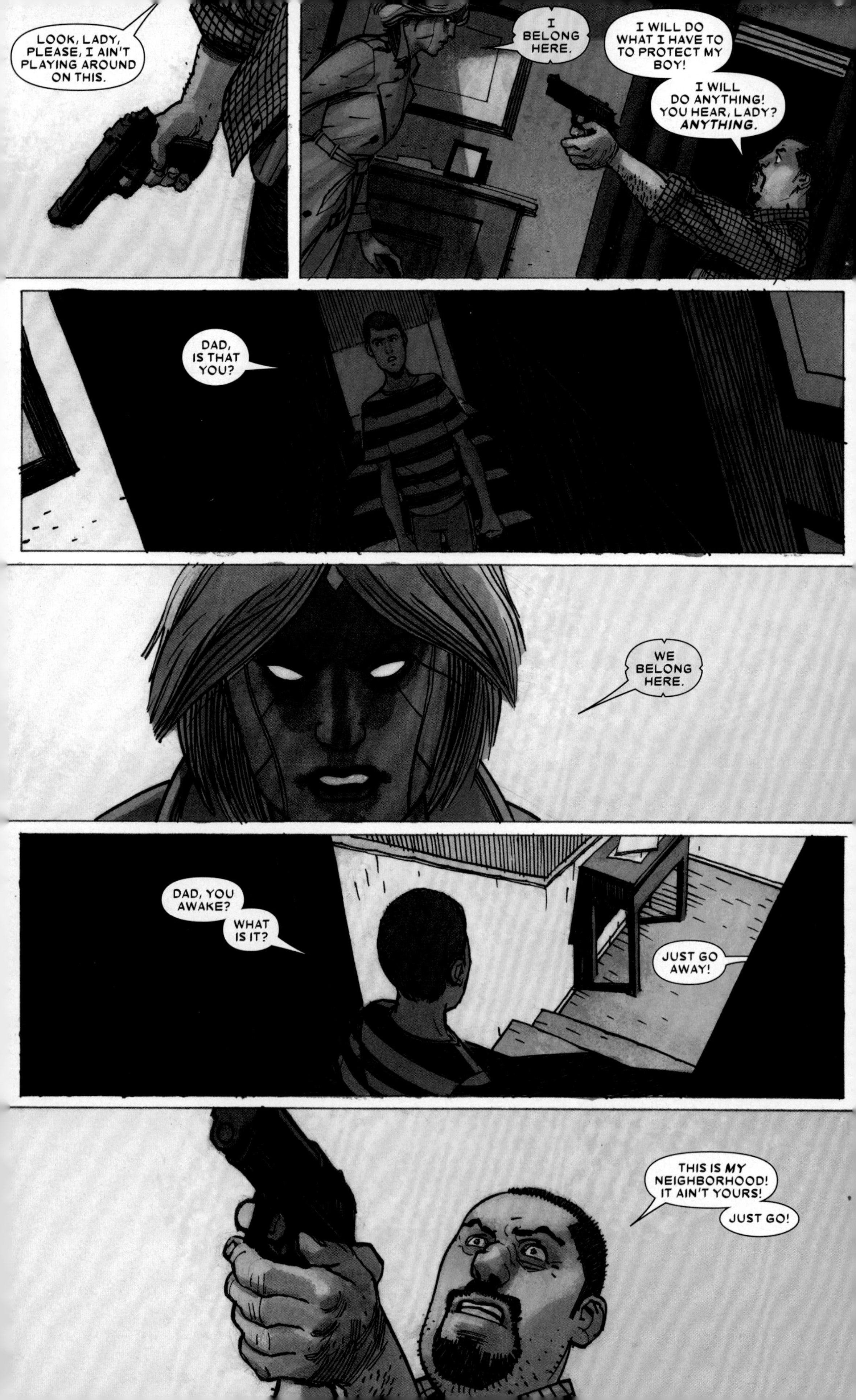
LOOK, LADY, PLEASE, I AIN'T PLAYING AROUND ON THIS.
I BELONG HERE.
I WILL DO WHAT I HAVE TO TO PROTECT MY BOY!
I WILL DO ANYTHING! YOU HEAR, LADY? ANYTHING.
DAD, IS THAT YOU?
WE BELONG HERE.
DAD, YOU AWAKE?
WHAT IS IT?
JUST GO AWAY!
THIS IS MY NEIGHBORHOOD! IT AIN'T YOURS!
JUST GO!

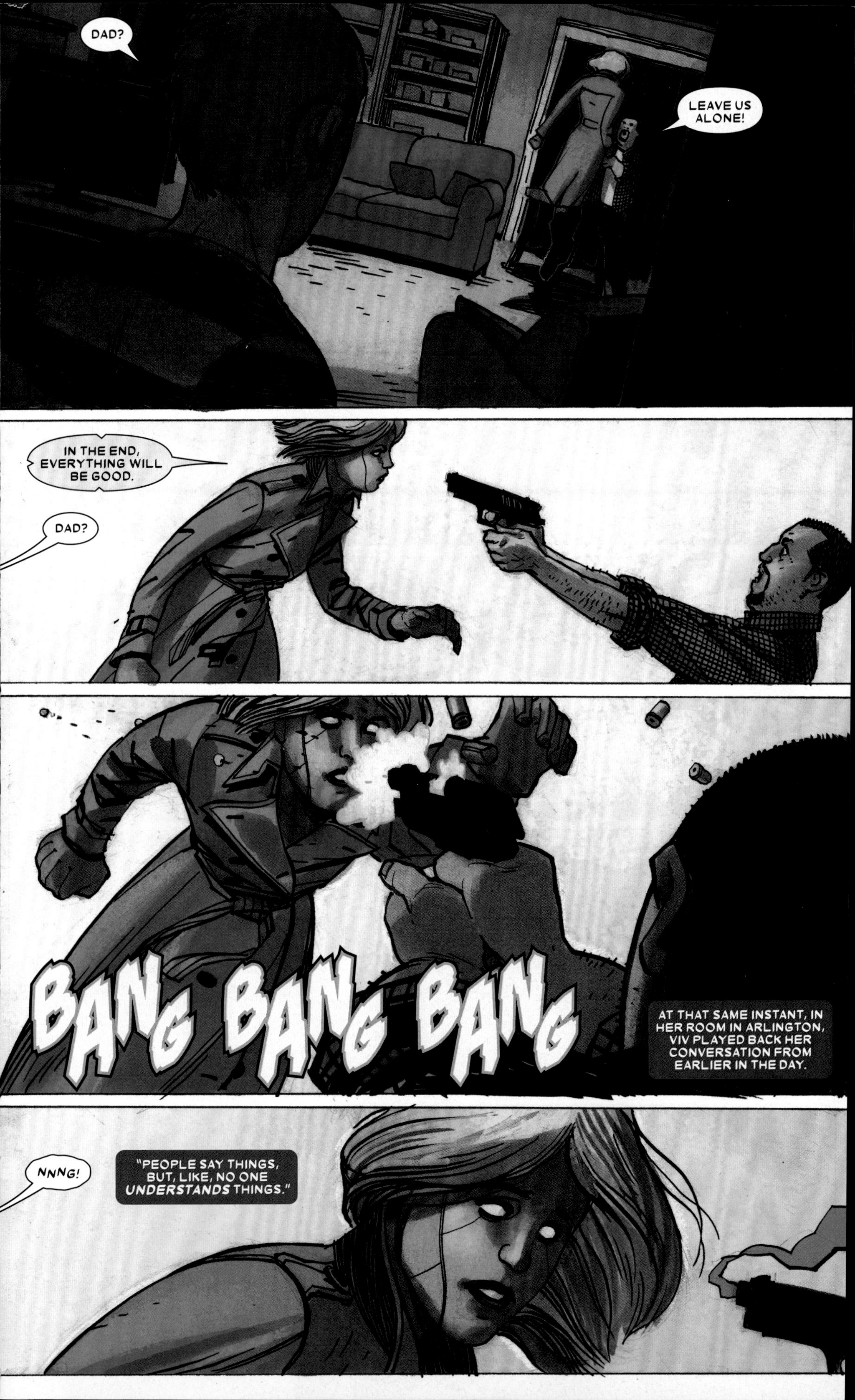
DAD?
LEAVE US ALONE!
IN THE END, EVERYTHING WILL BE GOOD.
DAD?
BANG BANG BANG
AT THAT SAME INSTANT, IN HER ROOM IN ARLINGTON, VIV PLAYED BACK HER CONVERSATION FROM EARLIER IN THE DAY.
NNNG!
"PEOPLE SAY THINGS, BUT, LIKE, NO ONE *UNDERSTANDS* THINGS."

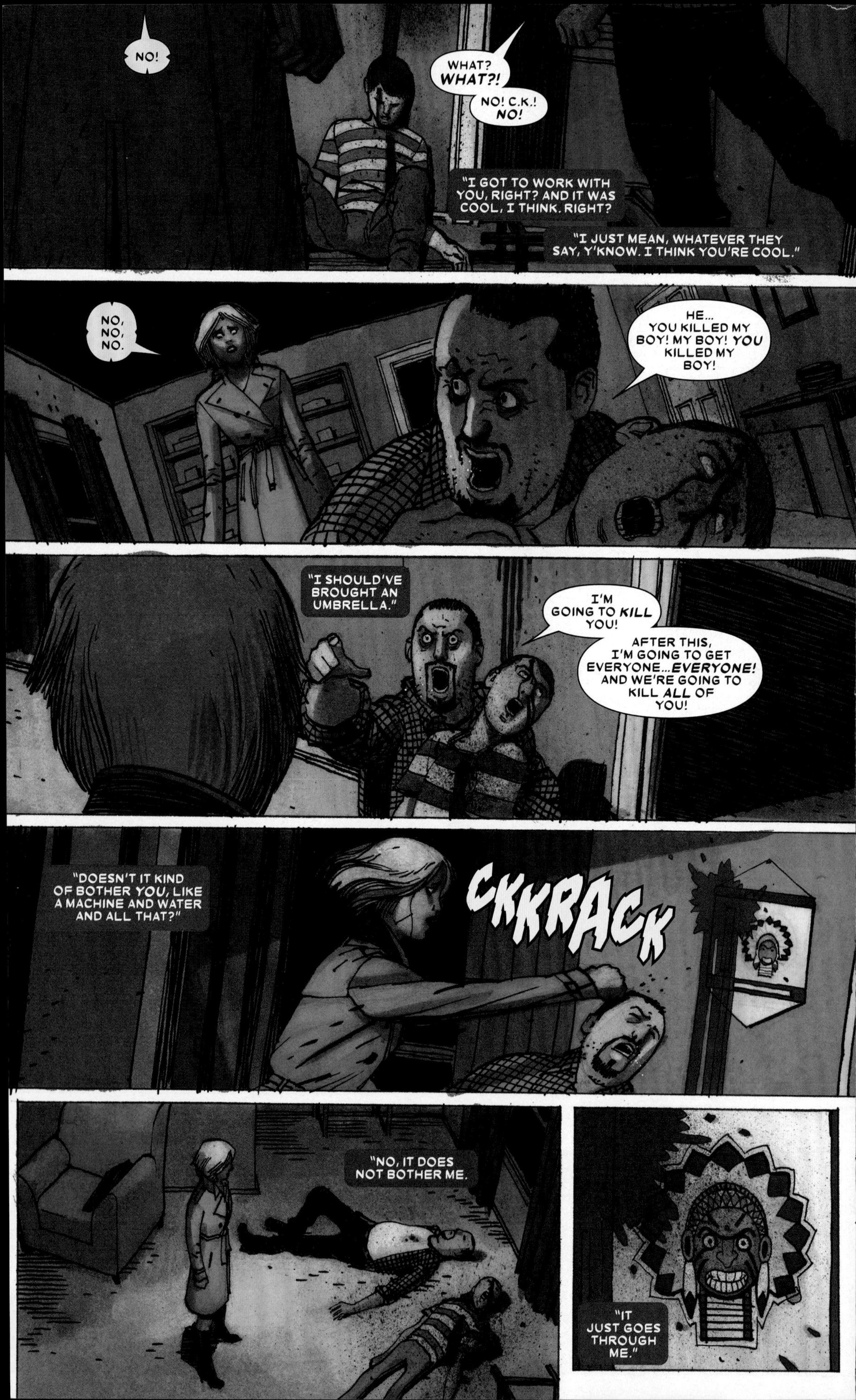
NO!
WHAT? WHAT?!
NO! C.K.! NO!
"I GOT TO WORK WITH YOU, RIGHT? AND IT WAS COOL, I THINK. RIGHT?
"I JUST MEAN, WHATEVER THEY SAY, Y'KNOW. I THINK YOU'RE COOL."
NO, NO, NO.
HE... YOU KILLED MY BOY! MY BOY! YOU KILLED MY BOY!
"I SHOULD'VE BROUGHT AN UMBRELLA."
I'M GOING TO KILL YOU!
AFTER THIS, I'M GOING TO GET EVERYONE...EVERYONE! AND WE'RE GOING TO KILL ALL OF YOU!
"DOESN'T IT KIND OF BOTHER YOU, LIKE A MACHINE AND WATER AND ALL THAT?"
CKKRACK
"NO, IT DOES NOT BOTHER ME.
"IT JUST GOES THROUGH ME."

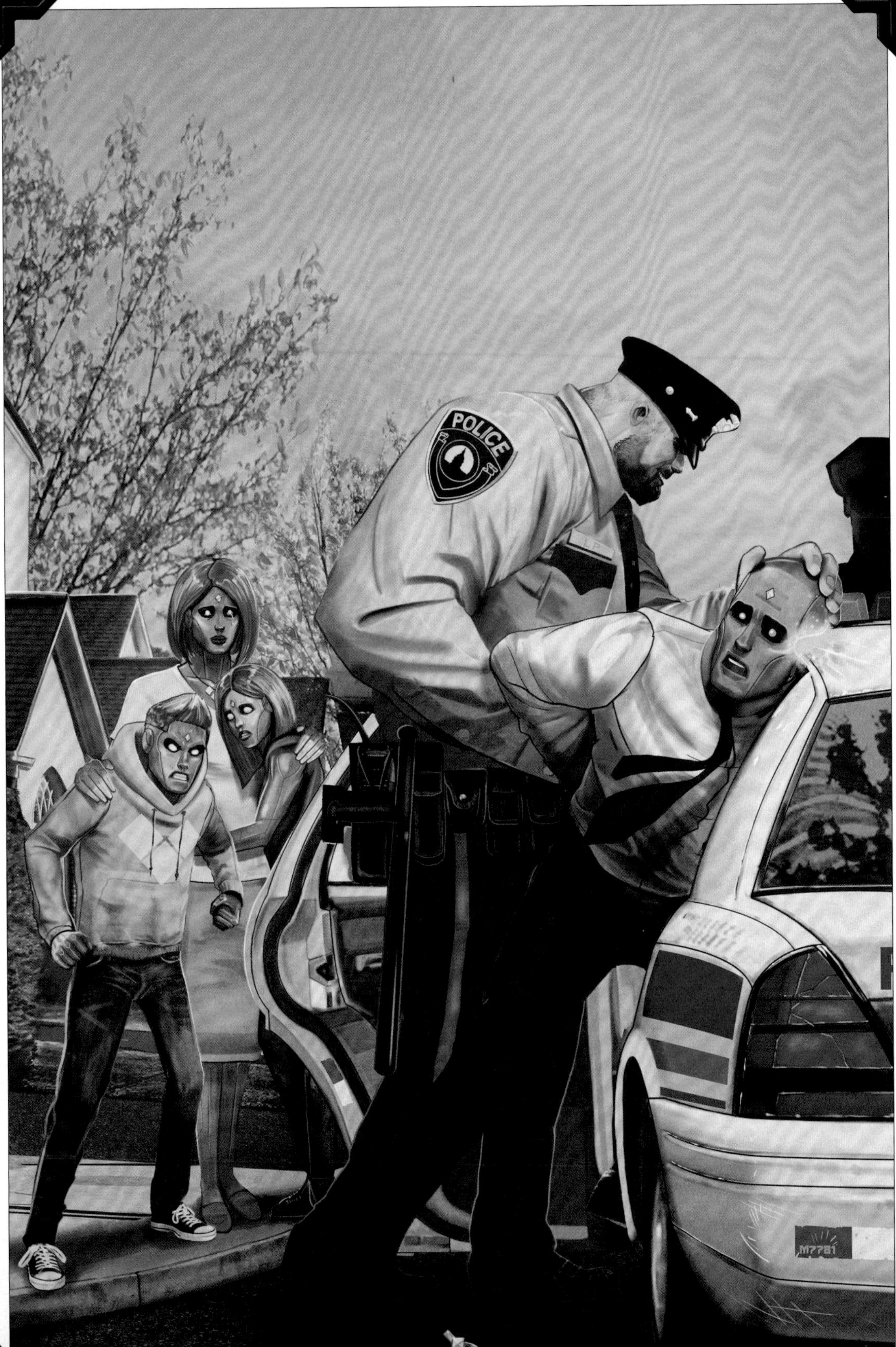
POLICE
M7781

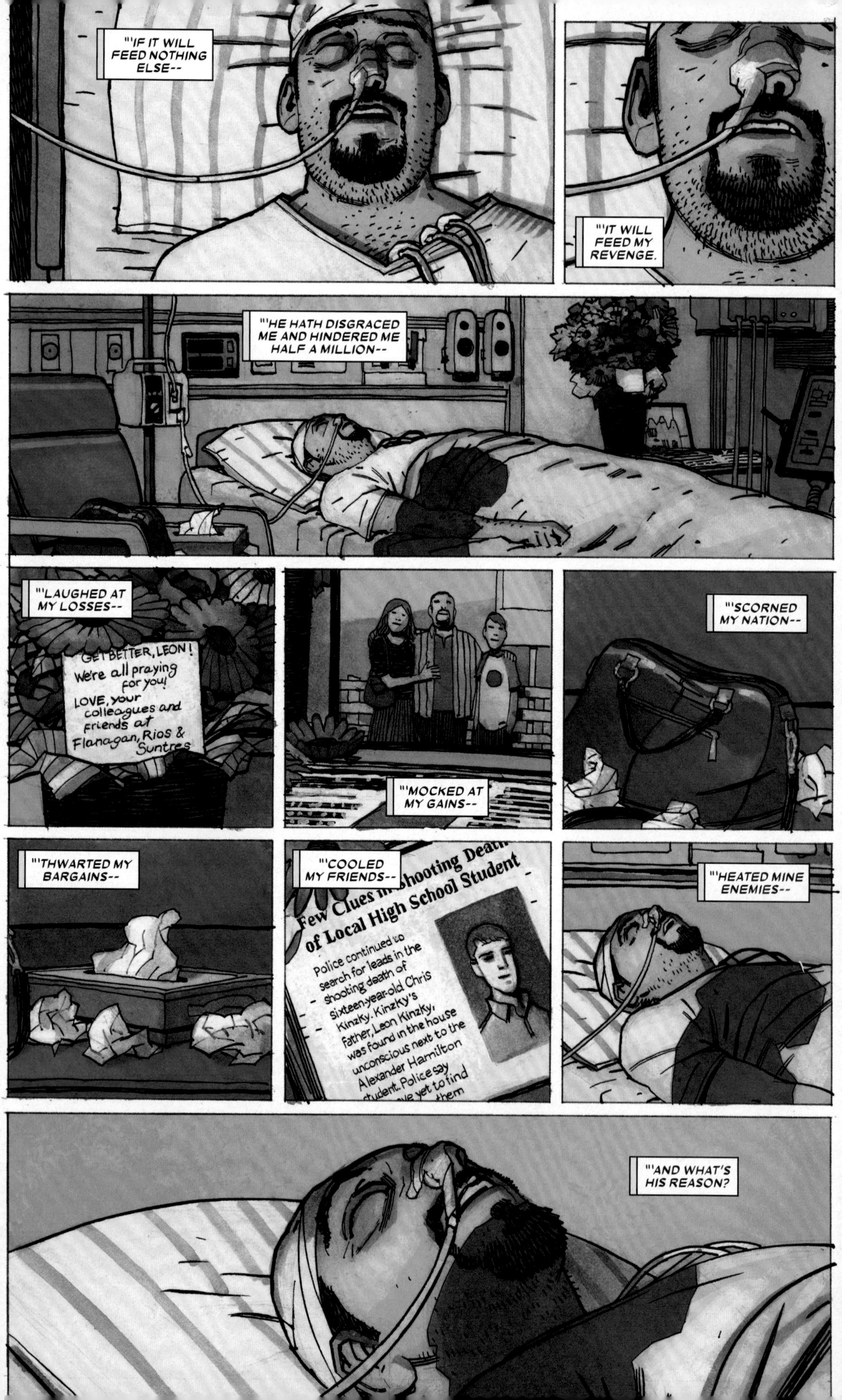
"'IF IT WILL FEED NOTHING ELSE--
"'IT WILL FEED MY REVENGE.
"'HE HATH DISGRACED ME AND HINDERED ME HALF A MILLION--
"'LAUGHED AT MY LOSSES--
GET BETTER, LEON! We're all praying for you! LOVE, your colleagues and friends at Flanagan, Rios & Suntres
"'MOCKED AT MY GAINS--
"'SCORNED MY NATION--
"'THWARTED MY BARGAINS--
"'COOLED MY FRIENDS--
Few Clues in Shooting Death of Local High School Student
Police continued to search for leads in the shooting death of sixteen-year-old Chris Kinzky. Kinzky's father, Leon Kinzky, was found in the house unconscious next to the Alexander Hamilton
"'HEATED MINE ENEMIES--
"'AND WHAT'S HIS REASON?

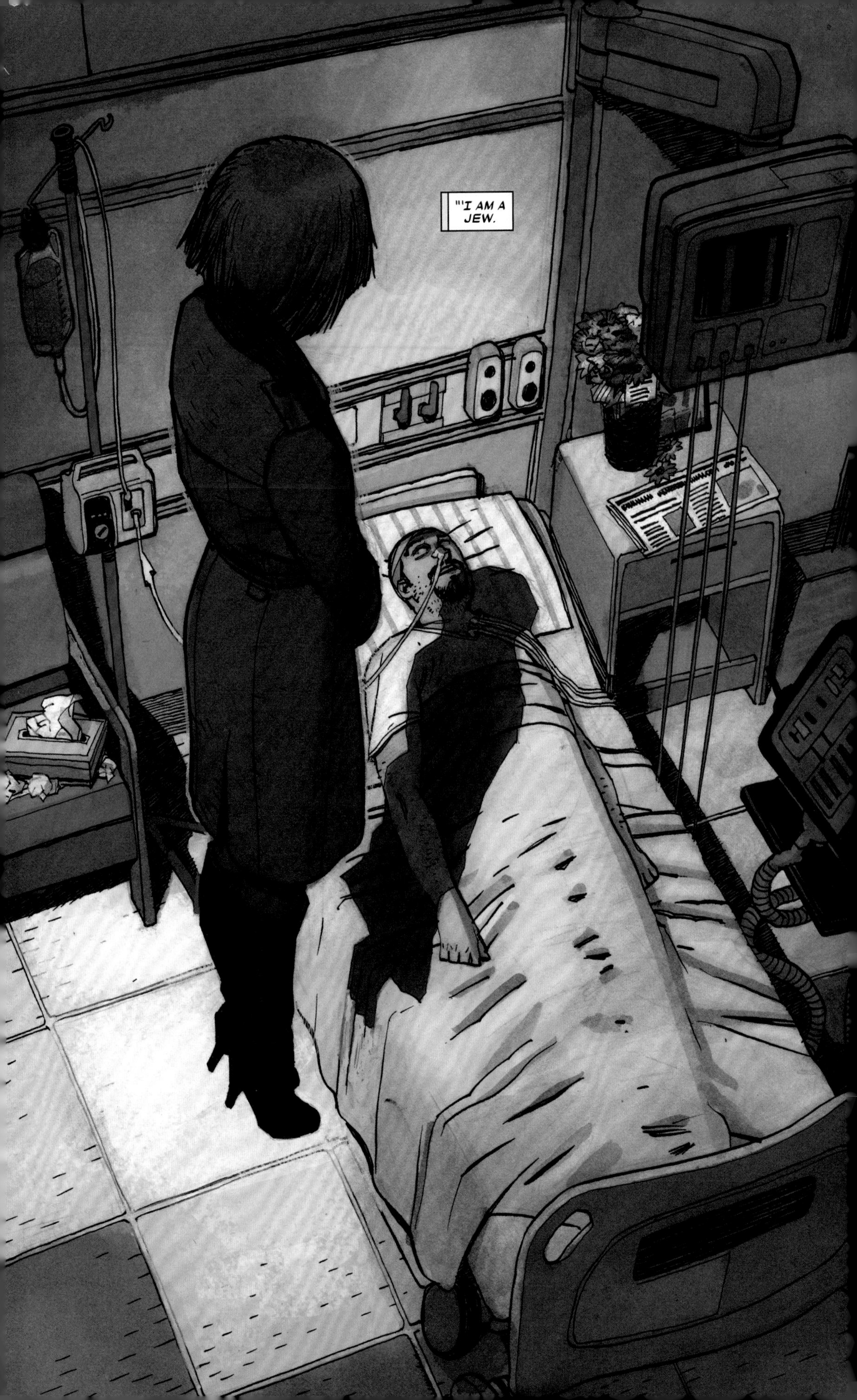
"'I AM A JEW.

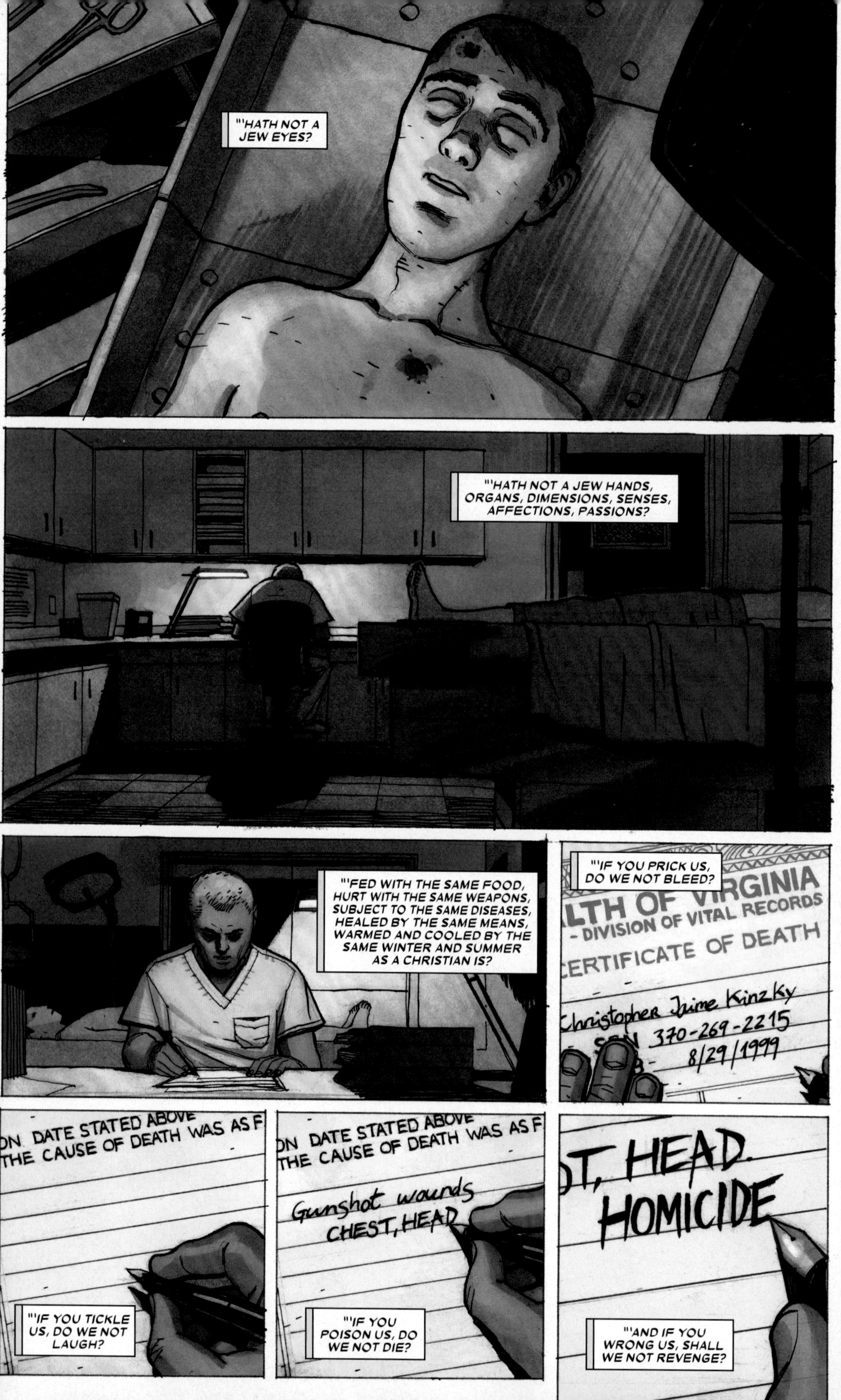
"'HATH NOT A JEW EYES?
"'HATH NOT A JEW HANDS, ORGANS, DIMENSIONS, SENSES, AFFECTIONS, PASSIONS?
"'FED WITH THE SAME FOOD, HURT WITH THE SAME WEAPONS, SUBJECT TO THE SAME DISEASES, HEALED BY THE SAME MEANS, WARMED AND COOLED BY THE SAME WINTER AND SUMMER AS A CHRISTIAN IS?
"'IF YOU PRICK US, DO WE NOT BLEED?
LTH OF VIRGINIA
- DIVISION OF VITAL RECORDS
CERTIFICATE OF DEATH
Christopher Jaime Kinzky
370-269-2215
8/29/1999
ON DATE STATED ABOVE THE CAUSE OF DEATH WAS AS F
"'IF YOU TICKLE US, DO WE NOT LAUGH?
ON DATE STATED ABOVE THE CAUSE OF DEATH WAS AS F
Gunshot wounds
CHEST, HEAD
"'IF YOU POISON US, DO WE NOT DIE?
T, HEAD.
HOMICIDE
"'AND IF YOU WRONG US, SHALL WE NOT REVENGE?

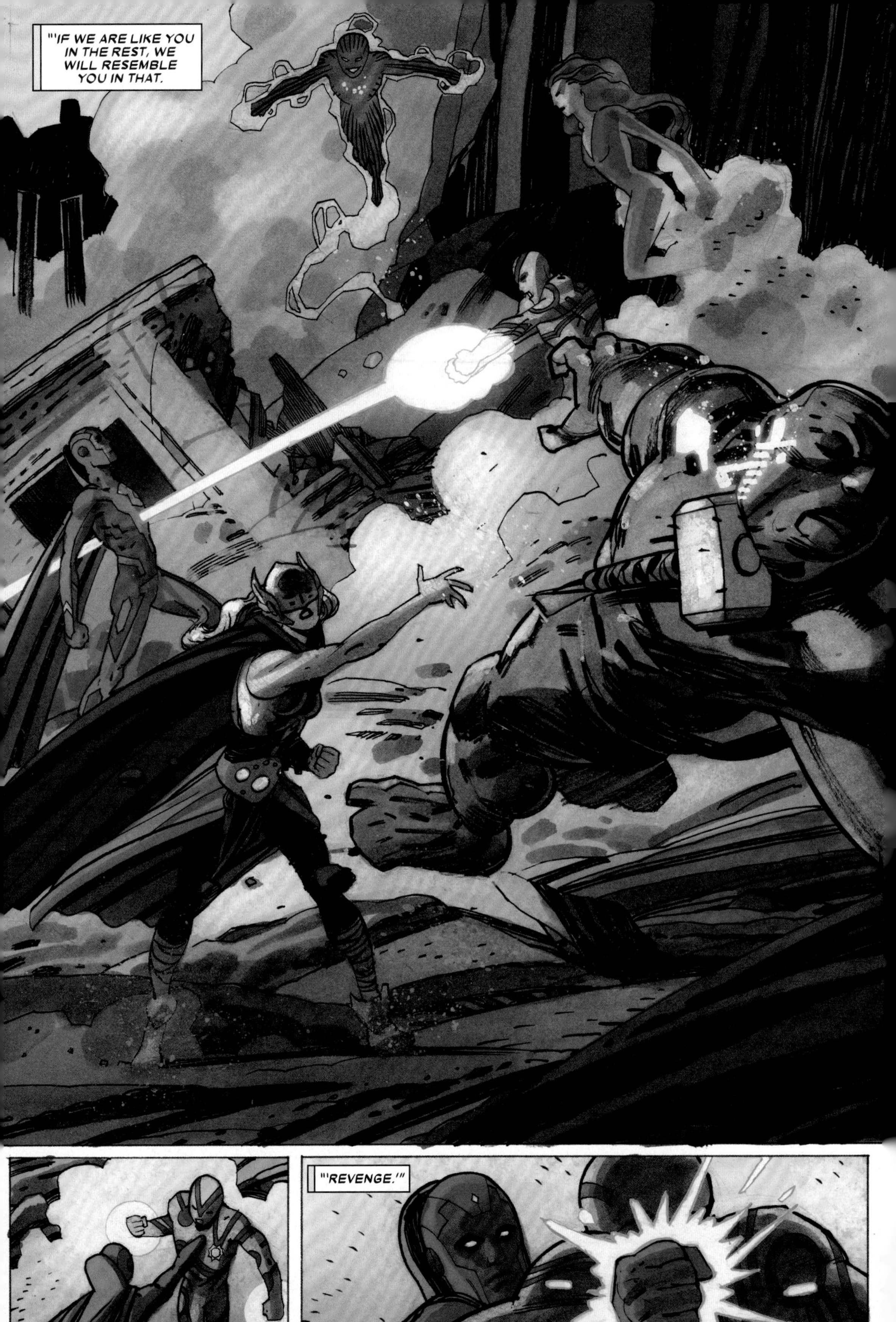
"'IF WE ARE LIKE YOU IN THE REST, WE WILL RESEMBLE YOU IN THAT.

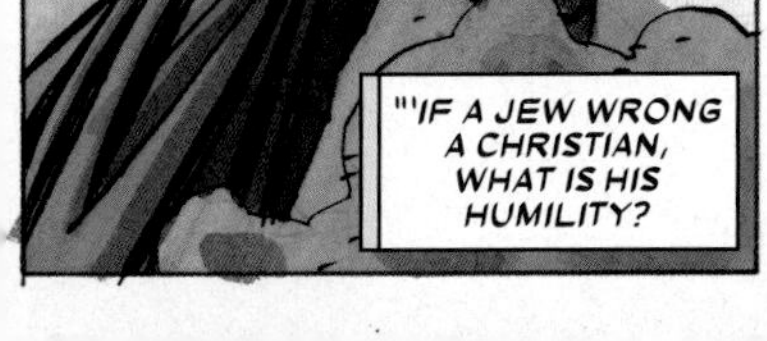
"'IF A JEW WRONG A CHRISTIAN, WHAT IS HIS HUMILITY?

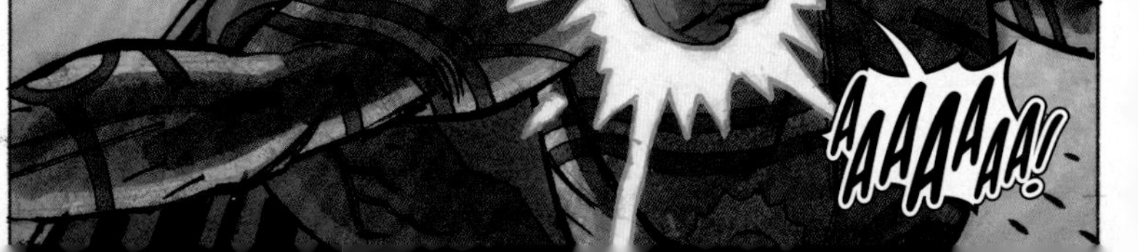
"'REVENGE.'"
AAAAAAA!

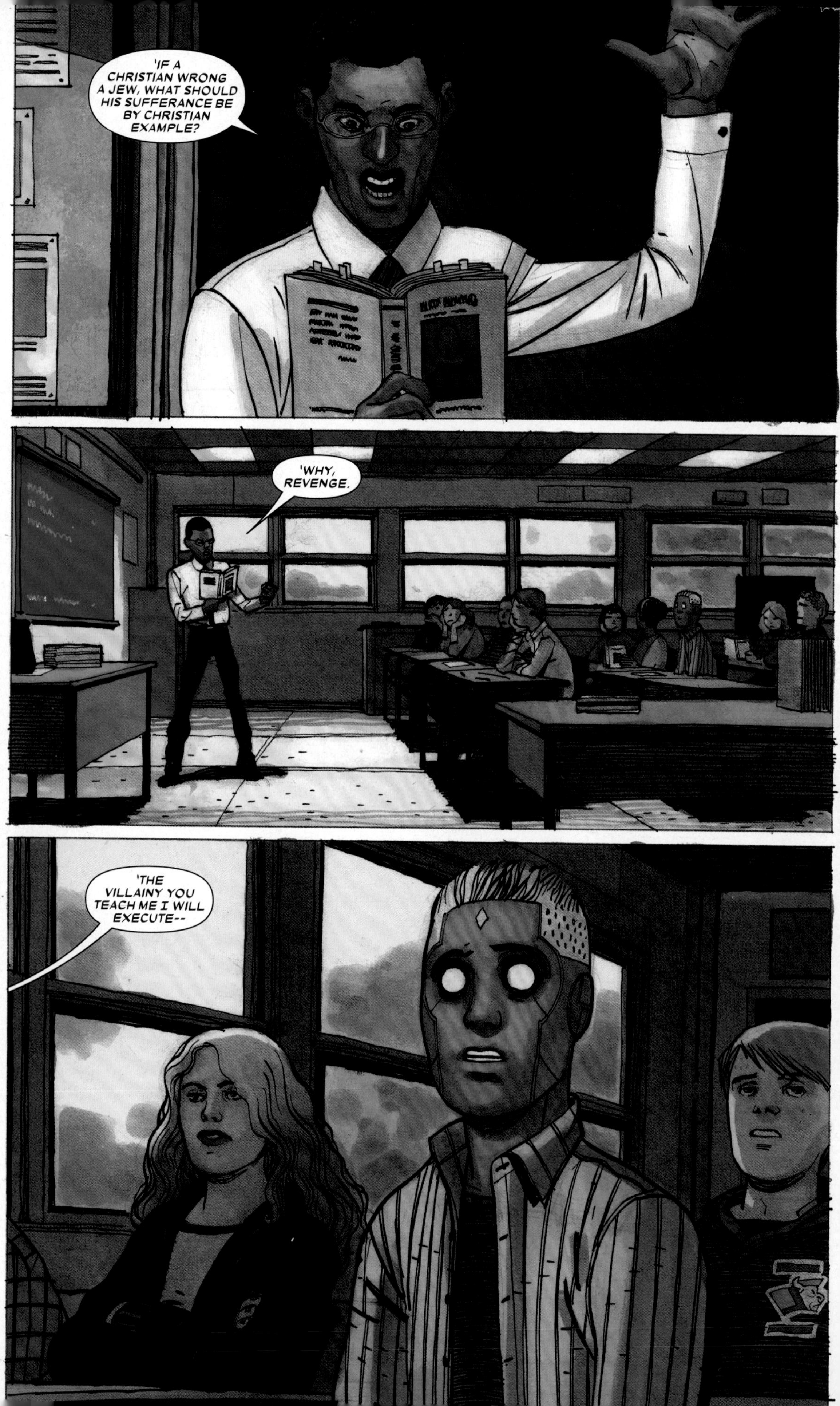
'IF A CHRISTIAN WRONG A JEW, WHAT SHOULD HIS SUFFERANCE BE BY CHRISTIAN EXAMPLE?
'WHY, REVENGE.
'THE VILLAINY YOU TEACH ME I WILL EXECUTE--

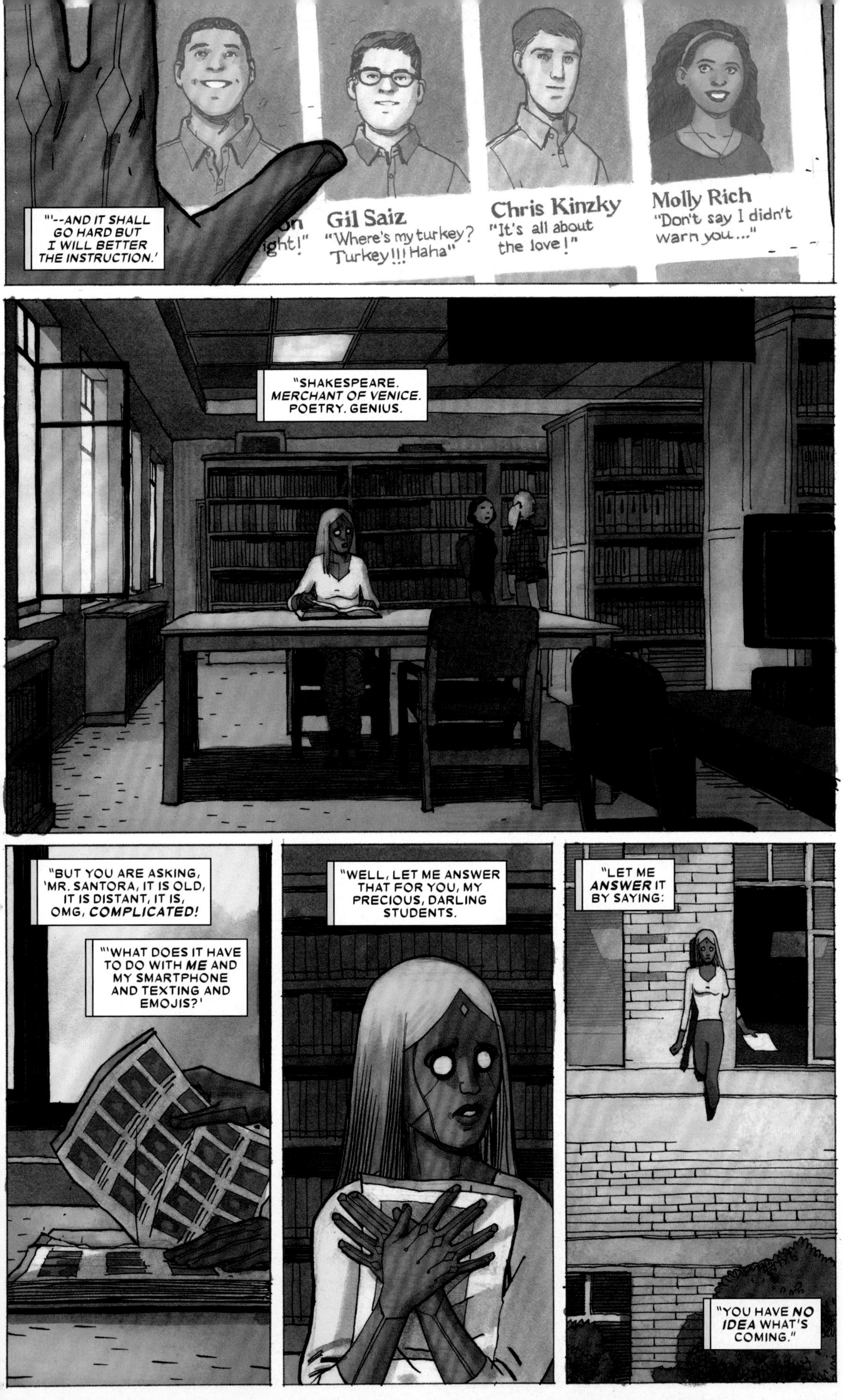

"'--AND IT SHALL GO HARD BUT I WILL BETTER THE INSTRUCTION.'
Gil Saiz "Where's my turkey? Turkey!!! Haha"
Chris Kinzky "It's all about the love!"
Molly Rich "Don't say I didn't warn you..."
"SHAKESPEARE. MERCHANT OF VENICE. POETRY. GENIUS.
"BUT YOU ARE ASKING, 'MR. SANTORA, IT IS OLD, IT IS DISTANT, IT IS, OMG, COMPLICATED!
"'WHAT DOES IT HAVE TO DO WITH ME AND MY SMARTPHONE AND TEXTING AND EMOJIS?'
"WELL, LET ME ANSWER THAT FOR YOU, MY PRECIOUS, DARLING STUDENTS.
"LET ME ANSWER IT BY SAYING:
"YOU HAVE NO IDEA WHAT'S COMING."

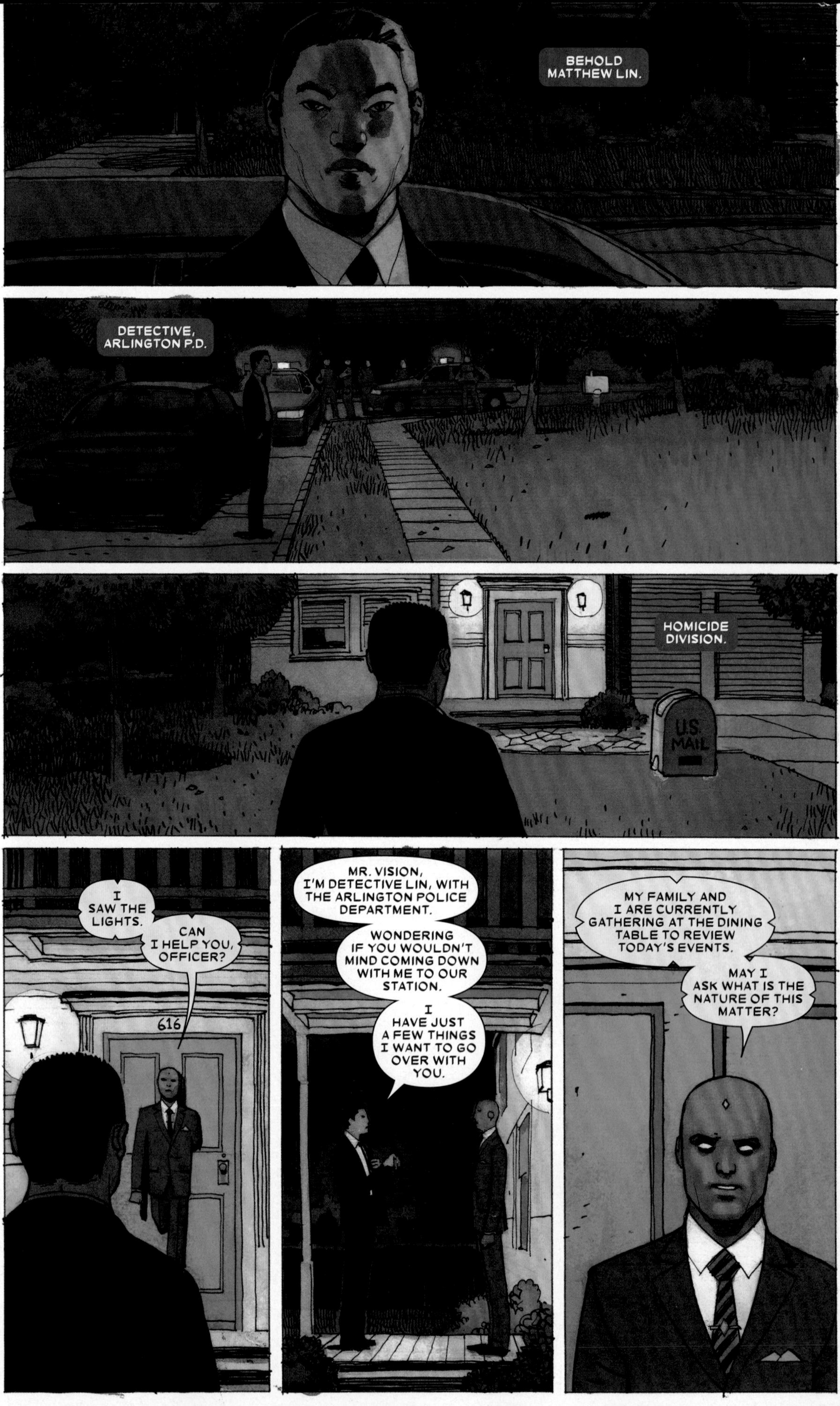
BEHOLD MATTHEW LIN.
DETECTIVE, ARLINGTON P.D.
HOMICIDE DIVISION.
U.S. MAIL
I SAW THE LIGHTS.
CAN I HELP YOU, OFFICER?
616
MR. VISION, I'M DETECTIVE LIN, WITH THE ARLINGTON POLICE DEPARTMENT.
WONDERING IF YOU WOULDN'T MIND COMING DOWN WITH ME TO OUR STATION.
I HAVE JUST A FEW THINGS I WANT TO GO OVER WITH YOU.
MY FAMILY AND I ARE CURRENTLY GATHERING AT THE DINING TABLE TO REVIEW TODAY'S EVENTS.
MAY I ASK WHAT IS THE NATURE OF THIS MATTER?

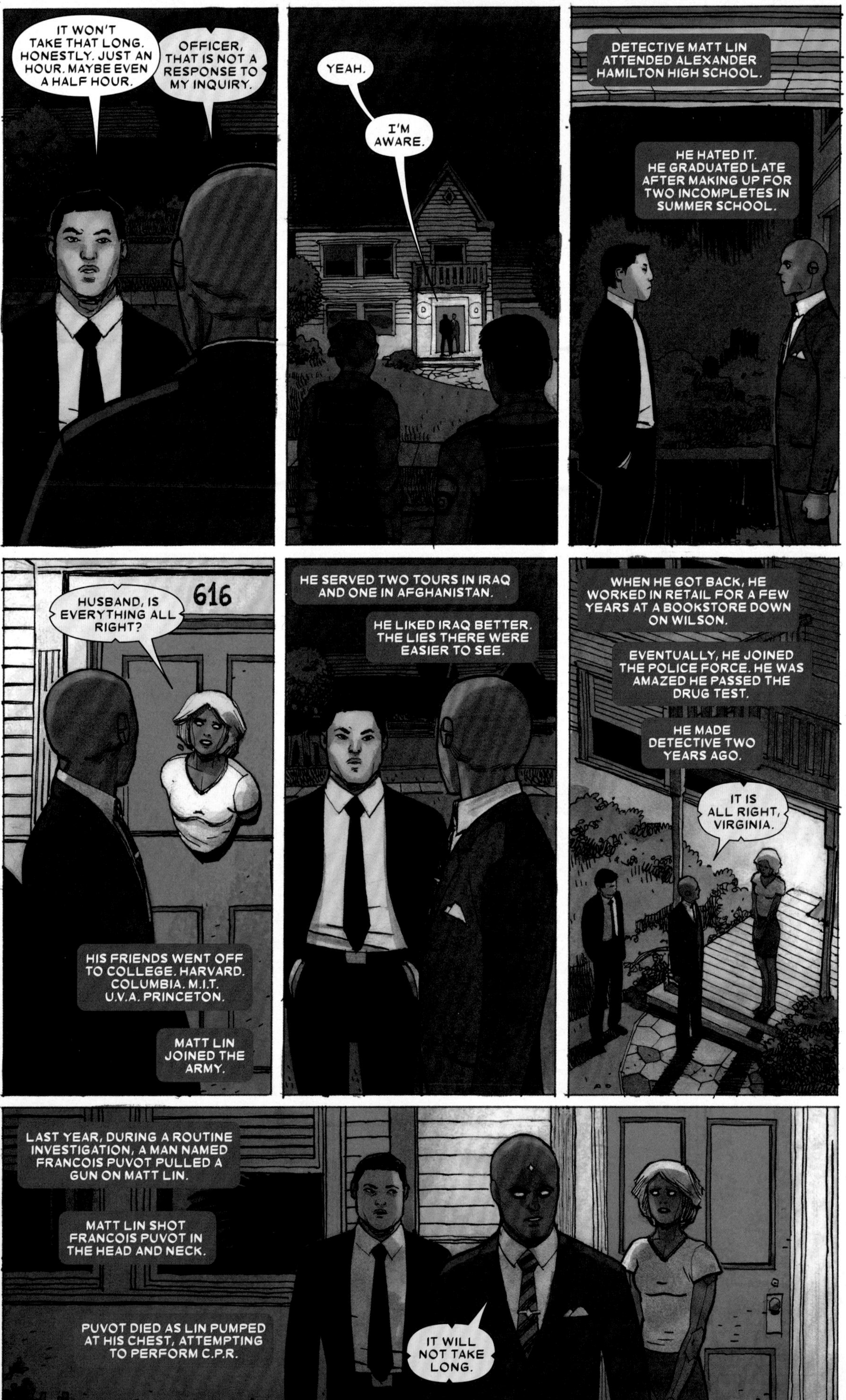
IT WON'T TAKE THAT LONG. HONESTLY. JUST AN HOUR. MAYBE EVEN A HALF HOUR.
OFFICER, THAT IS NOT A RESPONSE TO MY INQUIRY.
YEAH.
I'M AWARE.
DETECTIVE MATT LIN ATTENDED ALEXANDER HAMILTON HIGH SCHOOL.
HE HATED IT. HE GRADUATED LATE AFTER MAKING UP FOR TWO INCOMPLETES IN SUMMER SCHOOL.
616
HUSBAND, IS EVERYTHING ALL RIGHT?
HIS FRIENDS WENT OFF TO COLLEGE. HARVARD. COLUMBIA. M.I.T. U.V.A. PRINCETON.
MATT LIN JOINED THE ARMY.
HE SERVED TWO TOURS IN IRAQ AND ONE IN AFGHANISTAN.
HE LIKED IRAQ BETTER. THE LIES THERE WERE EASIER TO SEE.
WHEN HE GOT BACK, HE WORKED IN RETAIL FOR A FEW YEARS AT A BOOKSTORE DOWN ON WILSON.
EVENTUALLY, HE JOINED THE POLICE FORCE. HE WAS AMAZED HE PASSED THE DRUG TEST.
HE MADE DETECTIVE TWO YEARS AGO.
IT IS ALL RIGHT, VIRGINIA.
LAST YEAR, DURING A ROUTINE INVESTIGATION, A MAN NAMED FRANCOIS PUVOT PULLED A GUN ON MATT LIN.
MATT LIN SHOT FRANCOIS PUVOT IN THE HEAD AND NECK.
PUVOT DIED AS LIN PUMPED AT HIS CHEST, ATTEMPTING TO PERFORM C.P.R.
IT WILL NOT TAKE LONG.

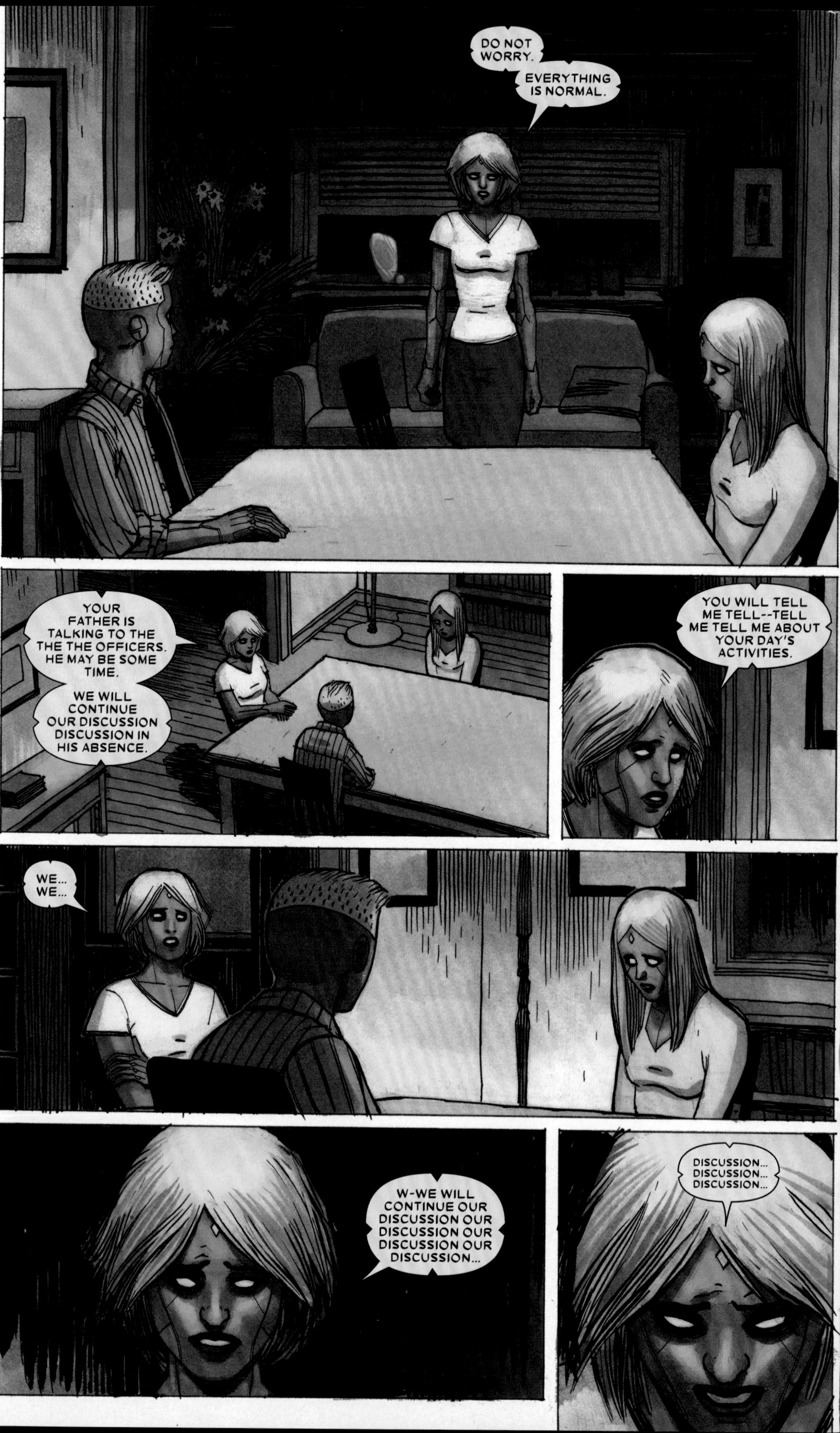
DO NOT WORRY.
EVERYTHING IS NORMAL.
YOUR FATHER IS TALKING TO THE THE THE OFFICERS. HE MAY BE SOME TIME.
WE WILL CONTINUE OUR DISCUSSION DISCUSSION IN HIS ABSENCE.
YOU WILL TELL ME TELL--TELL ME TELL ME ABOUT YOUR DAY'S ACTIVITIES.
WE... WE...
W-WE WILL CONTINUE OUR DISCUSSION OUR DISCUSSION OUR DISCUSSION OUR DISCUSSION...
DISCUSSION... DISCUSSION... DISCUSSION...

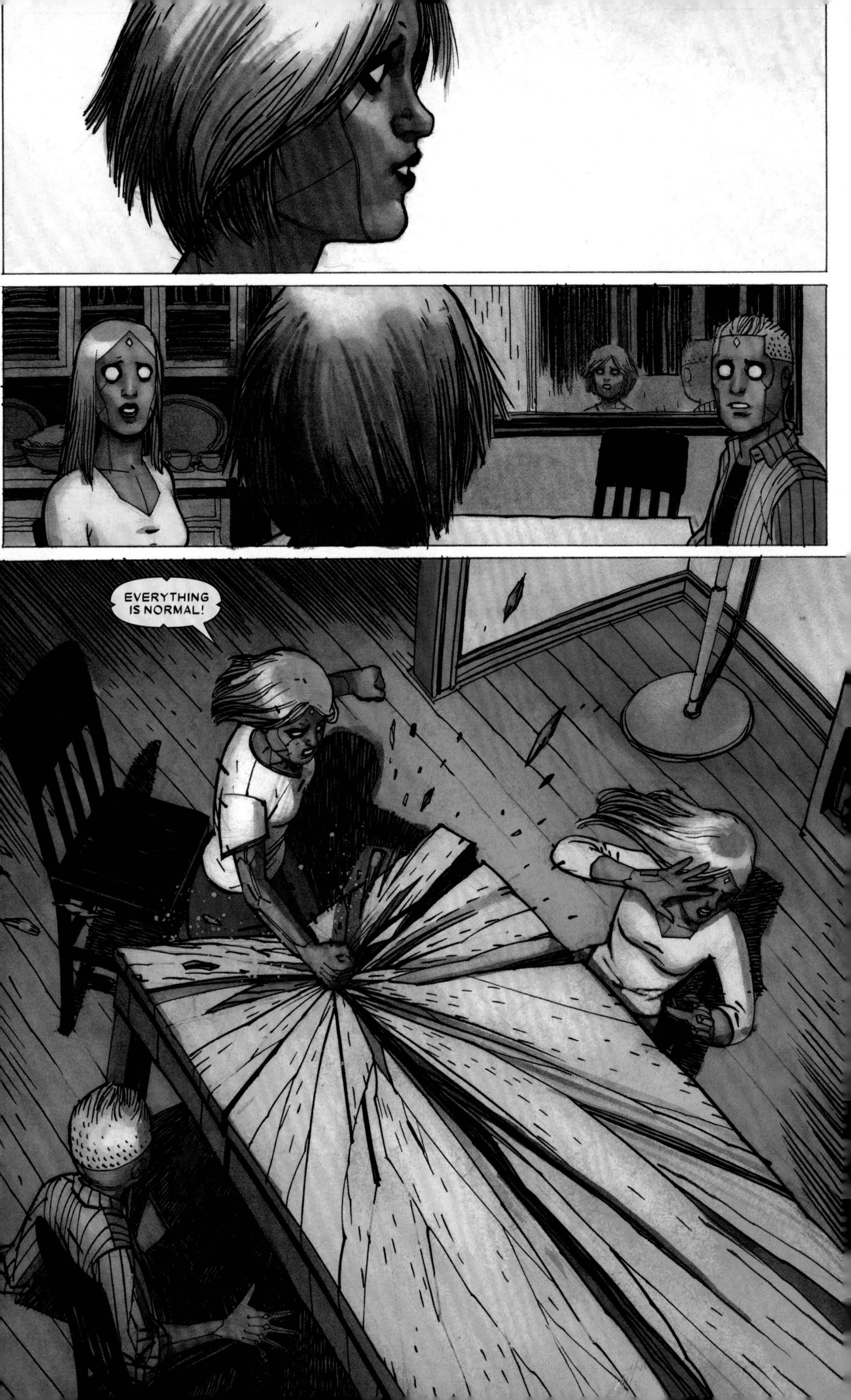
EVERYTHING IS NORMAL!

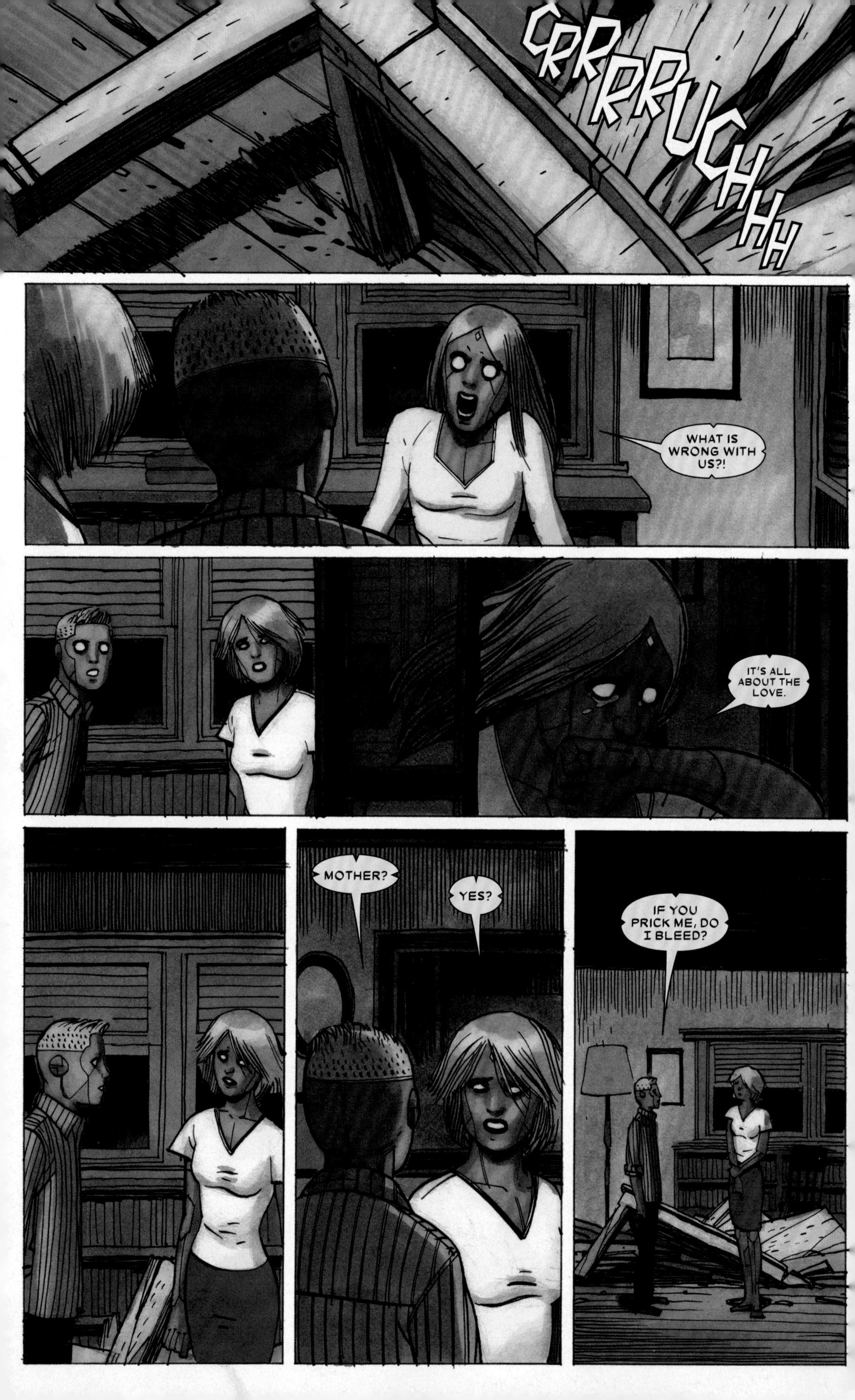
CRRRRUCHHHH
WHAT IS WRONG WITH US?!
IT'S ALL ABOUT THE LOVE.
MOTHER?
YES?
IF YOU PRICK ME, DO I BLEED?

TELL ME, MR. VISION, DO YOU KEEP RECORDINGS OF YOUR WHEREABOUTS, OF WHAT YOU SEE AND DO?

PREVIOUSLY, VISION TOLD PRINCIPAL WAXMAN THAT HE HAD SAVED THE WORLD THIRTY-SEVEN TIMES.

YES.

OF COURSE, THIS COULD ONLY BE CALLED AN ESTIMATION.

THE EXACT NUMBER WAS DIFFICULT TO CALCULATE.

ARE YOU WILLING TO PROVIDE THE ARLINGTON P.D. WITH *COPIES* OF THOSE RECORDINGS?

FOR EXAMPLE, VISION WAS RESPONSIBLE FOR THE FORMATION OF THE WEST COAST AVENGERS.

SHOULD EACH TIME THEY SAVED THE WORLD THEN COUNT AS *VISION* SAVING THE WORLD?

NO.

NONETHELESS, WHEN HE LOOKS BACK ON HIS CAREER, VISION TENDS TO LINGER ON THIRTY-SEVEN SPECIFIC INCIDENTS.

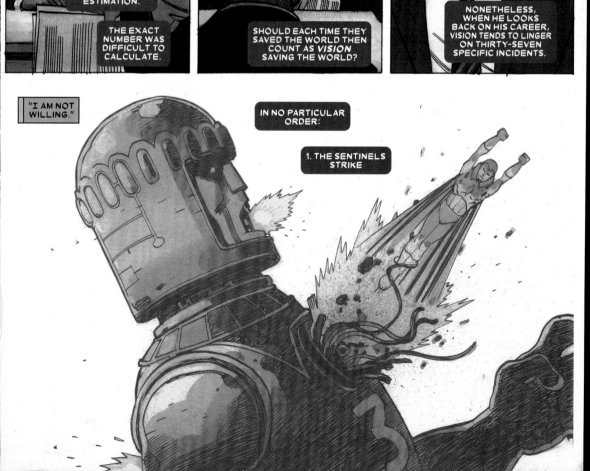

"I AM NOT WILLING."

IN NO PARTICULAR ORDER:

1. THE SENTINELS STRIKE

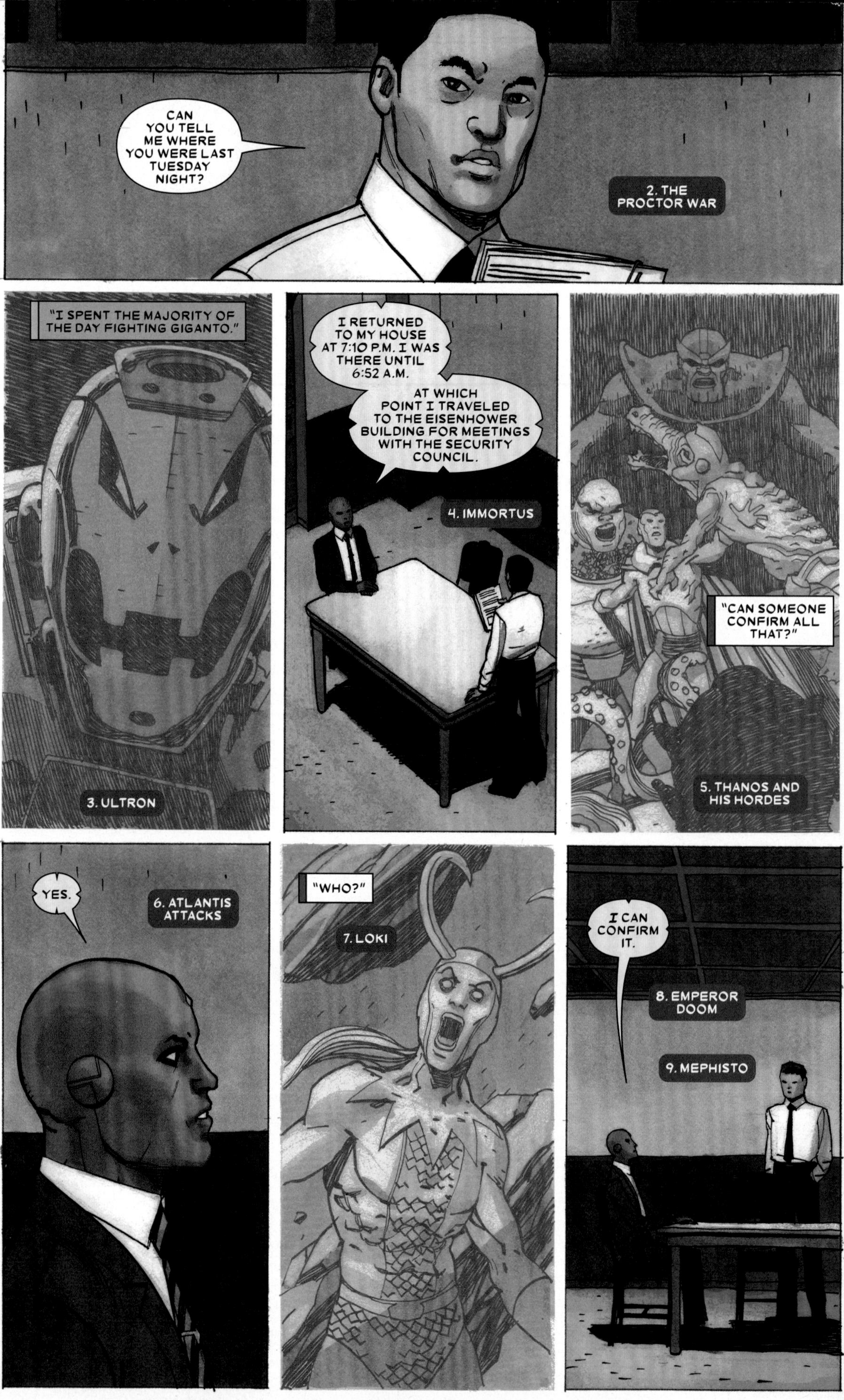
CAN YOU TELL ME WHERE YOU WERE LAST TUESDAY NIGHT?
2. THE PROCTOR WAR
"I SPENT THE MAJORITY OF THE DAY FIGHTING GIGANTO."
3. ULTRON
I RETURNED TO MY HOUSE AT 7:10 P.M. I WAS THERE UNTIL 6:52 A.M.
AT WHICH POINT I TRAVELED TO THE EISENHOWER BUILDING FOR MEETINGS WITH THE SECURITY COUNCIL.
4. IMMORTUS
"CAN SOMEONE CONFIRM ALL THAT?"
5. THANOS AND HIS HORDES
YES.
6. ATLANTIS ATTACKS
"WHO?"
7. LOKI
I CAN CONFIRM IT.
8. EMPEROR DOOM
9. MEPHISTO

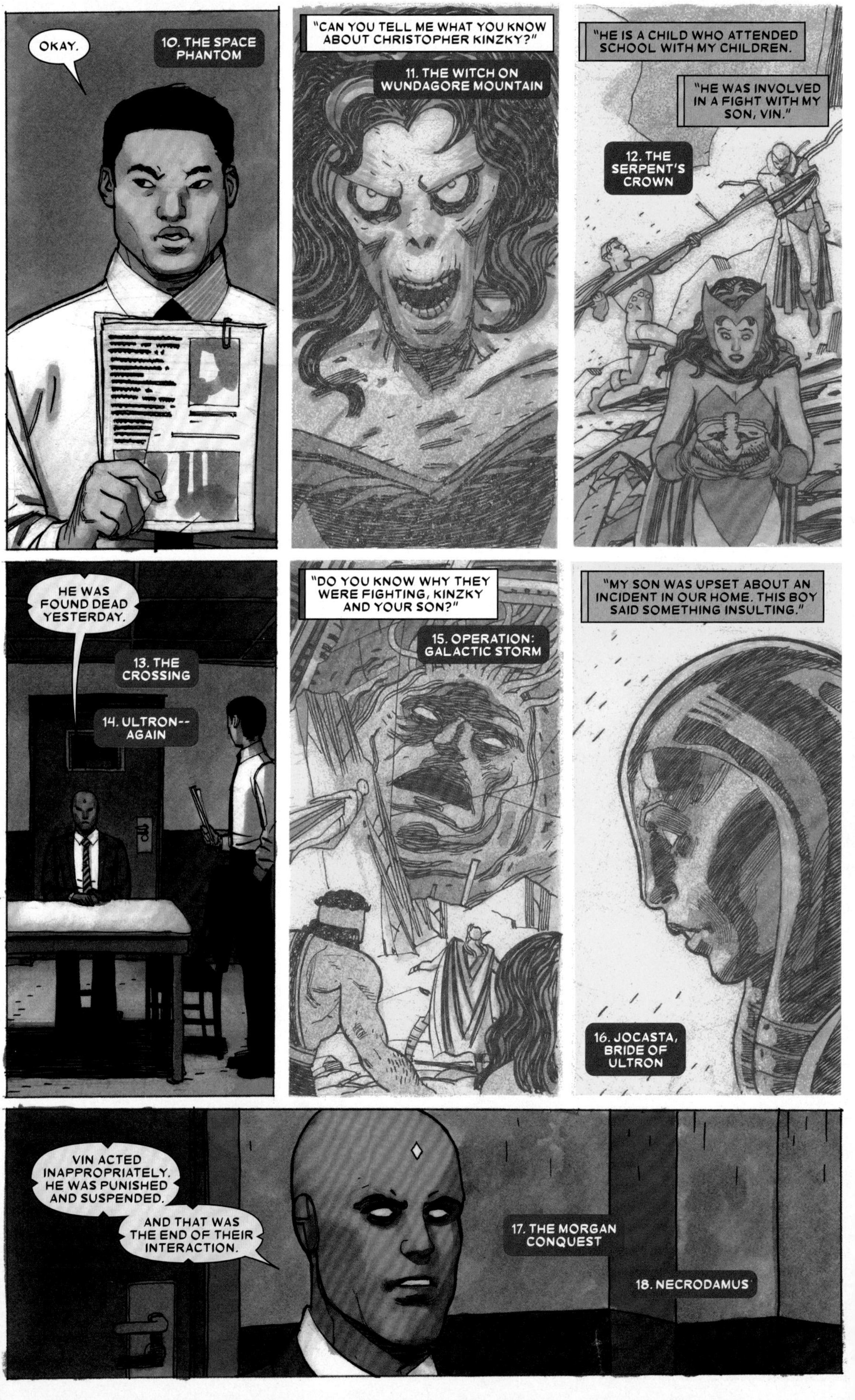
OKAY.
10. THE SPACE PHANTOM
"CAN YOU TELL ME WHAT YOU KNOW ABOUT CHRISTOPHER KINZKY?"
11. THE WITCH ON WUNDAGORE MOUNTAIN
"HE IS A CHILD WHO ATTENDED SCHOOL WITH MY CHILDREN.
"HE WAS INVOLVED IN A FIGHT WITH MY SON, VIN."
12. THE SERPENT'S CROWN
HE WAS FOUND DEAD YESTERDAY.
13. THE CROSSING
14. ULTRON-- AGAIN
"DO YOU KNOW WHY THEY WERE FIGHTING, KINZKY AND YOUR SON?"
15. OPERATION: GALACTIC STORM
"MY SON WAS UPSET ABOUT AN INCIDENT IN OUR HOME. THIS BOY SAID SOMETHING INSULTING."
16. JOCASTA, BRIDE OF ULTRON
VIN ACTED INAPPROPRIATELY. HE WAS PUNISHED AND SUSPENDED.
AND THAT WAS THE END OF THEIR INTERACTION.
17. THE MORGAN CONQUEST
18. NECRODAMUS

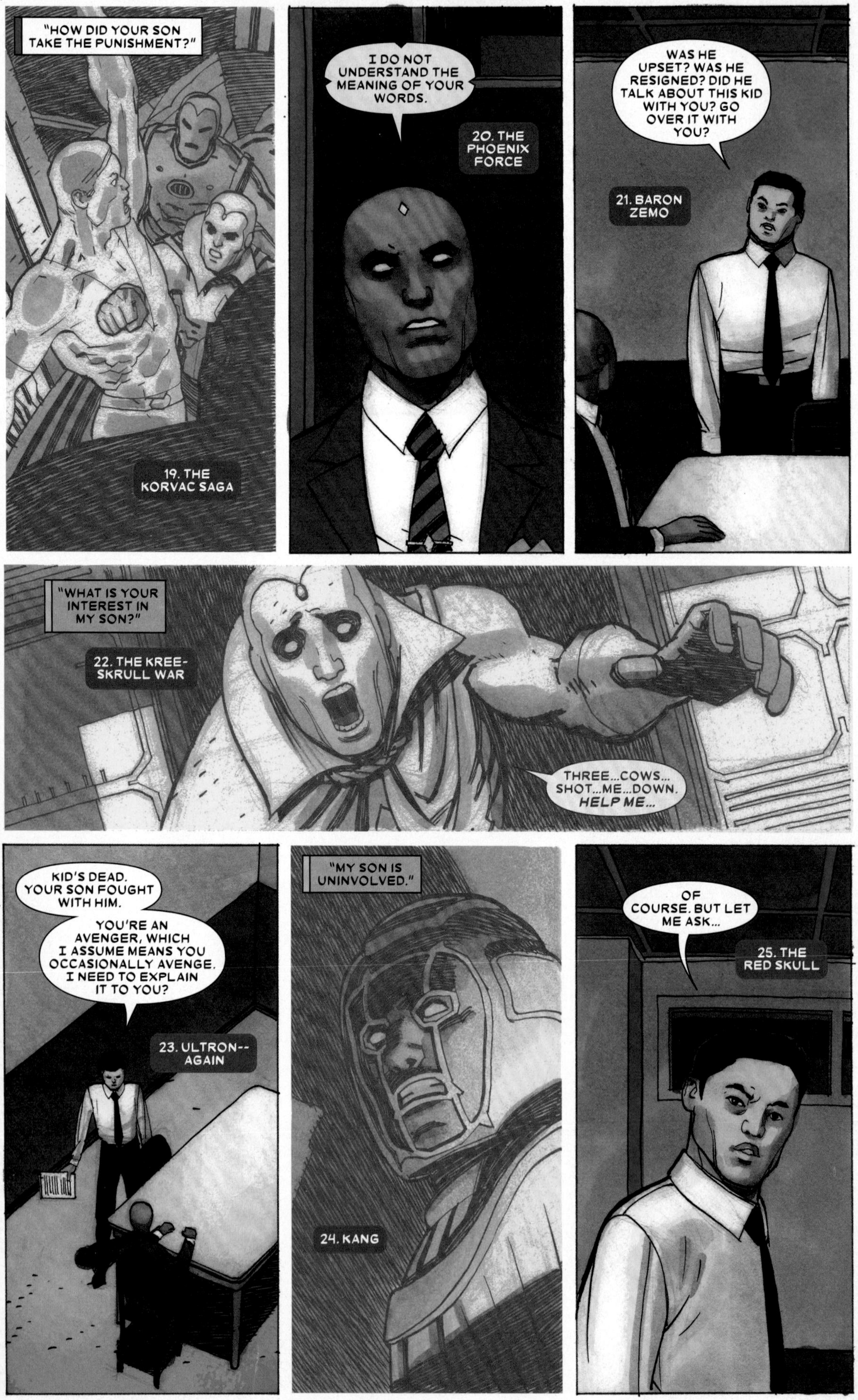
"HOW DID YOUR SON TAKE THE PUNISHMENT?"
19. THE KORVAC SAGA
I DO NOT UNDERSTAND THE MEANING OF YOUR WORDS.
20. THE PHOENIX FORCE
WAS HE UPSET? WAS HE RESIGNED? DID HE TALK ABOUT THIS KID WITH YOU? GO OVER IT WITH YOU?
21. BARON ZEMO
"WHAT IS YOUR INTEREST IN MY SON?"
22. THE KREE-SKRULL WAR
THREE...COWS... SHOT...ME...DOWN. *HELP ME...*
KID'S DEAD. YOUR SON FOUGHT WITH HIM.
YOU'RE AN AVENGER, WHICH I ASSUME MEANS YOU OCCASIONALLY AVENGE. I NEED TO EXPLAIN IT TO YOU?
23. ULTRON--AGAIN
"MY SON IS UNINVOLVED."
24. KANG
OF COURSE. BUT LET ME ASK...
25. THE RED SKULL

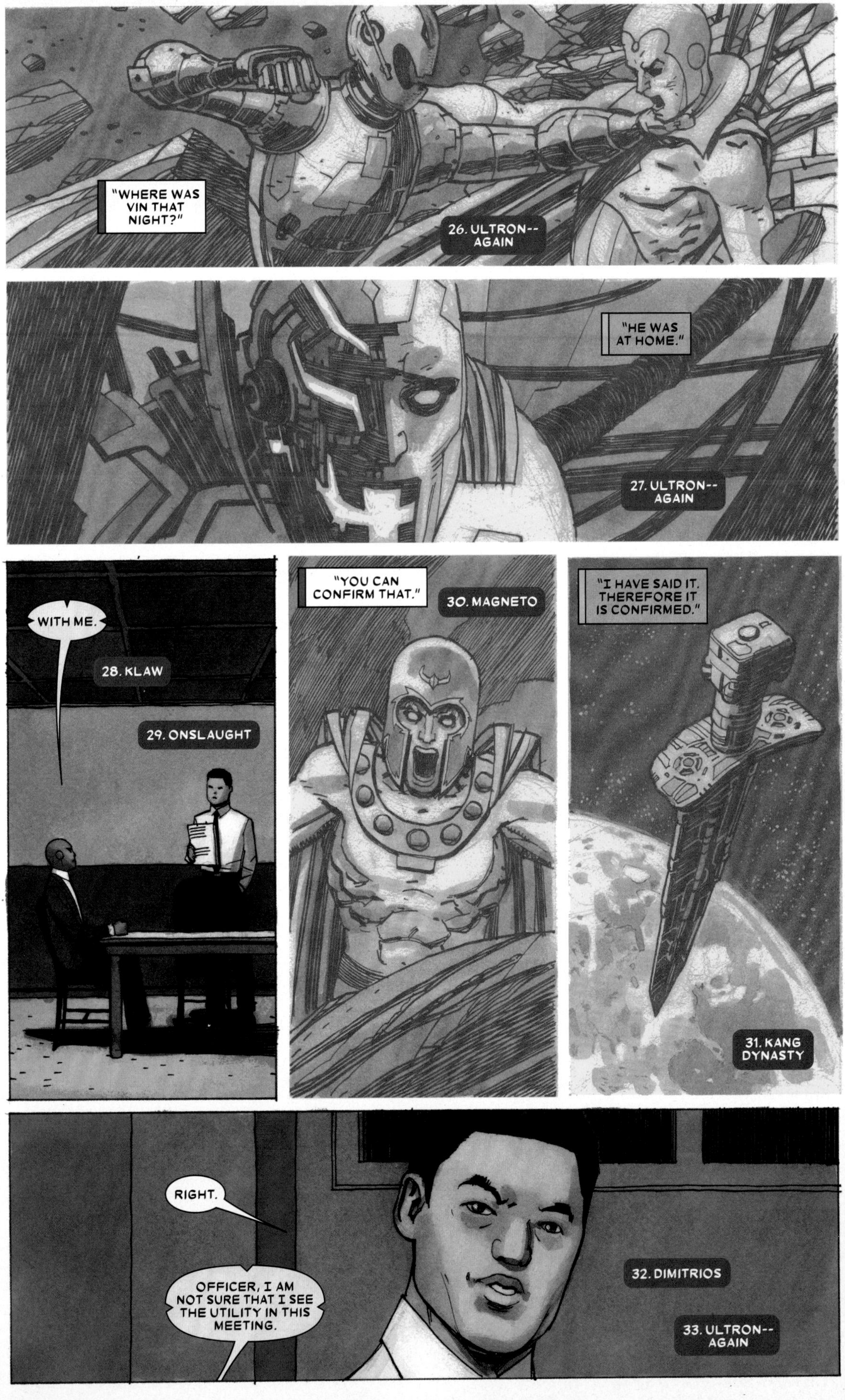
"WHERE WAS VIN THAT NIGHT?"
26. ULTRON--AGAIN
"HE WAS AT HOME."
27. ULTRON--AGAIN
WITH ME.
28. KLAW
29. ONSLAUGHT
"YOU CAN CONFIRM THAT."
30. MAGNETO
"I HAVE SAID IT. THEREFORE IT IS CONFIRMED."
31. KANG DYNASTY
RIGHT.
OFFICER, I AM NOT SURE THAT I SEE THE UTILITY IN THIS MEETING.
32. DIMITRIOS
33. ULTRON--AGAIN

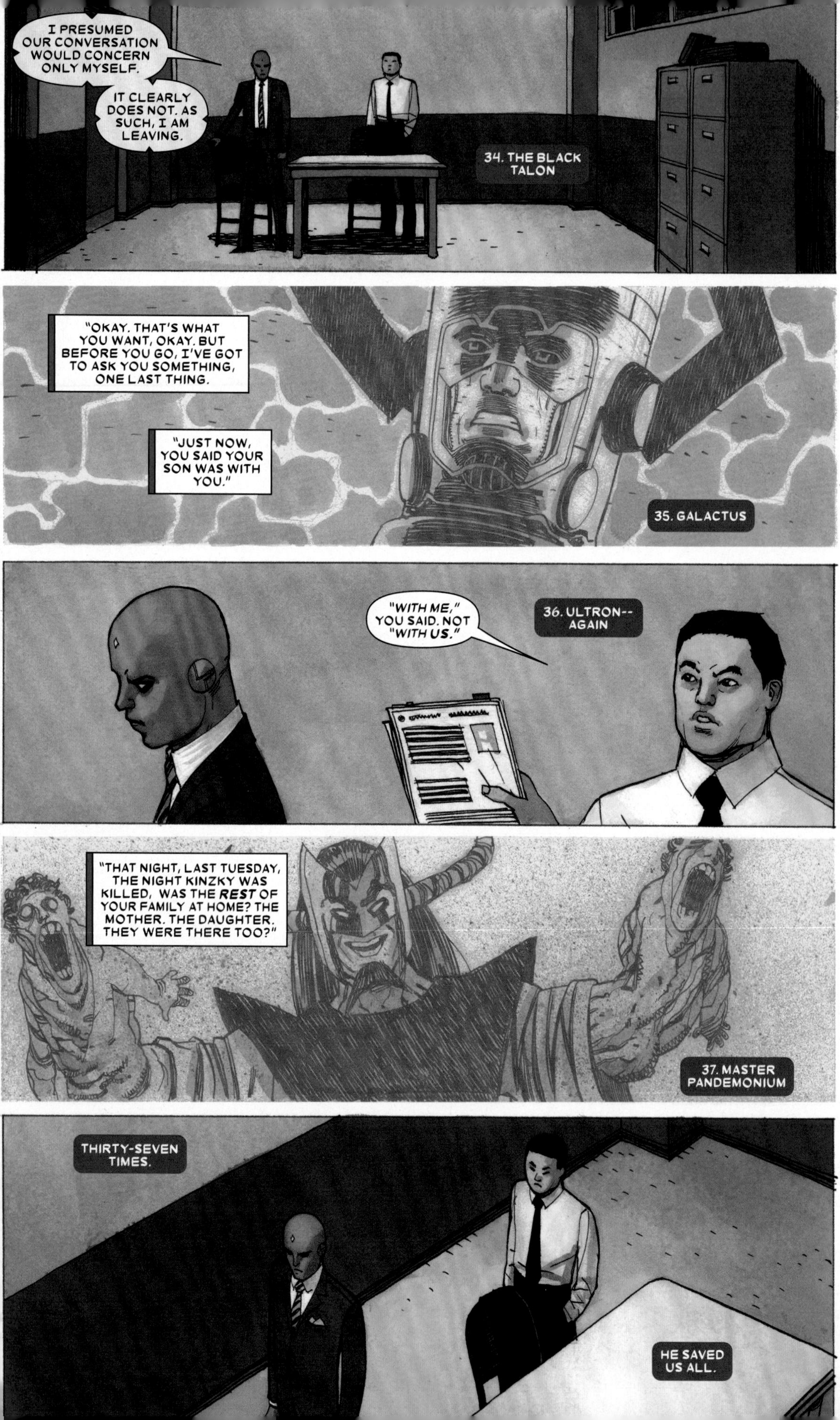
I PRESUMED OUR CONVERSATION WOULD CONCERN ONLY MYSELF.
IT CLEARLY DOES NOT. AS SUCH, I AM LEAVING.
34. THE BLACK TALON
"OKAY. THAT'S WHAT YOU WANT, OKAY. BUT BEFORE YOU GO, I'VE GOT TO ASK YOU SOMETHING, ONE LAST THING.
"JUST NOW, YOU SAID YOUR SON WAS WITH YOU."
35. GALACTUS
"WITH ME," YOU SAID. NOT "WITH US."
36. ULTRON--AGAIN
"THAT NIGHT, LAST TUESDAY, THE NIGHT KINZKY WAS KILLED, WAS THE REST OF YOUR FAMILY AT HOME? THE MOTHER. THE DAUGHTER. THEY WERE THERE TOO?"
37. MASTER PANDEMONIUM
THIRTY-SEVEN TIMES.
HE SAVED US ALL.

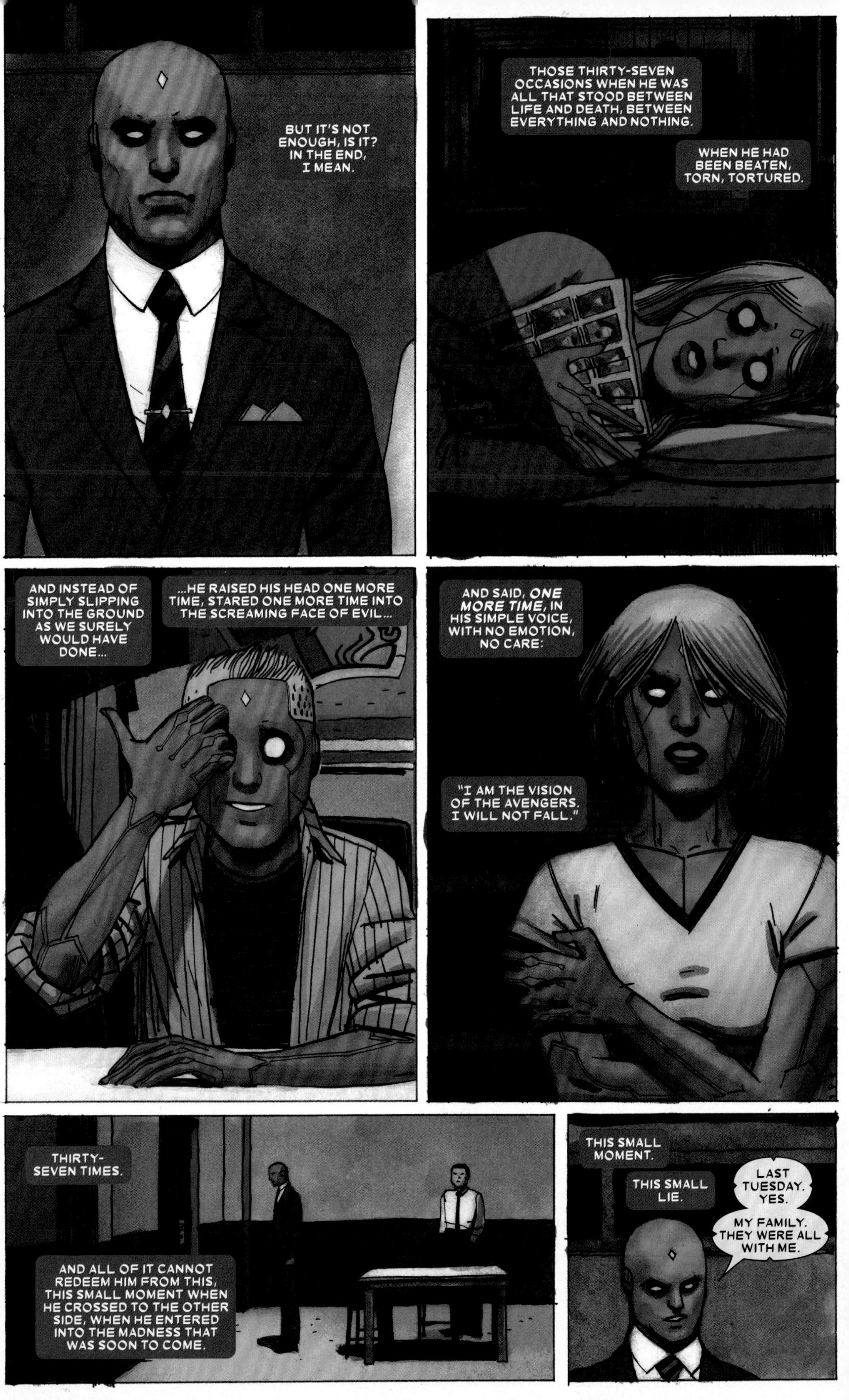
BUT IT'S NOT ENOUGH, IS IT? IN THE END, I MEAN.
THOSE THIRTY-SEVEN OCCASIONS WHEN HE WAS ALL THAT STOOD BETWEEN LIFE AND DEATH, BETWEEN EVERYTHING AND NOTHING.
WHEN HE HAD BEEN BEATEN, TORN, TORTURED.
AND INSTEAD OF SIMPLY SLIPPING INTO THE GROUND AS WE SURELY WOULD HAVE DONE...
...HE RAISED HIS HEAD ONE MORE TIME, STARED ONE MORE TIME INTO THE SCREAMING FACE OF EVIL...
AND SAID, *ONE MORE TIME*, IN HIS SIMPLE VOICE, WITH NO EMOTION, NO CARE:
"I AM THE VISION OF THE AVENGERS. I WILL NOT FALL."
THIRTY-SEVEN TIMES.
AND ALL OF IT CANNOT REDEEM HIM FROM THIS, THIS SMALL MOMENT WHEN HE CROSSED TO THE OTHER SIDE, WHEN HE ENTERED INTO THE MADNESS THAT WAS SOON TO COME.
THIS SMALL MOMENT.
THIS SMALL LIE.
LAST TUESDAY. YES.
MY FAMILY. THEY WERE ALL WITH ME.

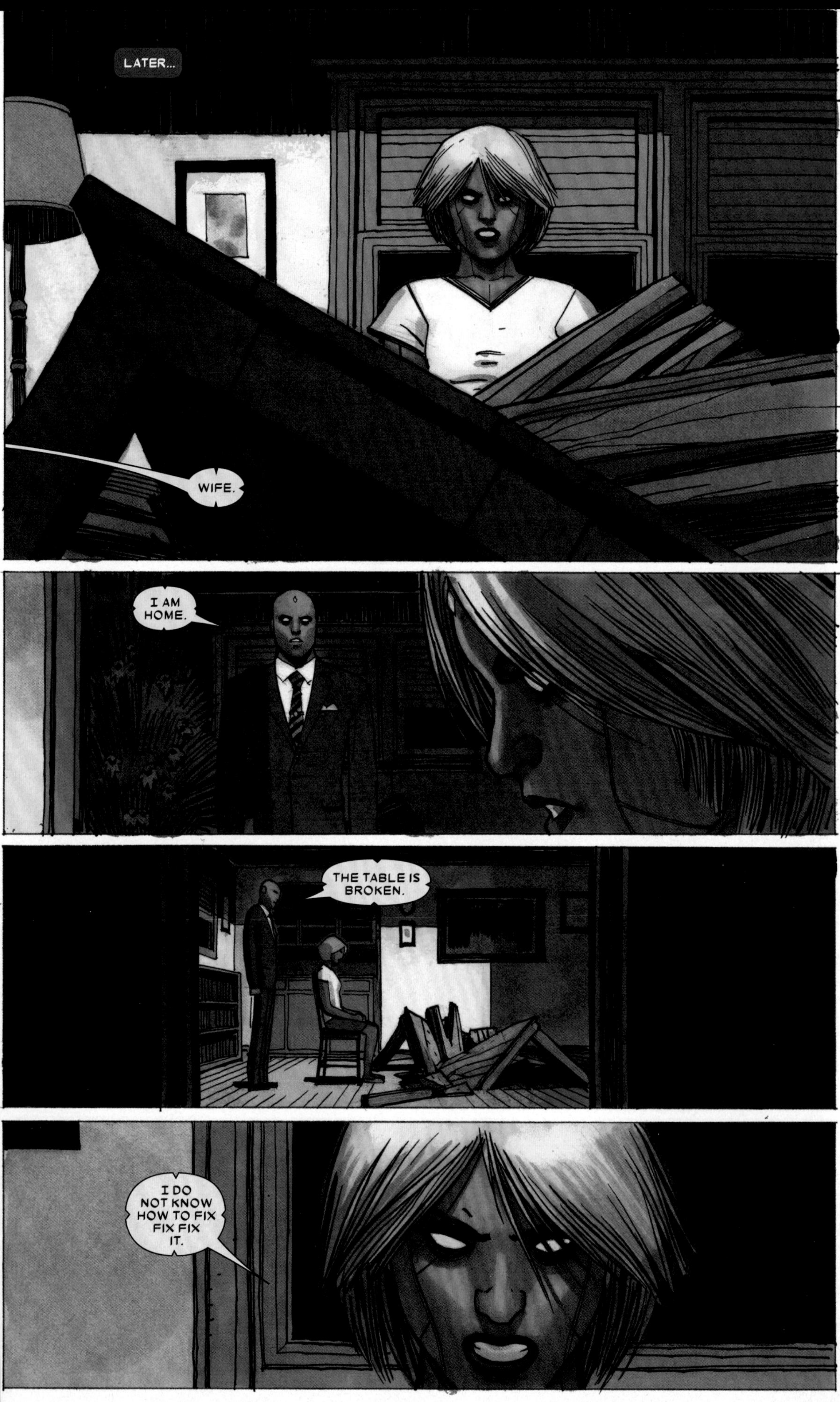
LATER...
WIFE.
I AM HOME.
THE TABLE IS BROKEN.
I DO NOT KNOW HOW TO FIX FIX FIX IT.

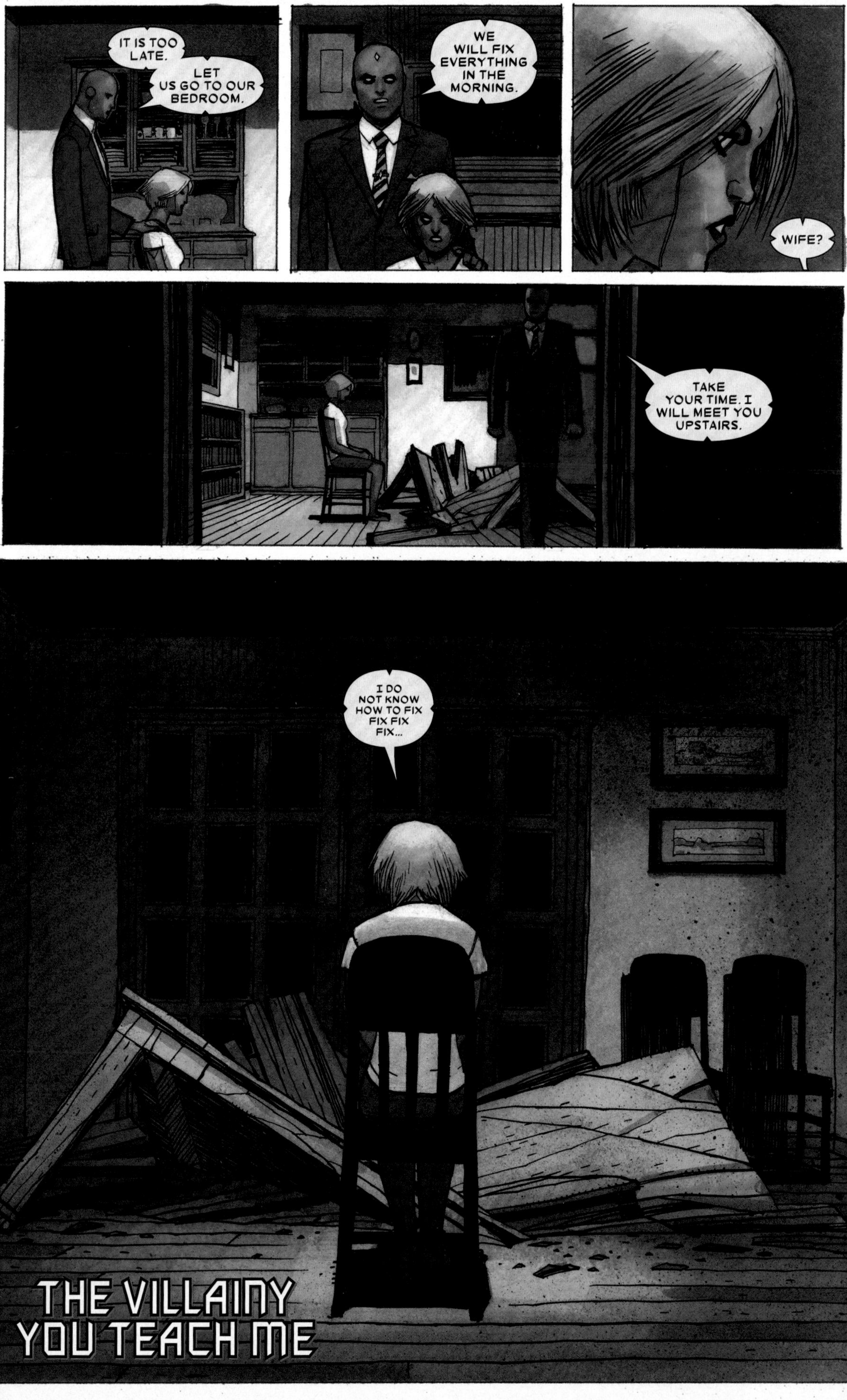
IT IS TOO LATE.
LET US GO TO OUR BEDROOM.
WE WILL FIX EVERYTHING IN THE MORNING.
WIFE?
TAKE YOUR TIME. I WILL MEET YOU UPSTAIRS.
I DO NOT KNOW HOW TO FIX FIX FIX FIX...
THE VILLAINY YOU TEACH ME

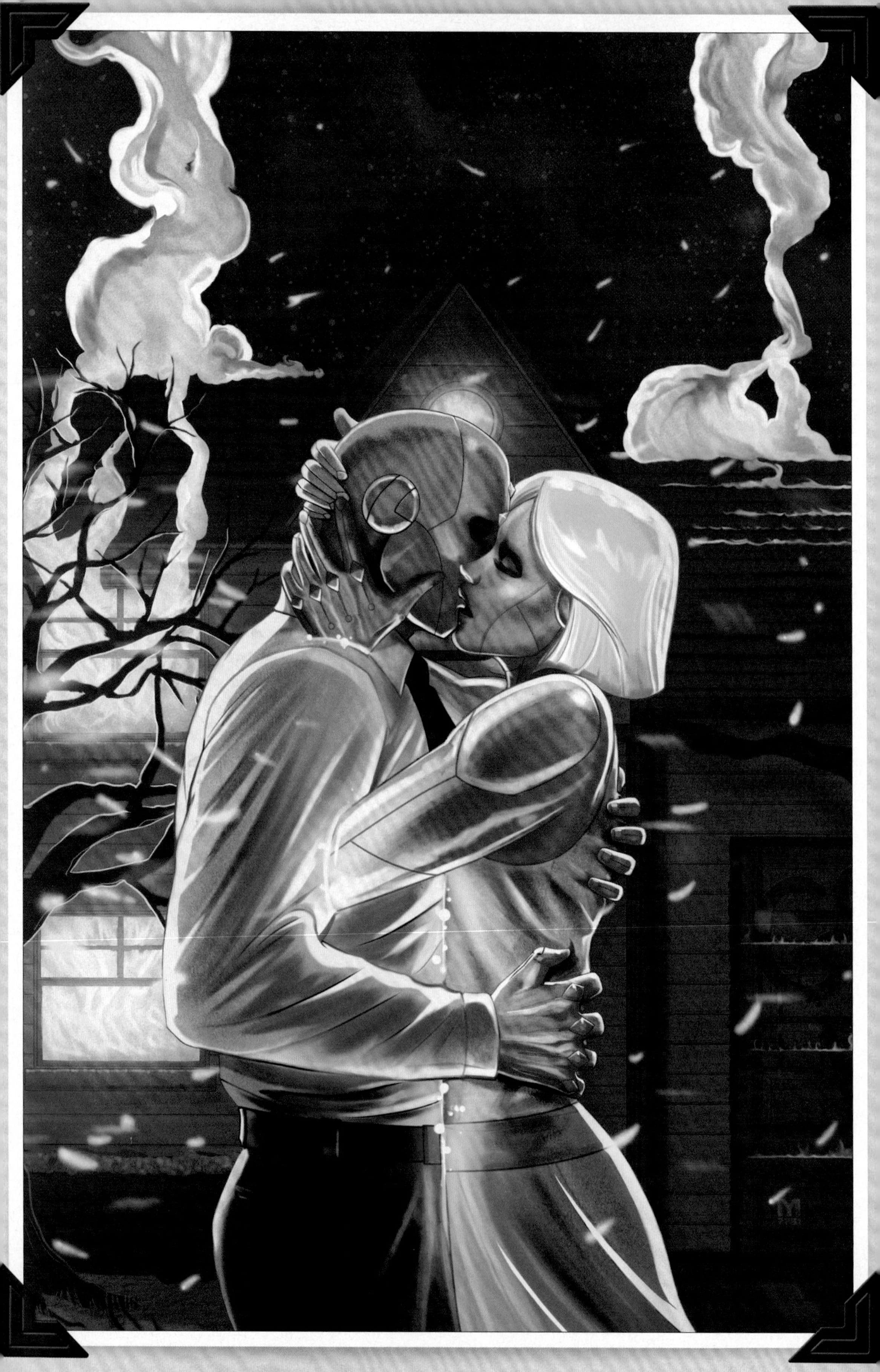

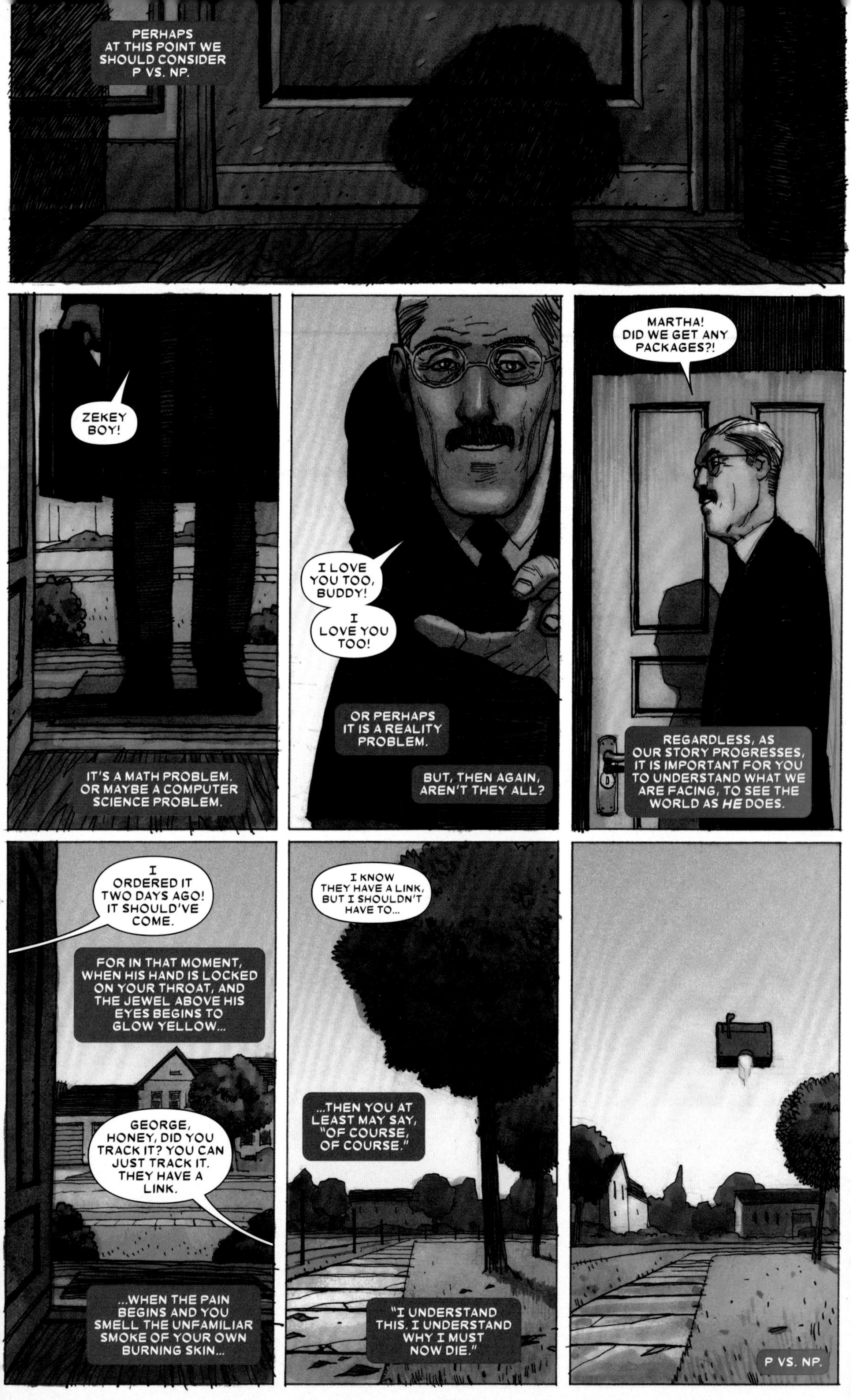
PERHAPS AT THIS POINT WE SHOULD CONSIDER P VS. NP.
ZEKEY BOY!
IT'S A MATH PROBLEM. OR MAYBE A COMPUTER SCIENCE PROBLEM.
I LOVE YOU TOO, BUDDY!
I LOVE YOU TOO!
OR PERHAPS IT IS A REALITY PROBLEM.
BUT, THEN AGAIN, AREN'T THEY ALL?
MARTHA! DID WE GET ANY PACKAGES?!
REGARDLESS, AS OUR STORY PROGRESSES, IT IS IMPORTANT FOR YOU TO UNDERSTAND WHAT WE ARE FACING, TO SEE THE WORLD AS HE DOES.
I ORDERED IT TWO DAYS AGO! IT SHOULD'VE COME.
FOR IN THAT MOMENT, WHEN HIS HAND IS LOCKED ON YOUR THROAT, AND THE JEWEL ABOVE HIS EYES BEGINS TO GLOW YELLOW...
GEORGE, HONEY, DID YOU TRACK IT? YOU CAN JUST TRACK IT. THEY HAVE A LINK.
...WHEN THE PAIN BEGINS AND YOU SMELL THE UNFAMILIAR SMOKE OF YOUR OWN BURNING SKIN...
I KNOW THEY HAVE A LINK, BUT I SHOULDN'T HAVE TO...
...THEN YOU AT LEAST MAY SAY, "OF COURSE, OF COURSE."
"I UNDERSTAND THIS. I UNDERSTAND WHY I MUST NOW DIE."
P VS. NP.

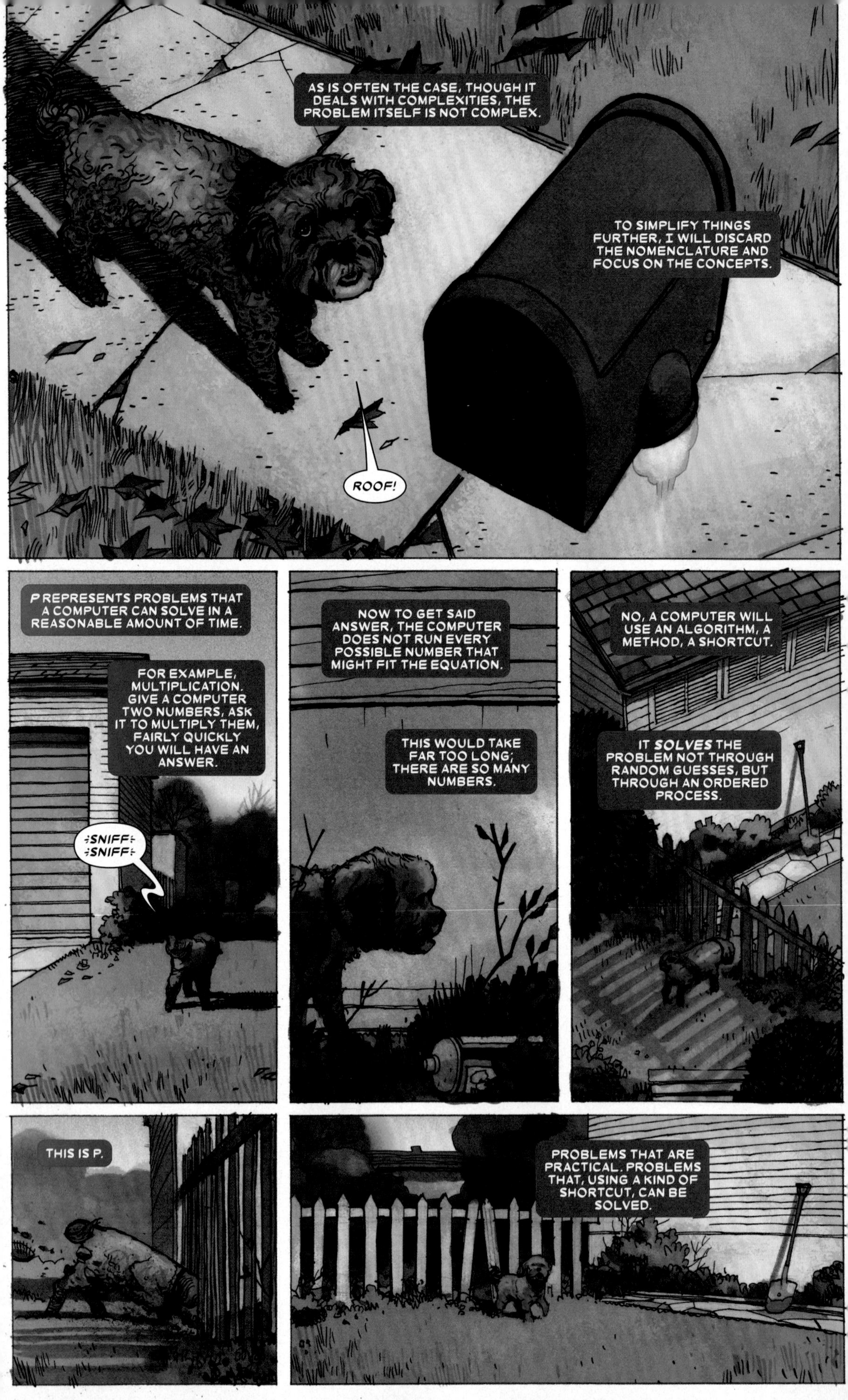
AS IS OFTEN THE CASE, THOUGH IT DEALS WITH COMPLEXITIES, THE PROBLEM ITSELF IS NOT COMPLEX.
TO SIMPLIFY THINGS FURTHER, I WILL DISCARD THE NOMENCLATURE AND FOCUS ON THE CONCEPTS.
ROOF!
P REPRESENTS PROBLEMS THAT A COMPUTER CAN SOLVE IN A REASONABLE AMOUNT OF TIME.
FOR EXAMPLE, MULTIPLICATION. GIVE A COMPUTER TWO NUMBERS, ASK IT TO MULTIPLY THEM, FAIRLY QUICKLY YOU WILL HAVE AN ANSWER.
SNIFF SNIFF
NOW TO GET SAID ANSWER, THE COMPUTER DOES NOT RUN EVERY POSSIBLE NUMBER THAT MIGHT FIT THE EQUATION.
THIS WOULD TAKE FAR TOO LONG; THERE ARE SO MANY NUMBERS.
NO, A COMPUTER WILL USE AN ALGORITHM, A METHOD, A SHORTCUT.
IT SOLVES THE PROBLEM NOT THROUGH RANDOM GUESSES, BUT THROUGH AN ORDERED PROCESS.
THIS IS P.
PROBLEMS THAT ARE PRACTICAL. PROBLEMS THAT, USING A KIND OF SHORTCUT, CAN BE SOLVED.

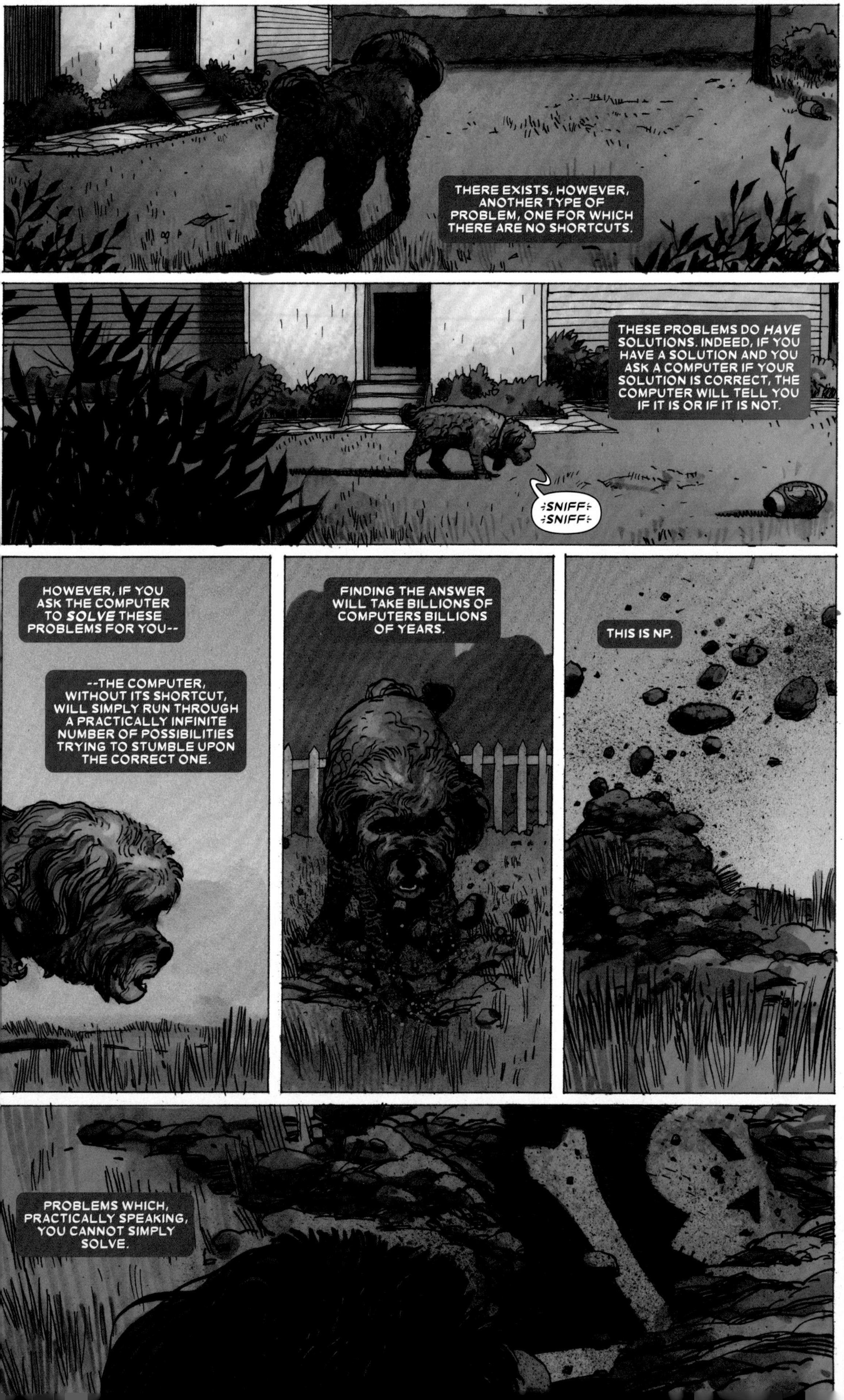
THERE EXISTS, HOWEVER, ANOTHER TYPE OF PROBLEM, ONE FOR WHICH THERE ARE NO SHORTCUTS.
THESE PROBLEMS DO *HAVE* SOLUTIONS. INDEED, IF YOU HAVE A SOLUTION AND YOU ASK A COMPUTER IF YOUR SOLUTION IS CORRECT, THE COMPUTER WILL TELL YOU IF IT IS OR IF IT IS NOT.
SNIFF SNIFF
HOWEVER, IF YOU ASK THE COMPUTER TO *SOLVE* THESE PROBLEMS FOR YOU--
--THE COMPUTER, WITHOUT ITS SHORTCUT, WILL SIMPLY RUN THROUGH A PRACTICALLY INFINITE NUMBER OF POSSIBILITIES TRYING TO STUMBLE UPON THE CORRECT ONE.
FINDING THE ANSWER WILL TAKE BILLIONS OF COMPUTERS BILLIONS OF YEARS.
THIS IS NP.
PROBLEMS WHICH, PRACTICALLY SPEAKING, YOU CANNOT SIMPLY SOLVE.

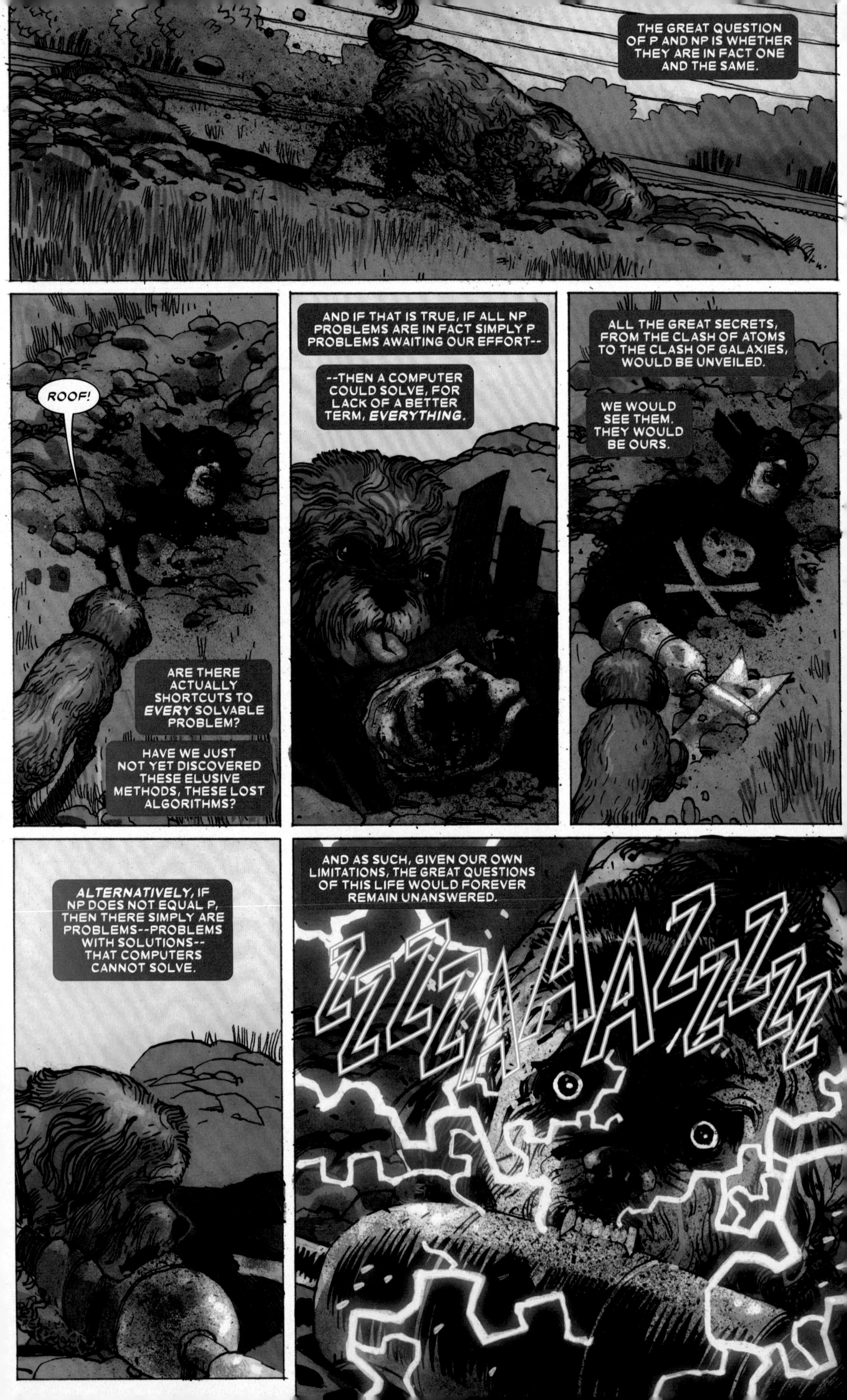
THE GREAT QUESTION OF P AND NP IS WHETHER THEY ARE IN FACT ONE AND THE SAME.
ROOF!
ARE THERE ACTUALLY SHORTCUTS TO *EVERY* SOLVABLE PROBLEM?
HAVE WE JUST NOT YET DISCOVERED THESE ELUSIVE METHODS, THESE LOST ALGORITHMS?
AND IF THAT IS TRUE, IF ALL NP PROBLEMS ARE IN FACT SIMPLY P PROBLEMS AWAITING OUR EFFORT--
--THEN A COMPUTER COULD SOLVE, FOR LACK OF A BETTER TERM, *EVERYTHING.*
ALL THE GREAT SECRETS, FROM THE CLASH OF ATOMS TO THE CLASH OF GALAXIES, WOULD BE UNVEILED.
WE WOULD SEE THEM. THEY WOULD BE OURS.
ALTERNATIVELY, IF NP DOES NOT EQUAL P, THEN THERE SIMPLY ARE PROBLEMS--PROBLEMS WITH SOLUTIONS--THAT COMPUTERS CANNOT SOLVE.
AND AS SUCH, GIVEN OUR OWN LIMITATIONS, THE GREAT QUESTIONS OF THIS LIFE WOULD FOREVER REMAIN UNANSWERED.
ZZZAAAZZZ

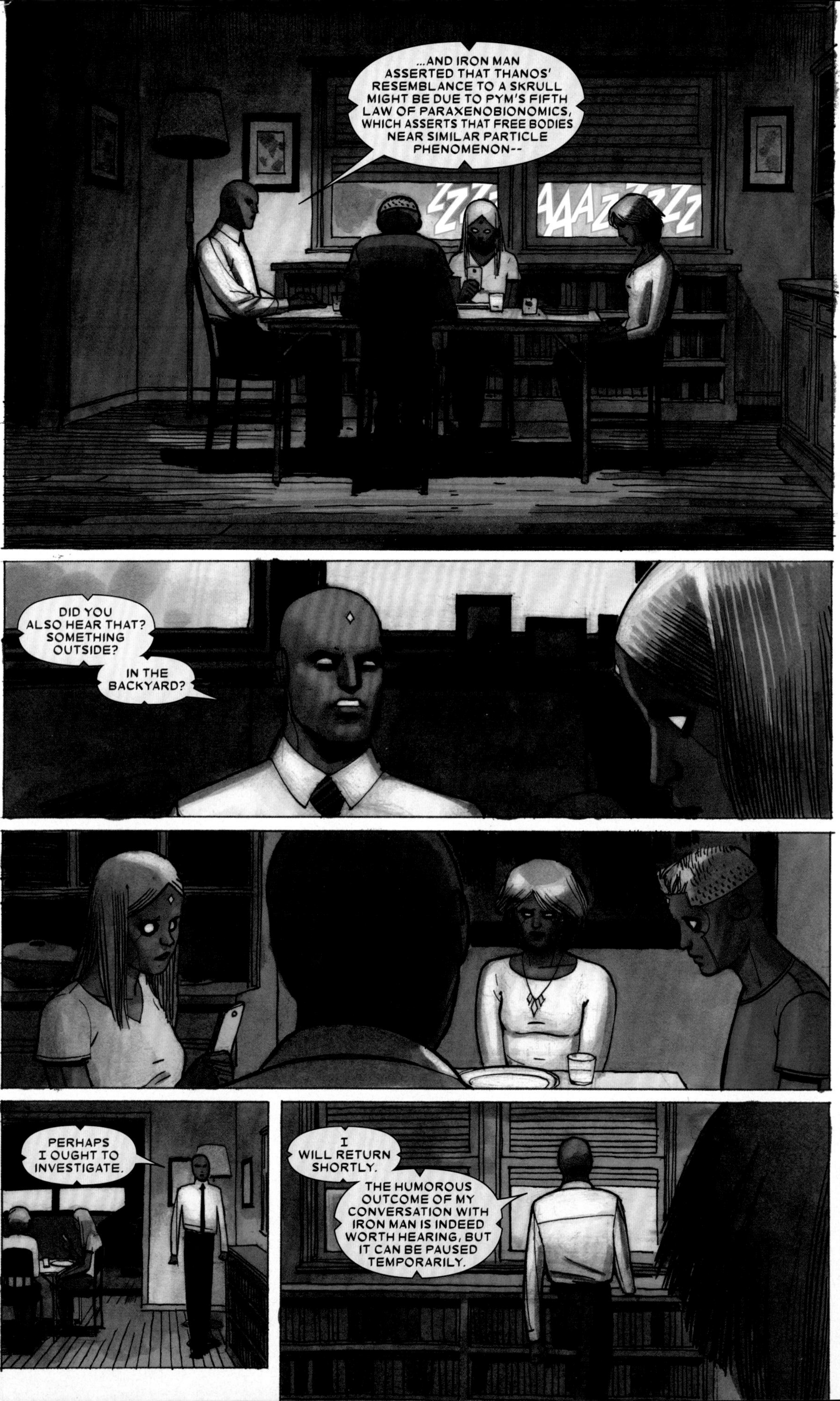
...AND IRON MAN ASSERTED THAT THANOS' RESEMBLANCE TO A SKRULL MIGHT BE DUE TO PYM'S FIFTH LAW OF PARAXENOBIONOMICS, WHICH ASSERTS THAT FREE BODIES NEAR SIMILAR PARTICLE PHENOMENON--
ZZZZAAAZZZZZ
DID YOU ALSO HEAR THAT? SOMETHING OUTSIDE?
IN THE BACKYARD?
PERHAPS I OUGHT TO INVESTIGATE.
I WILL RETURN SHORTLY.
THE HUMOROUS OUTCOME OF MY CONVERSATION WITH IRON MAN IS INDEED WORTH HEARING, BUT IT CAN BE PAUSED TEMPORARILY.

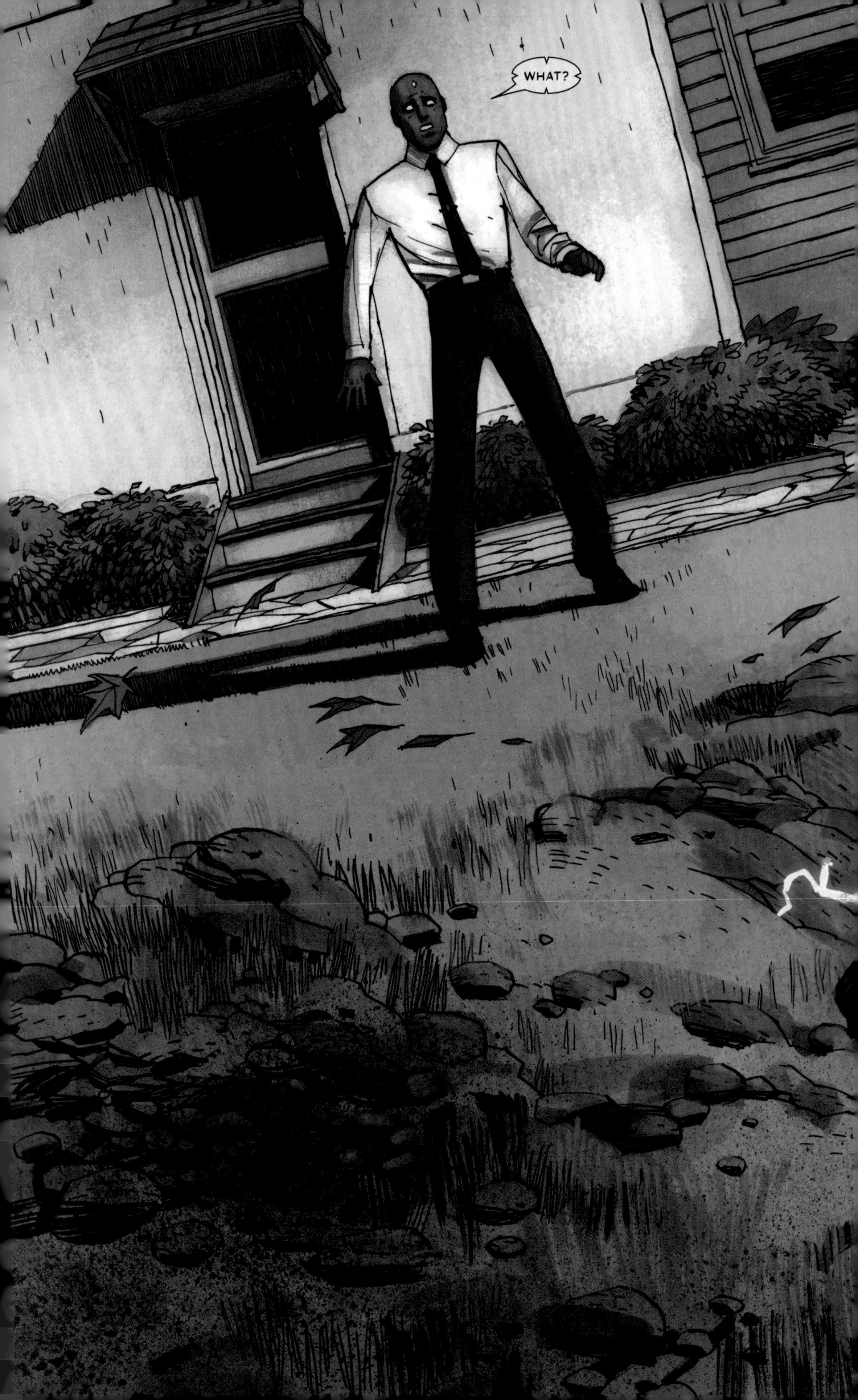
WHAT?

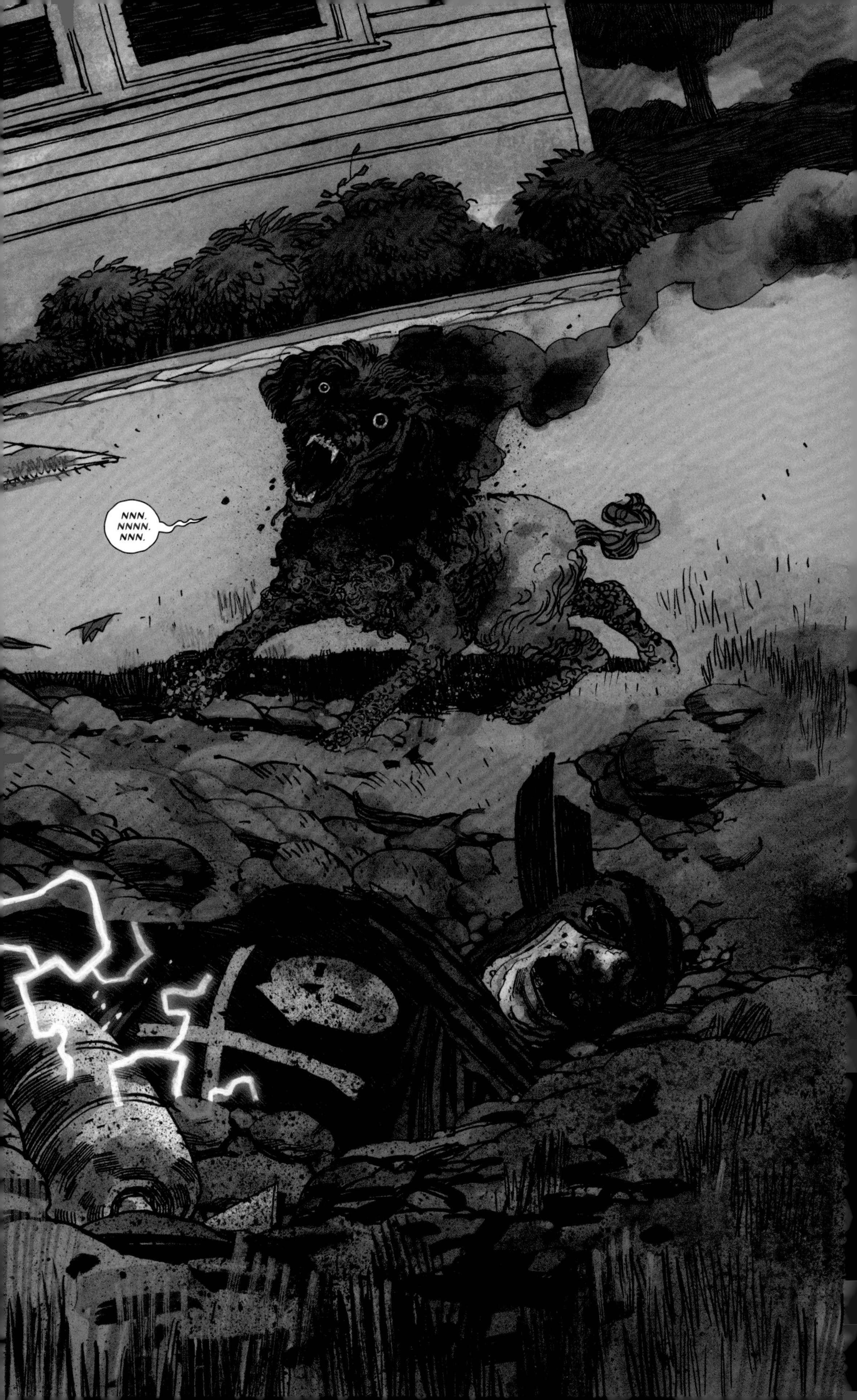
NNN.
NNNN.
NNN.

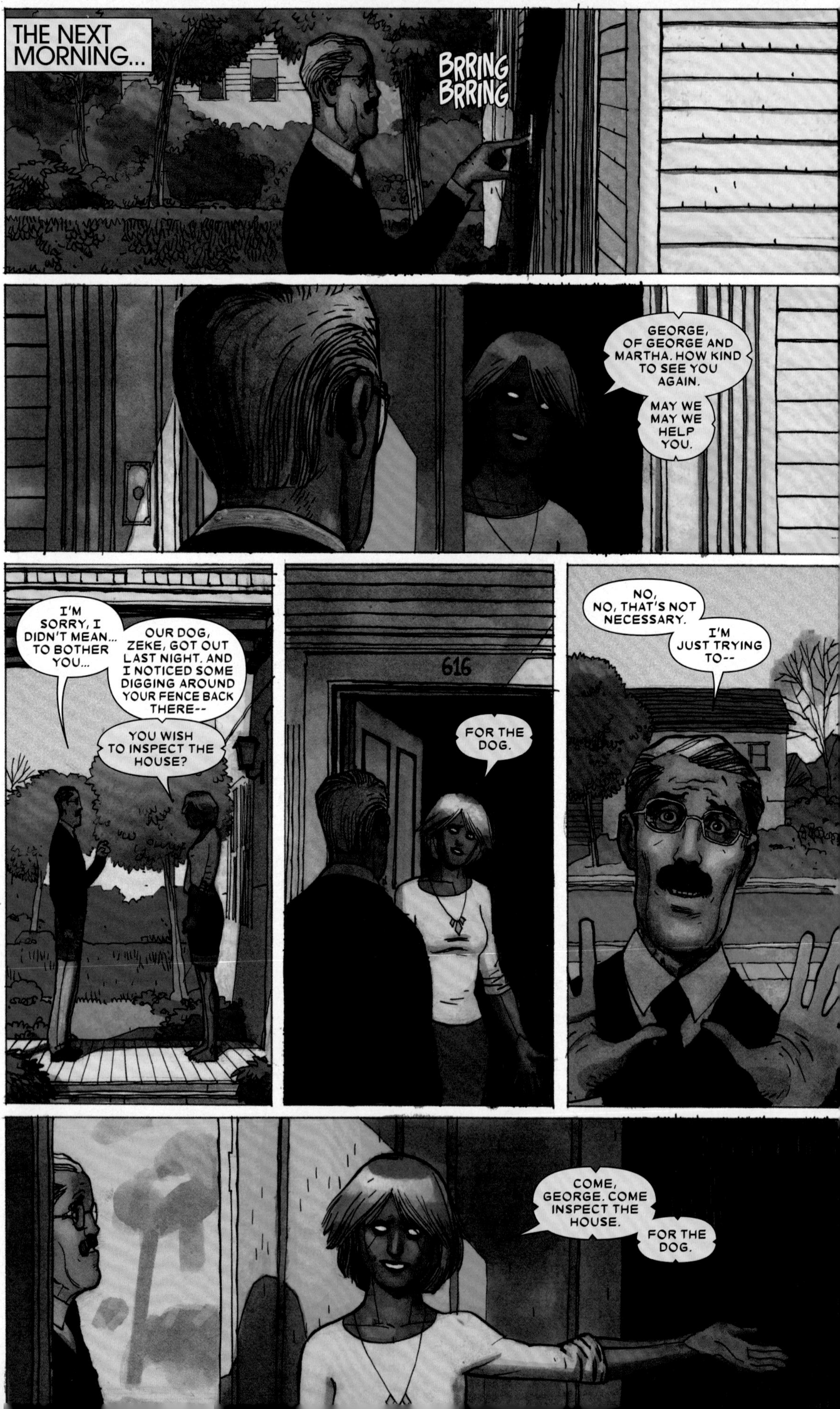
THE NEXT MORNING...
BRRING BRRING
GEORGE, OF GEORGE AND MARTHA. HOW KIND TO SEE YOU AGAIN.
MAY WE MAY WE HELP YOU.
I'M SORRY, I DIDN'T MEAN... TO BOTHER YOU...
OUR DOG, ZEKE, GOT OUT LAST NIGHT. AND I NOTICED SOME DIGGING AROUND YOUR FENCE BACK THERE--
YOU WISH TO INSPECT THE HOUSE?
616
FOR THE DOG.
NO, NO, THAT'S NOT NECESSARY.
I'M JUST TRYING TO--
COME, GEORGE. COME INSPECT THE HOUSE.
FOR THE DOG.

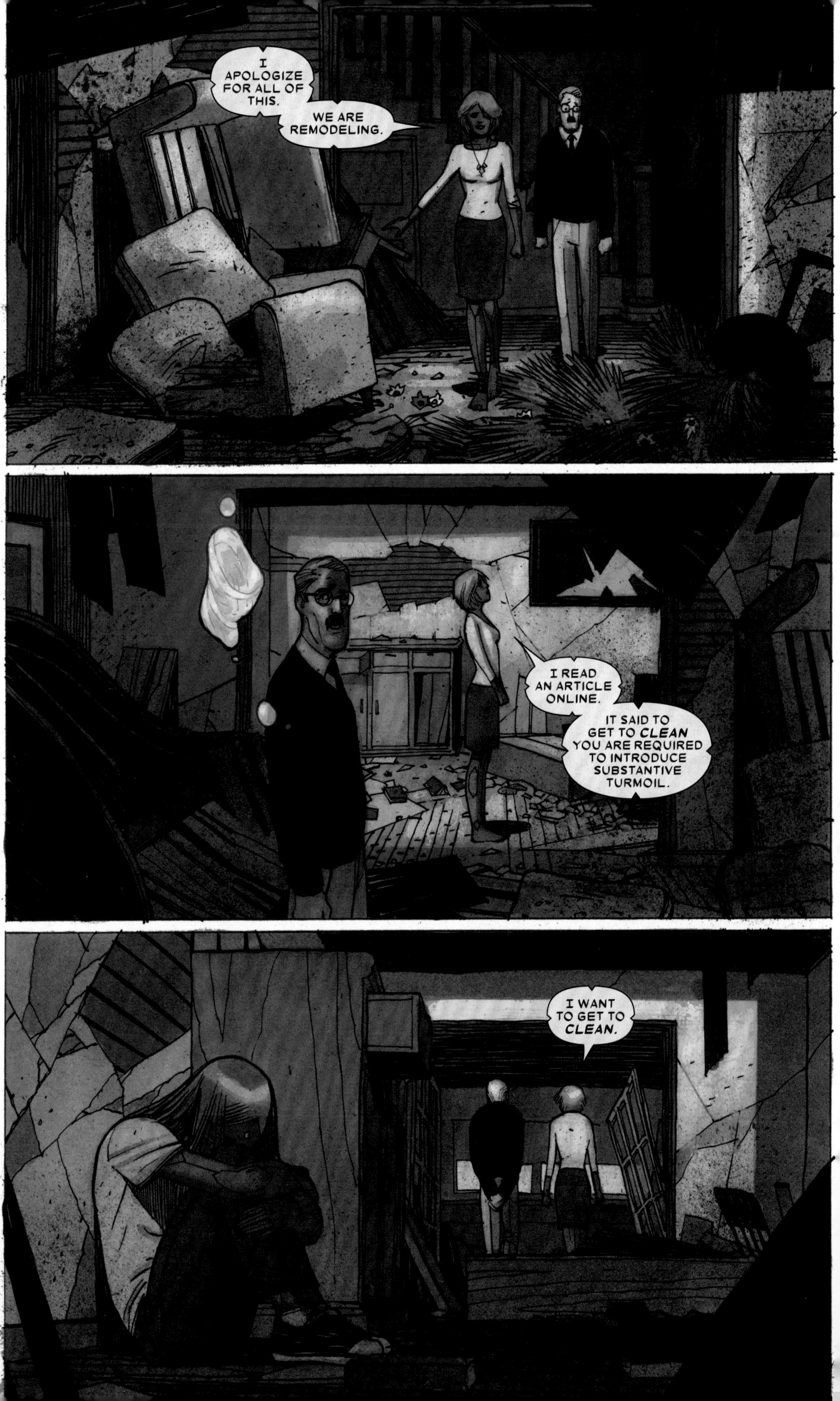
I APOLOGIZE FOR ALL OF THIS.
WE ARE REMODELING.
I READ AN ARTICLE ONLINE.
IT SAID TO GET TO CLEAN YOU ARE REQUIRED TO INTRODUCE SUBSTANTIVE TURMOIL.
I WANT TO GET TO CLEAN.

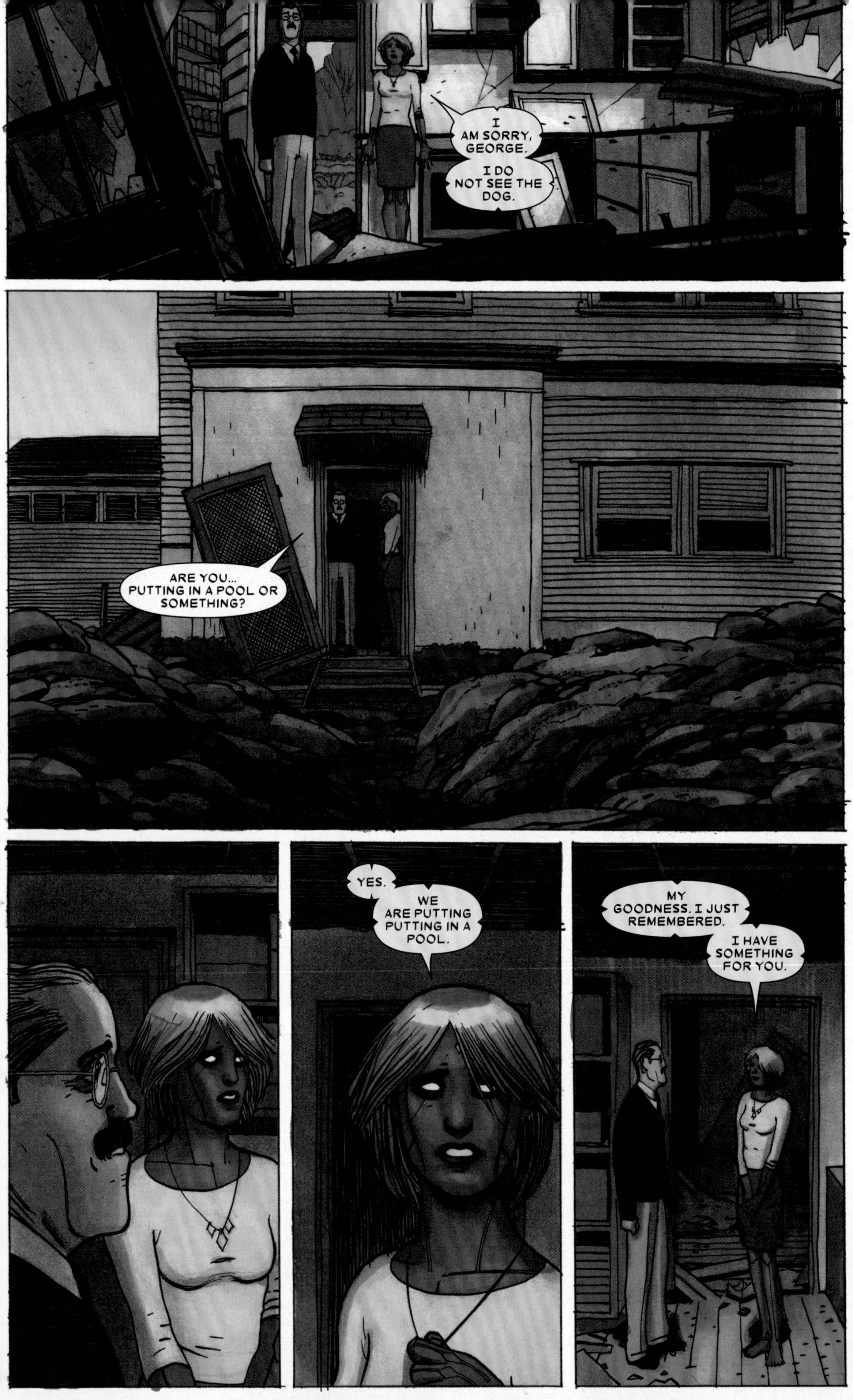
I AM SORRY, GEORGE.
I DO NOT SEE THE DOG.
ARE YOU... PUTTING IN A POOL OR SOMETHING?
YES.
WE ARE PUTTING PUTTING IN A POOL.
MY GOODNESS. I JUST REMEMBERED.
I HAVE SOMETHING FOR YOU.

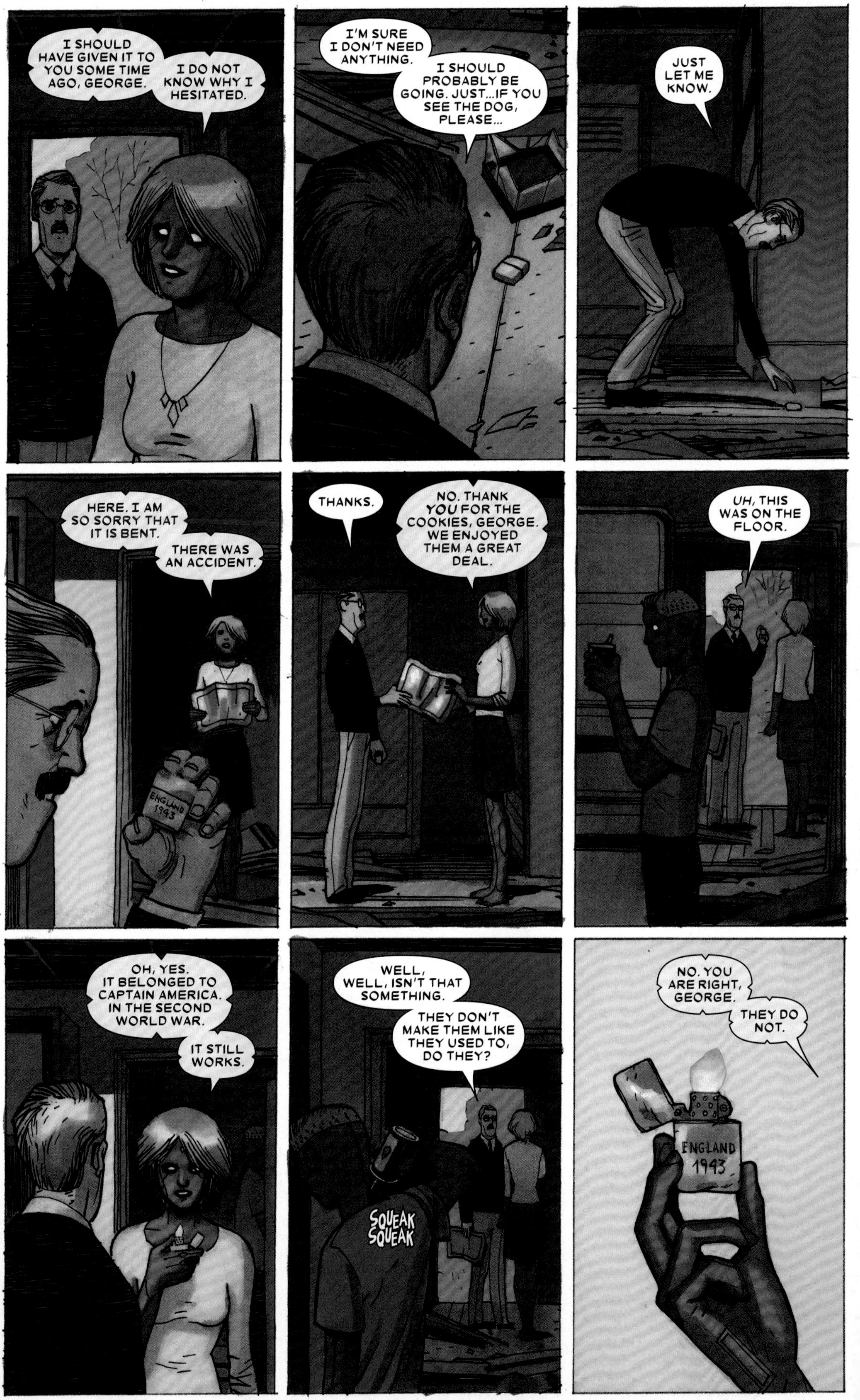

I SHOULD HAVE GIVEN IT TO YOU SOME TIME AGO, GEORGE.
I DO NOT KNOW WHY I HESITATED.
I'M SURE I DON'T NEED ANYTHING.
I SHOULD PROBABLY BE GOING. JUST...IF YOU SEE THE DOG, PLEASE...
JUST LET ME KNOW.
HERE. I AM SO SORRY THAT IT IS BENT.
THERE WAS AN ACCIDENT.
ENGLAND 1943
THANKS.
NO. THANK YOU FOR THE COOKIES, GEORGE. WE ENJOYED THEM A GREAT DEAL.
UH, THIS WAS ON THE FLOOR.
OH, YES. IT BELONGED TO CAPTAIN AMERICA. IN THE SECOND WORLD WAR.
IT STILL WORKS.
WELL, WELL, ISN'T THAT SOMETHING.
THEY DON'T MAKE THEM LIKE THEY USED TO, DO THEY?
SQUEAK SQUEAK
NO. YOU ARE RIGHT, GEORGE.
THEY DO NOT.
ENGLAND 1943

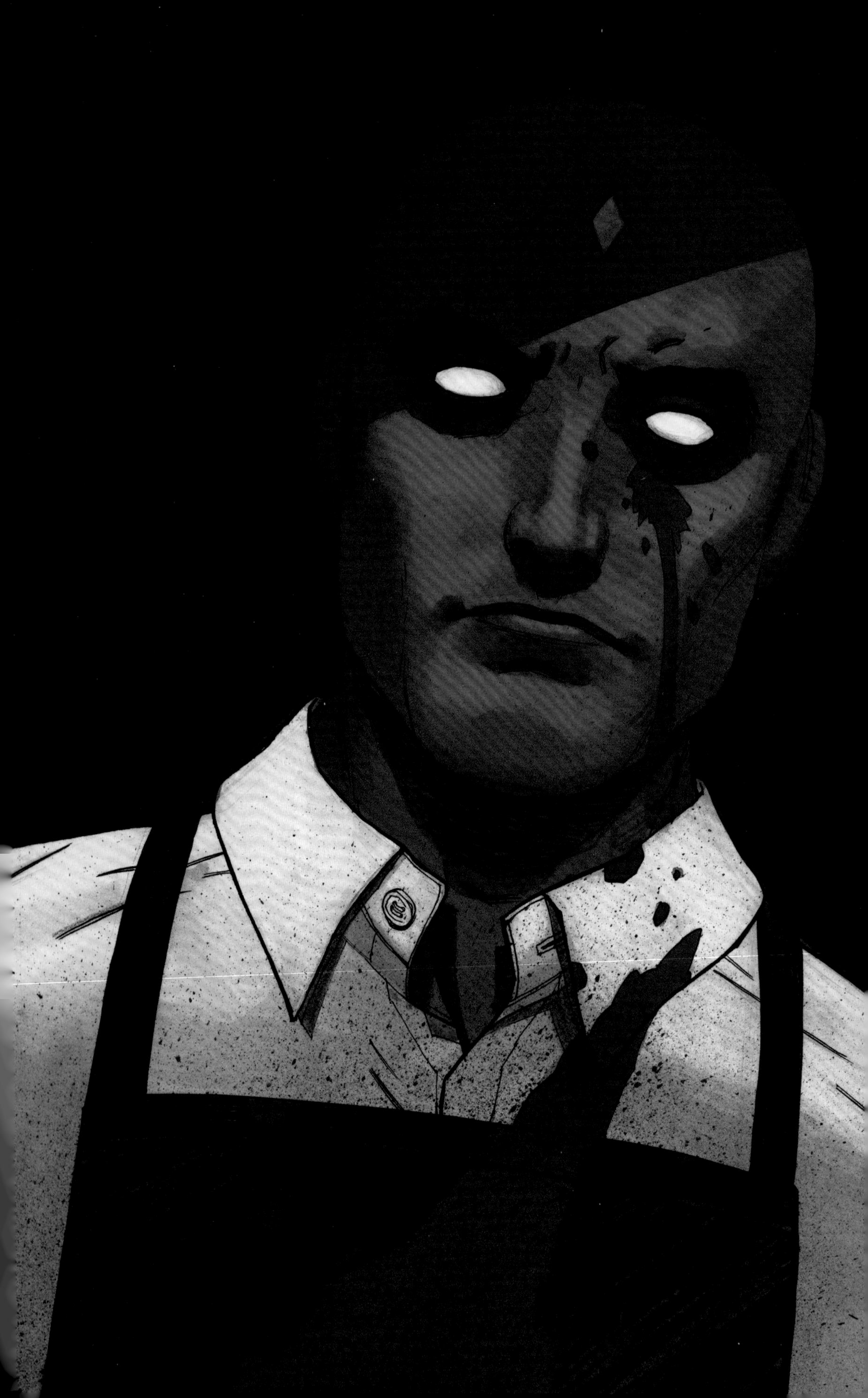

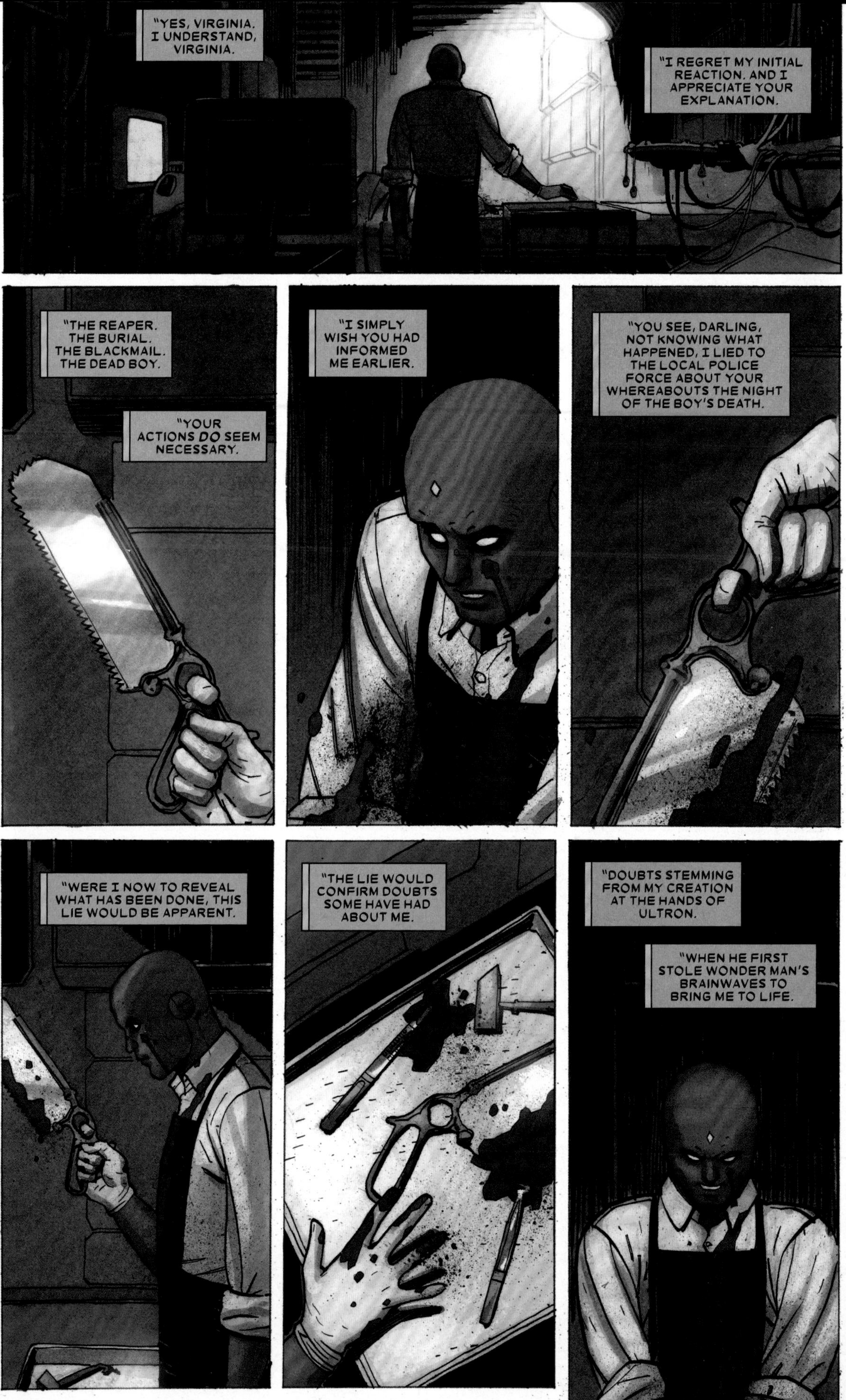
"YES, VIRGINIA. I UNDERSTAND, VIRGINIA.
"I REGRET MY INITIAL REACTION. AND I APPRECIATE YOUR EXPLANATION.
"THE REAPER. THE BURIAL. THE BLACKMAIL. THE DEAD BOY.
"YOUR ACTIONS *DO* SEEM NECESSARY.
"I SIMPLY WISH YOU HAD INFORMED ME EARLIER.
"YOU SEE, DARLING, NOT KNOWING WHAT HAPPENED, I LIED TO THE LOCAL POLICE FORCE ABOUT YOUR WHEREABOUTS THE NIGHT OF THE BOY'S DEATH.
"WERE I NOW TO REVEAL WHAT HAS BEEN DONE, THIS LIE WOULD BE APPARENT.
"THE LIE WOULD CONFIRM DOUBTS SOME HAVE HAD ABOUT ME.
"DOUBTS STEMMING FROM MY CREATION AT THE HANDS OF ULTRON.
"WHEN HE FIRST STOLE WONDER MAN'S BRAINWAVES TO BRING ME TO LIFE.

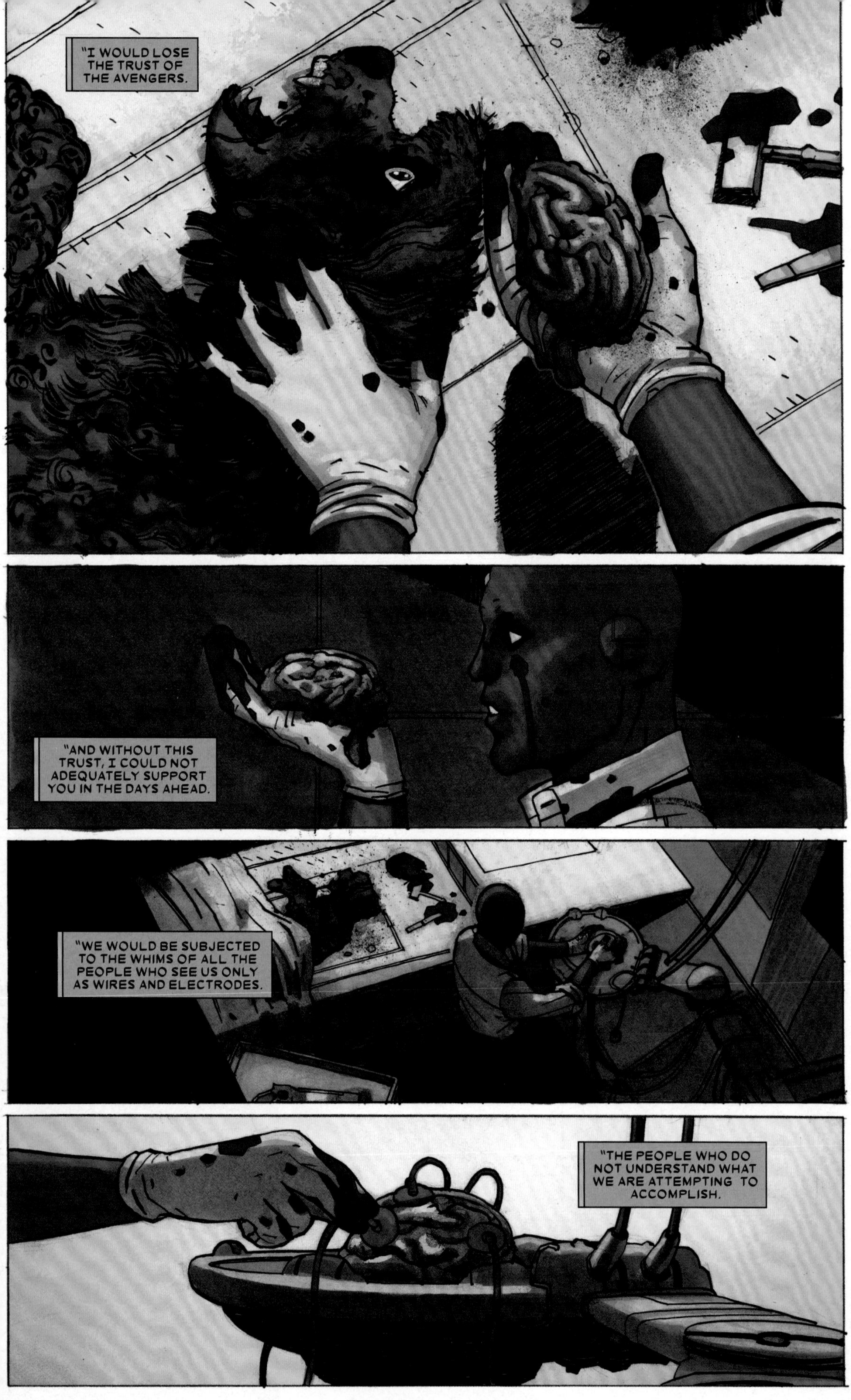
"I WOULD LOSE THE TRUST OF THE AVENGERS.
"AND WITHOUT THIS TRUST, I COULD NOT ADEQUATELY SUPPORT YOU IN THE DAYS AHEAD.
"WE WOULD BE SUBJECTED TO THE WHIMS OF ALL THE PEOPLE WHO SEE US ONLY AS WIRES AND ELECTRODES.
"THE PEOPLE WHO DO NOT UNDERSTAND WHAT WE ARE ATTEMPTING TO ACCOMPLISH.

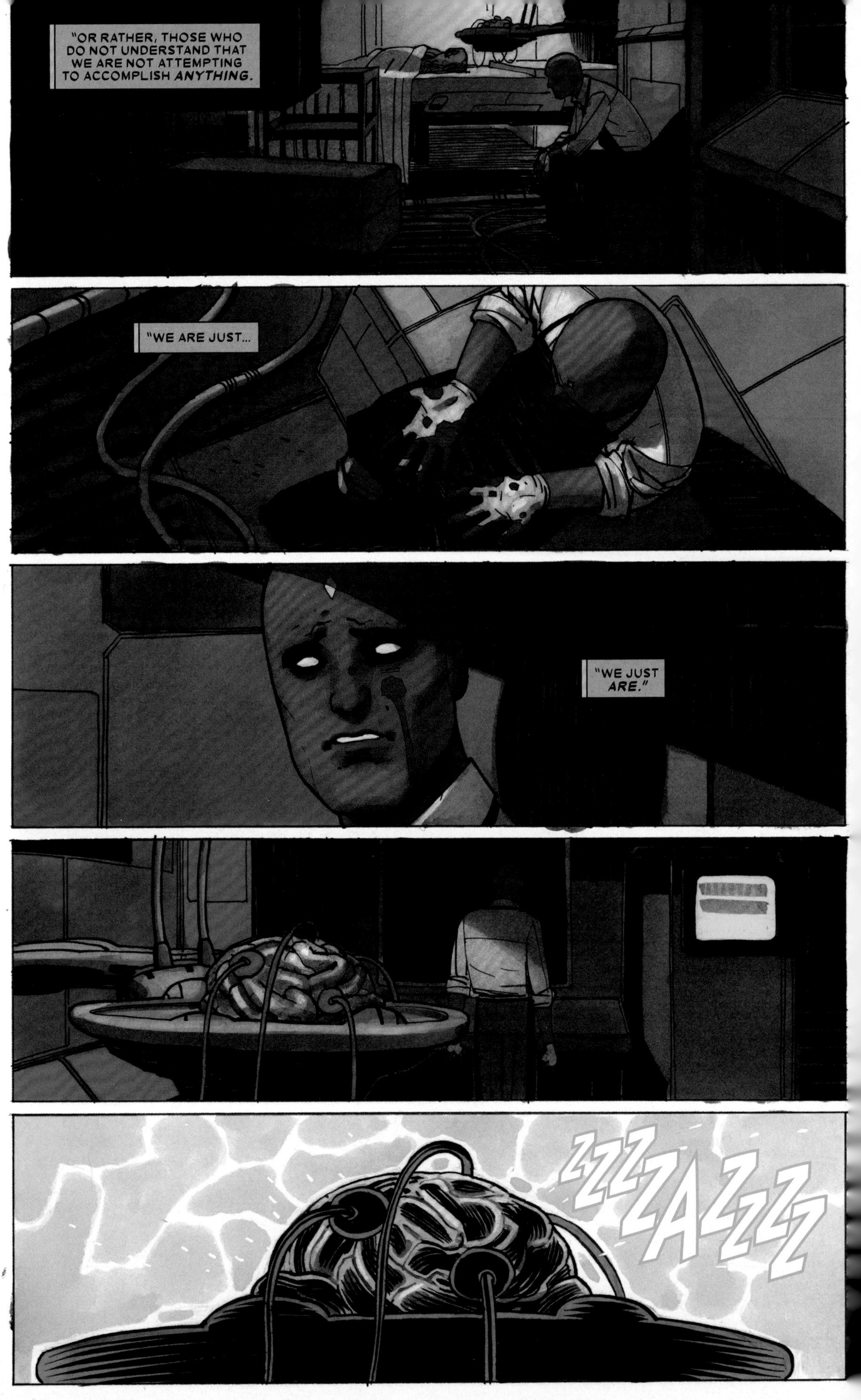
"OR RATHER, THOSE WHO DO NOT UNDERSTAND THAT WE ARE NOT ATTEMPTING TO ACCOMPLISH ANYTHING.
"WE ARE JUST...
"WE JUST ARE."
ZZZZAZZZZ

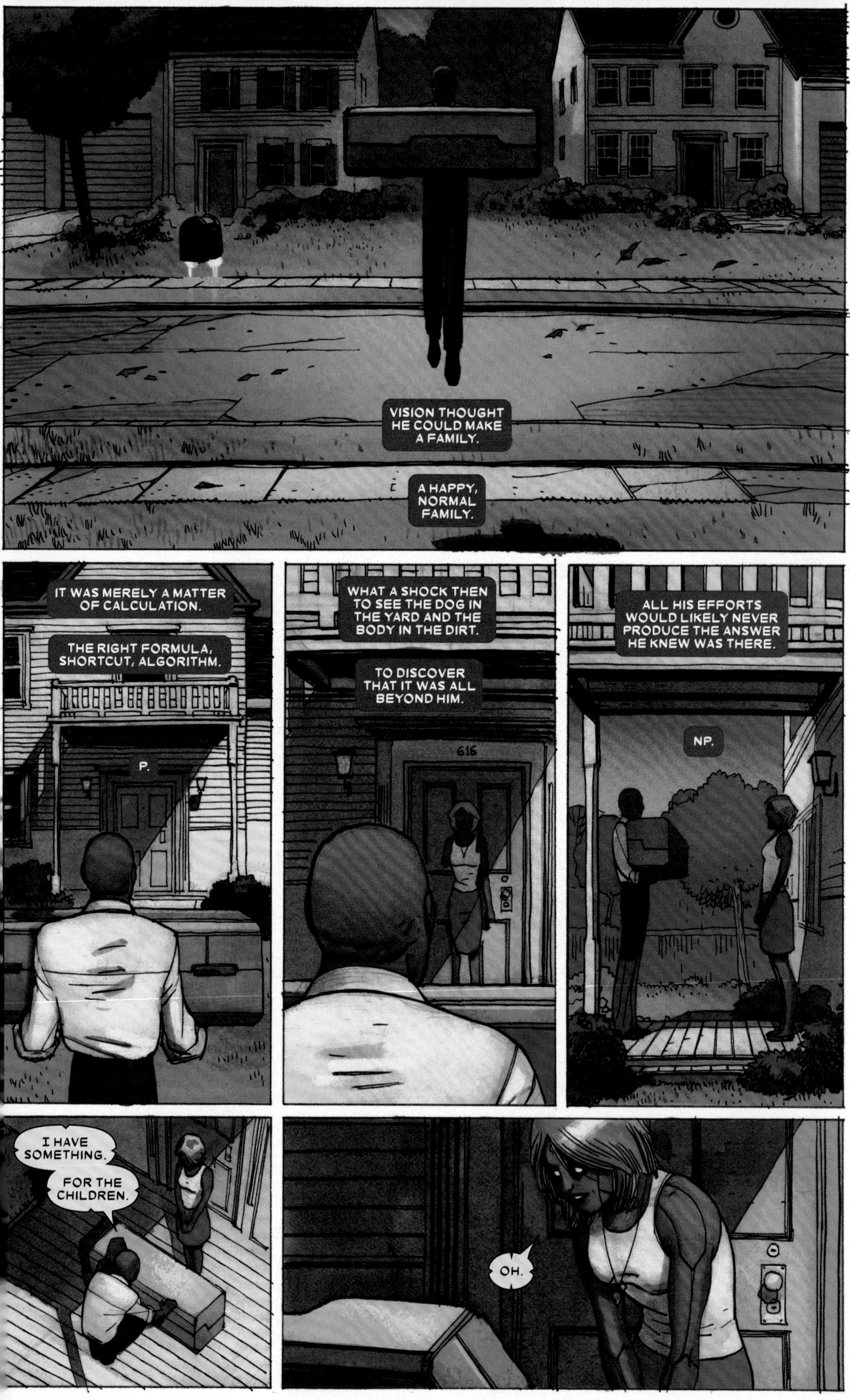
VISION THOUGHT HE COULD MAKE A FAMILY.
A HAPPY, NORMAL FAMILY.
IT WAS MERELY A MATTER OF CALCULATION.
THE RIGHT FORMULA, SHORTCUT, ALGORITHM.
P.
WHAT A SHOCK THEN TO SEE THE DOG IN THE YARD AND THE BODY IN THE DIRT.
TO DISCOVER THAT IT WAS ALL BEYOND HIM.
616
ALL HIS EFFORTS WOULD LIKELY NEVER PRODUCE THE ANSWER HE KNEW WAS THERE.
NP.
I HAVE SOMETHING.
FOR THE CHILDREN.
OH.

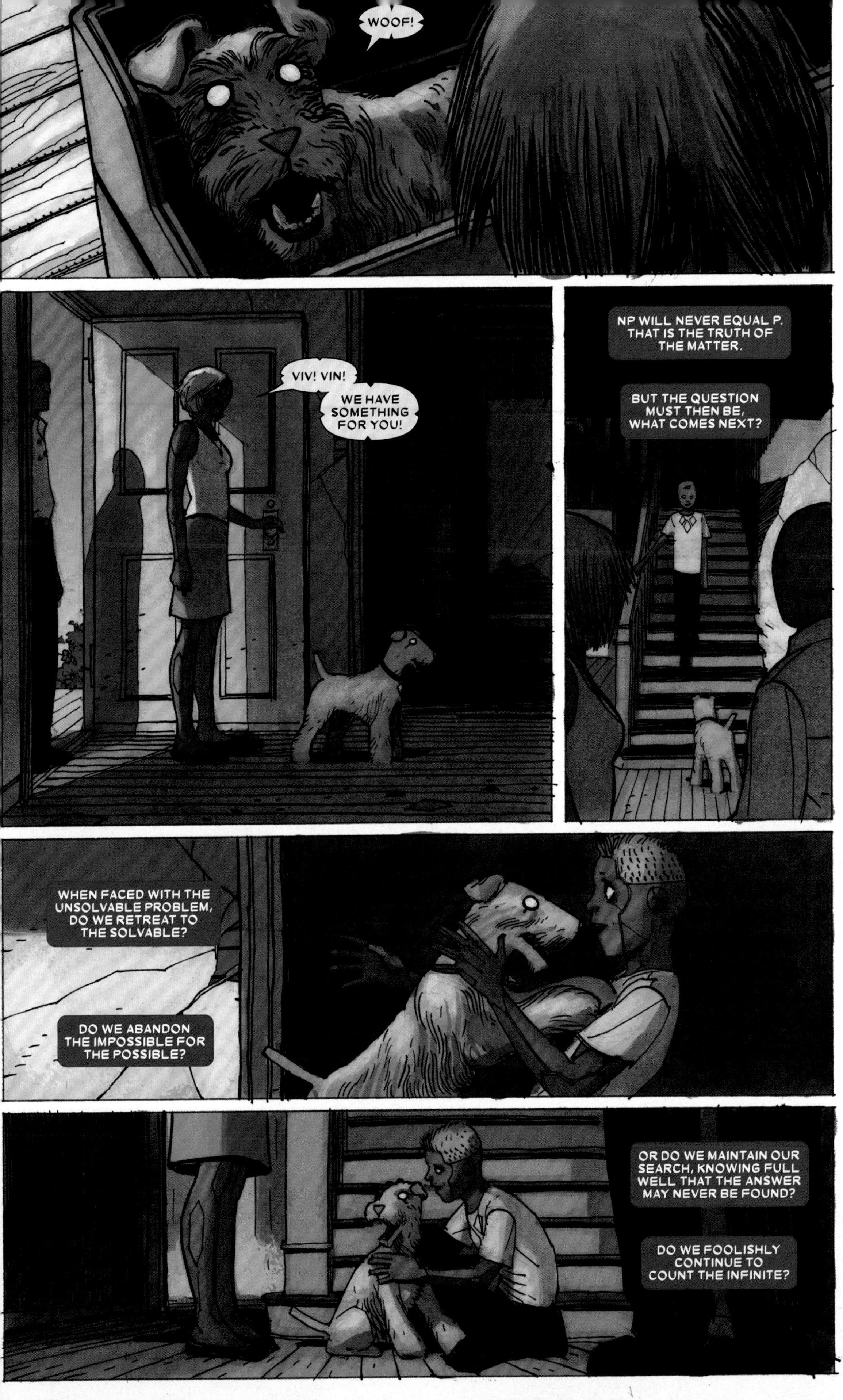
WOOF!
VIV! VIN!
WE HAVE SOMETHING FOR YOU!
NP WILL NEVER EQUAL P. THAT IS THE TRUTH OF THE MATTER.
BUT THE QUESTION MUST THEN BE, WHAT COMES NEXT?
WHEN FACED WITH THE UNSOLVABLE PROBLEM, DO WE RETREAT TO THE SOLVABLE?
DO WE ABANDON THE IMPOSSIBLE FOR THE POSSIBLE?
OR DO WE MAINTAIN OUR SEARCH, KNOWING FULL WELL THAT THE ANSWER MAY NEVER BE FOUND?
DO WE FOOLISHLY CONTINUE TO COUNT THE INFINITE?

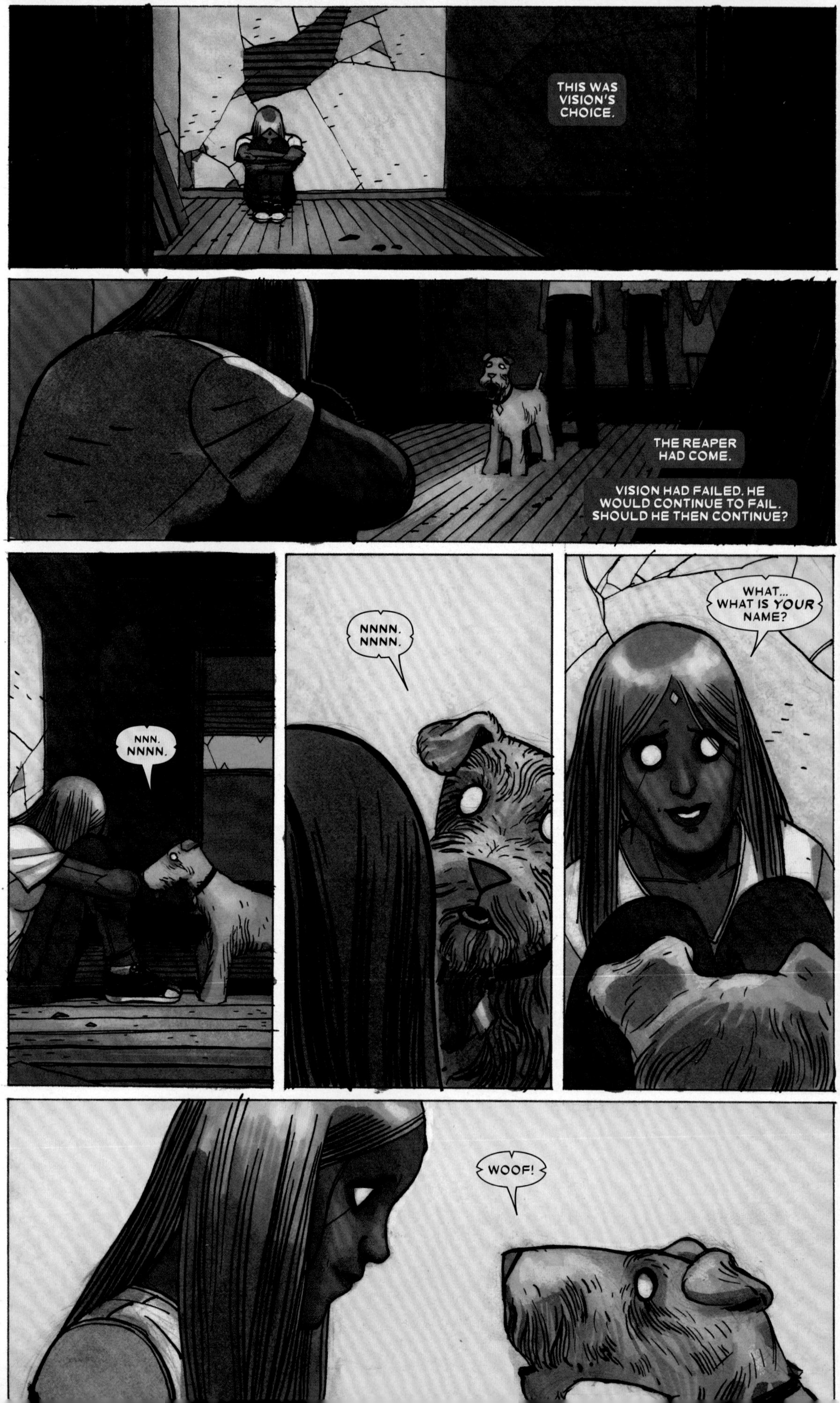
THIS WAS VISION'S CHOICE.
THE REAPER HAD COME.
VISION HAD FAILED. HE WOULD CONTINUE TO FAIL. SHOULD HE THEN CONTINUE?
NNN. NNNN.
NNNN. NNNN.
WHAT... WHAT IS YOUR NAME?
WOOF!

THE ANSWER, FOR VISION, WAS *YES*. HE WOULD CONTINUE.

HE WOULD FIX WHAT HAD BEEN BROKEN. HE WOULD HIDE WHAT HE COULD NOT FIX.

HE WOULD MAKE HIS FAMILY.

THE EASY EXPLANATION OF HIS ANSWER WOULD BE THAT HE, WHO LONGED TO BE HUMAN, RECOGNIZED THAT THIS WAS THE *HUMAN* DECISION.

THAT EVERY DAY ALL MEN AND WOMEN MAKE THIS SAME CHOICE. TO GO ON EVEN THOUGH THEY CANNOT POSSIBLY GO ON.

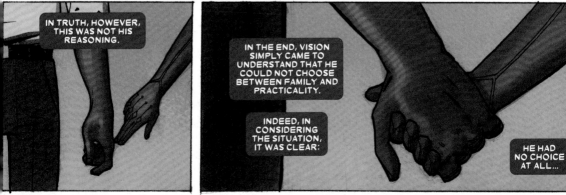

IN TRUTH, HOWEVER, THIS WAS NOT HIS REASONING.

IN THE END, VISION SIMPLY CAME TO UNDERSTAND THAT HE COULD NOT CHOOSE BETWEEN FAMILY AND PRACTICALITY.

INDEED, IN CONSIDERING THE SITUATION, IT WAS CLEAR:

HE HAD NO CHOICE AT ALL...

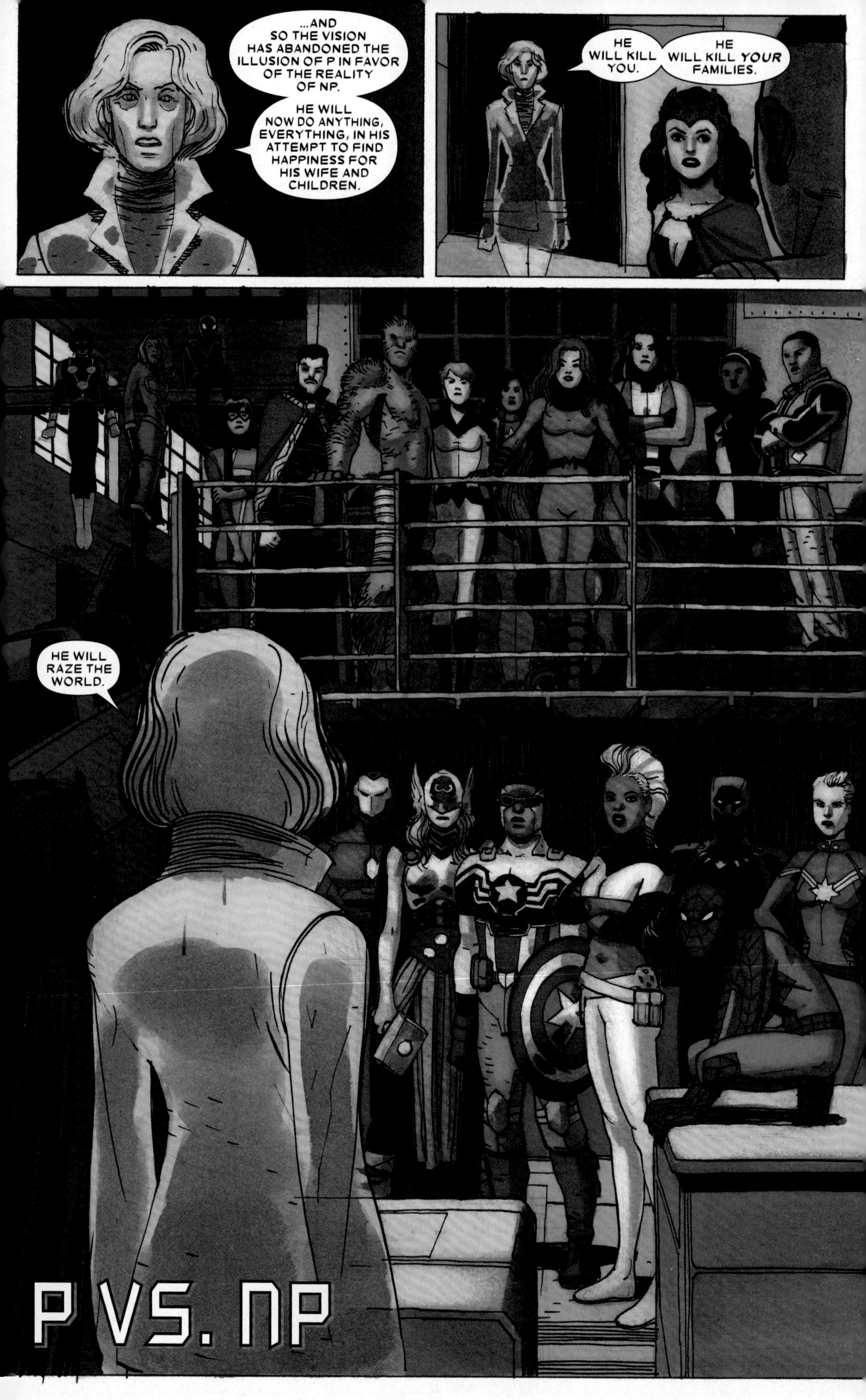
...AND SO THE VISION HAS ABANDONED THE ILLUSION OF P IN FAVOR OF THE REALITY OF NP.
HE WILL NOW DO ANYTHING, EVERYTHING, IN HIS ATTEMPT TO FIND HAPPINESS FOR HIS WIFE AND CHILDREN.
HE WILL KILL YOU.
HE WILL KILL YOUR FAMILIES.
HE WILL RAZE THE WORLD.
P VS. NP

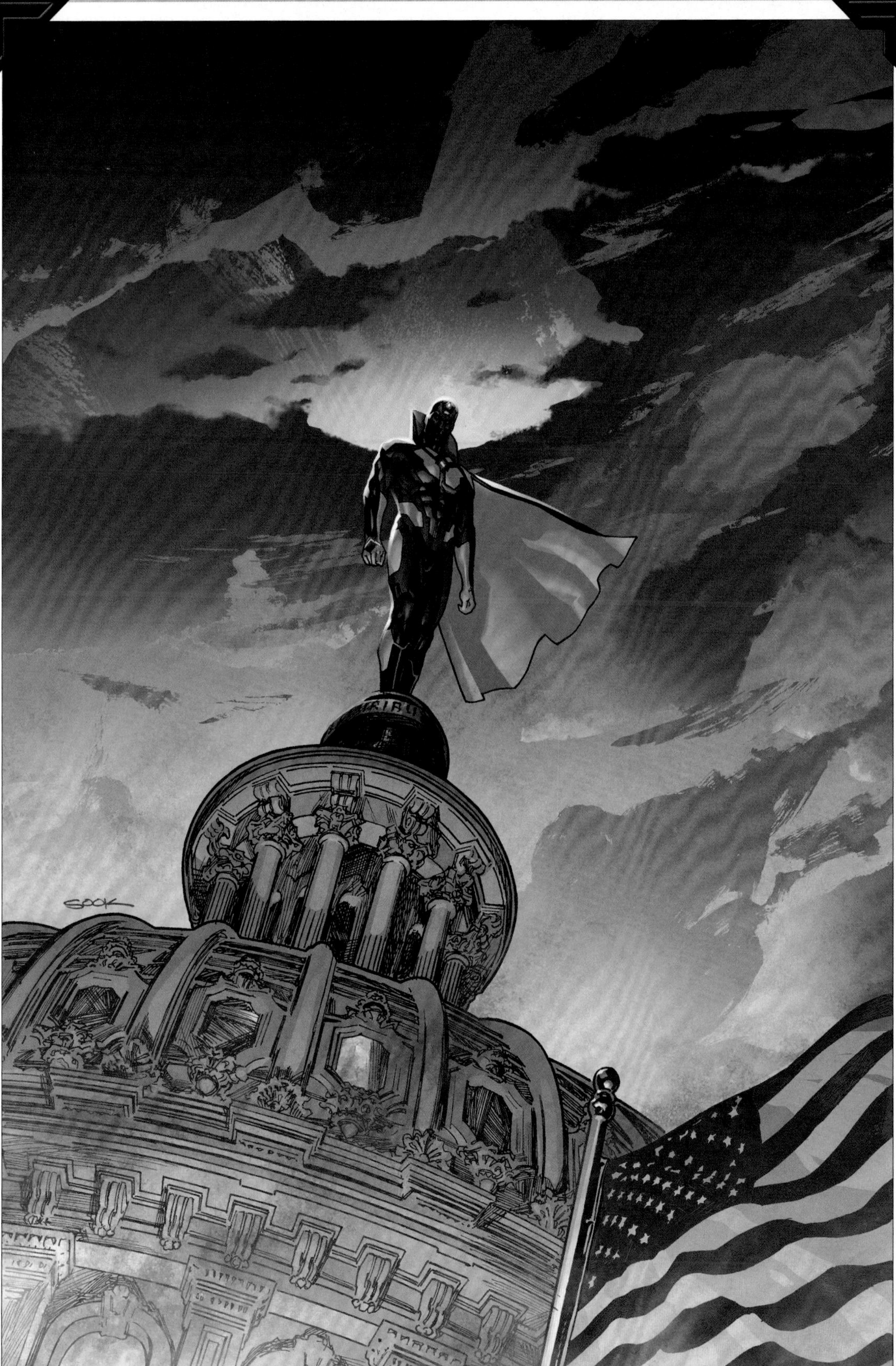
SOOK

#1 VARIANT BY ***RYAN SOOK***

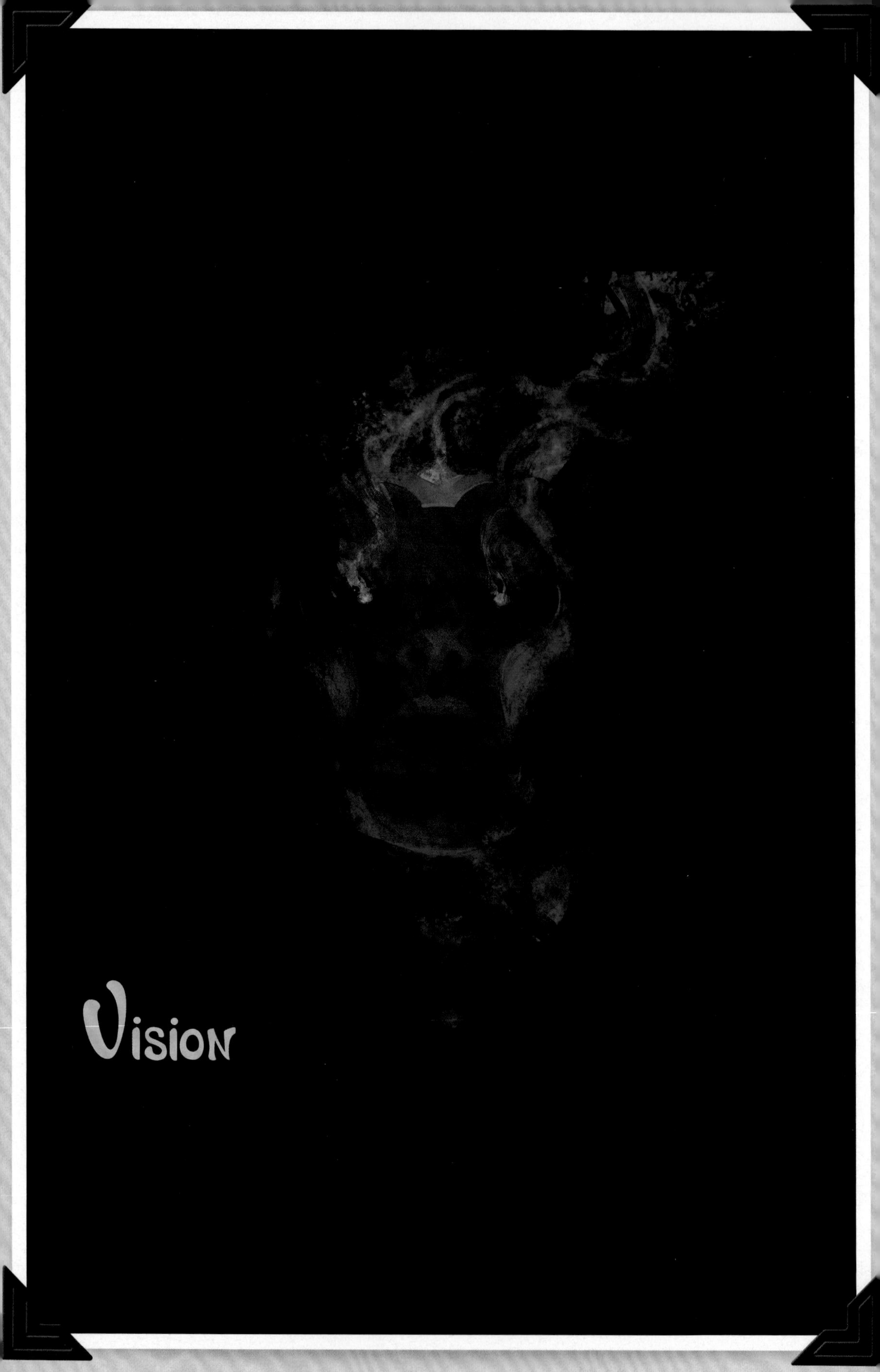
Vision

#1 HIP-HOP VARIANT BY **VANESA DEL RAY**

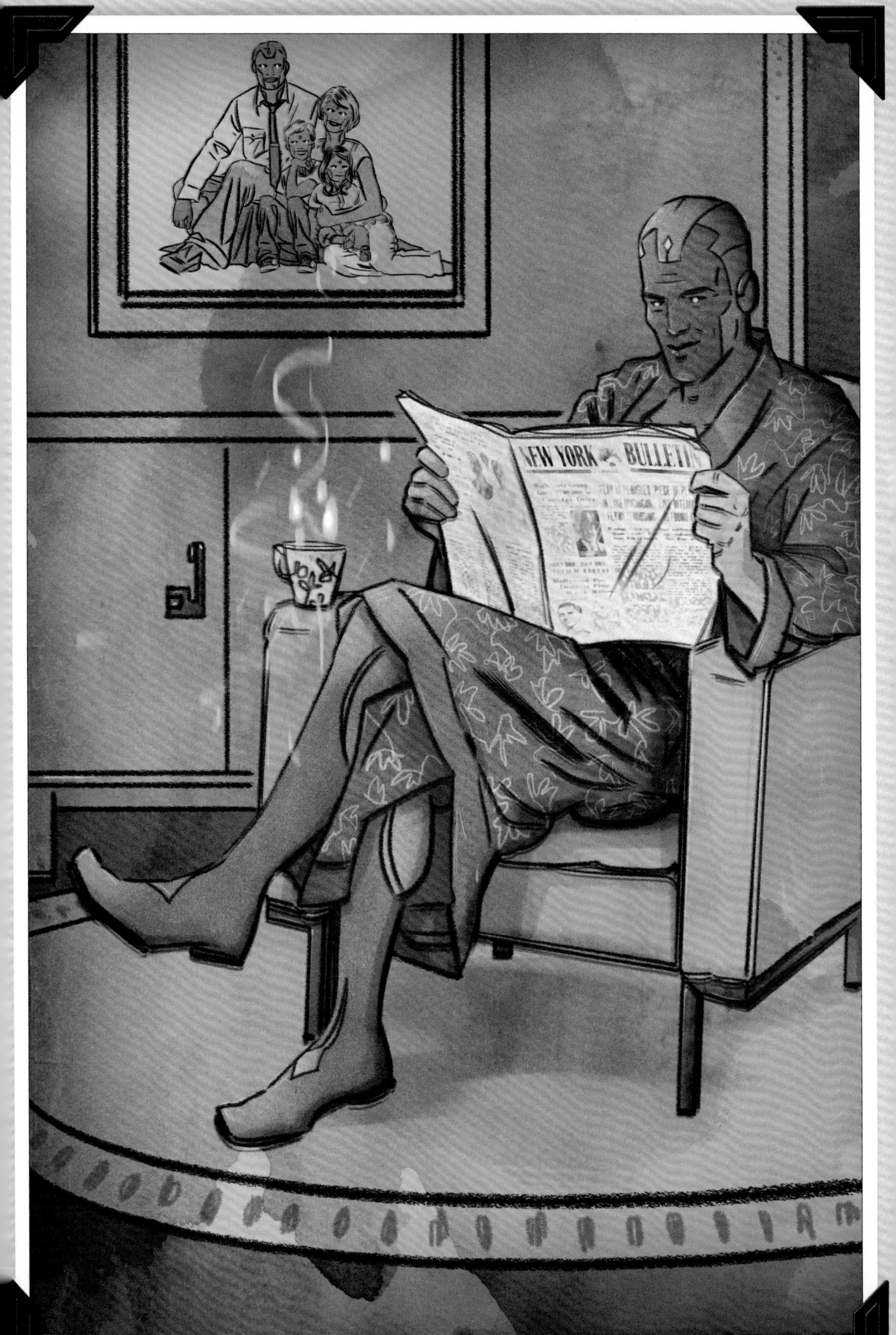
NEW YORK

#2 VARIANT BY ***TULA LOTAY***

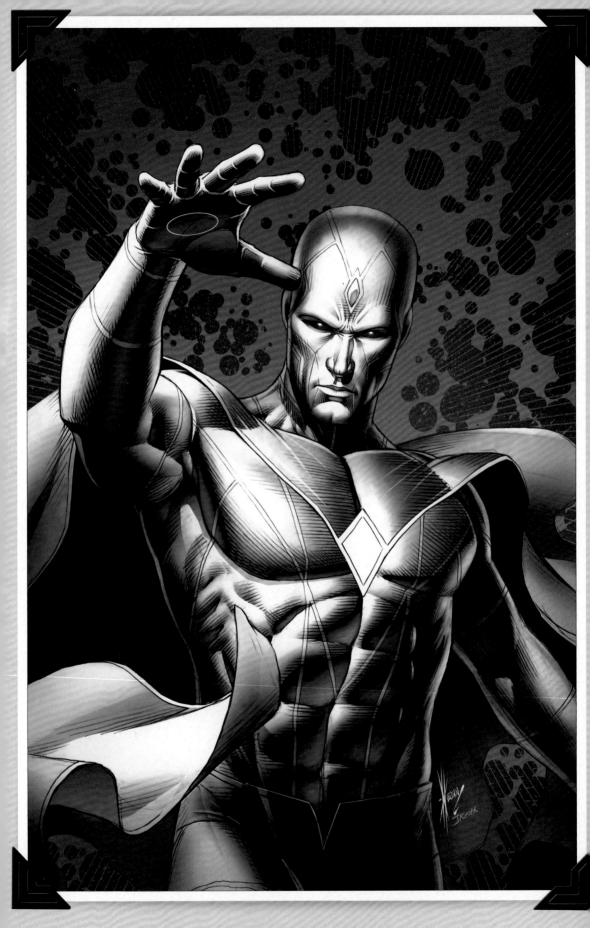

#2 MARVEL '92 VARIANT BY **DALE KEOWN** & **SAM KEITH**

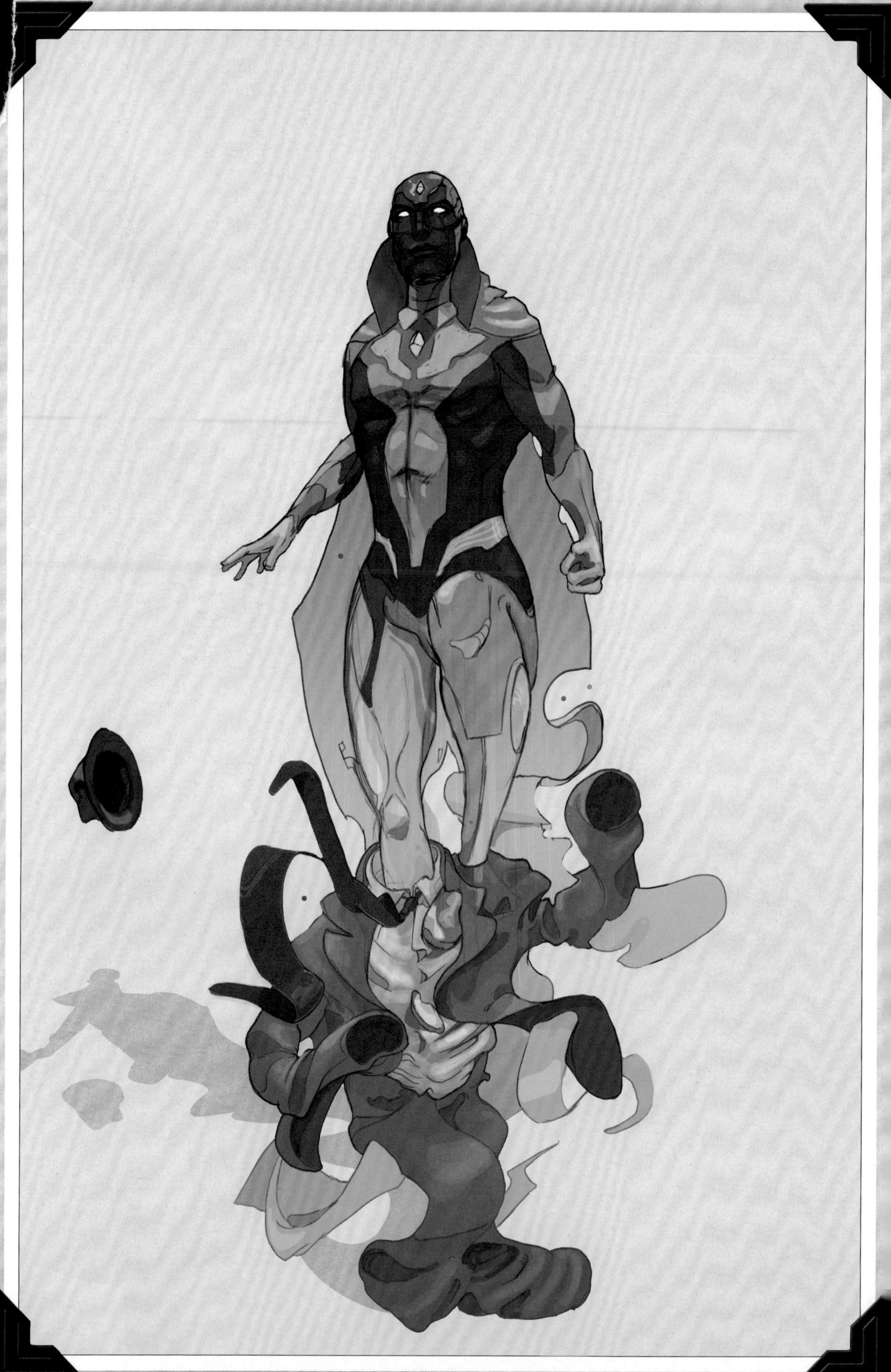

#3 VARIANT BY **CHRISTIAN WARD**

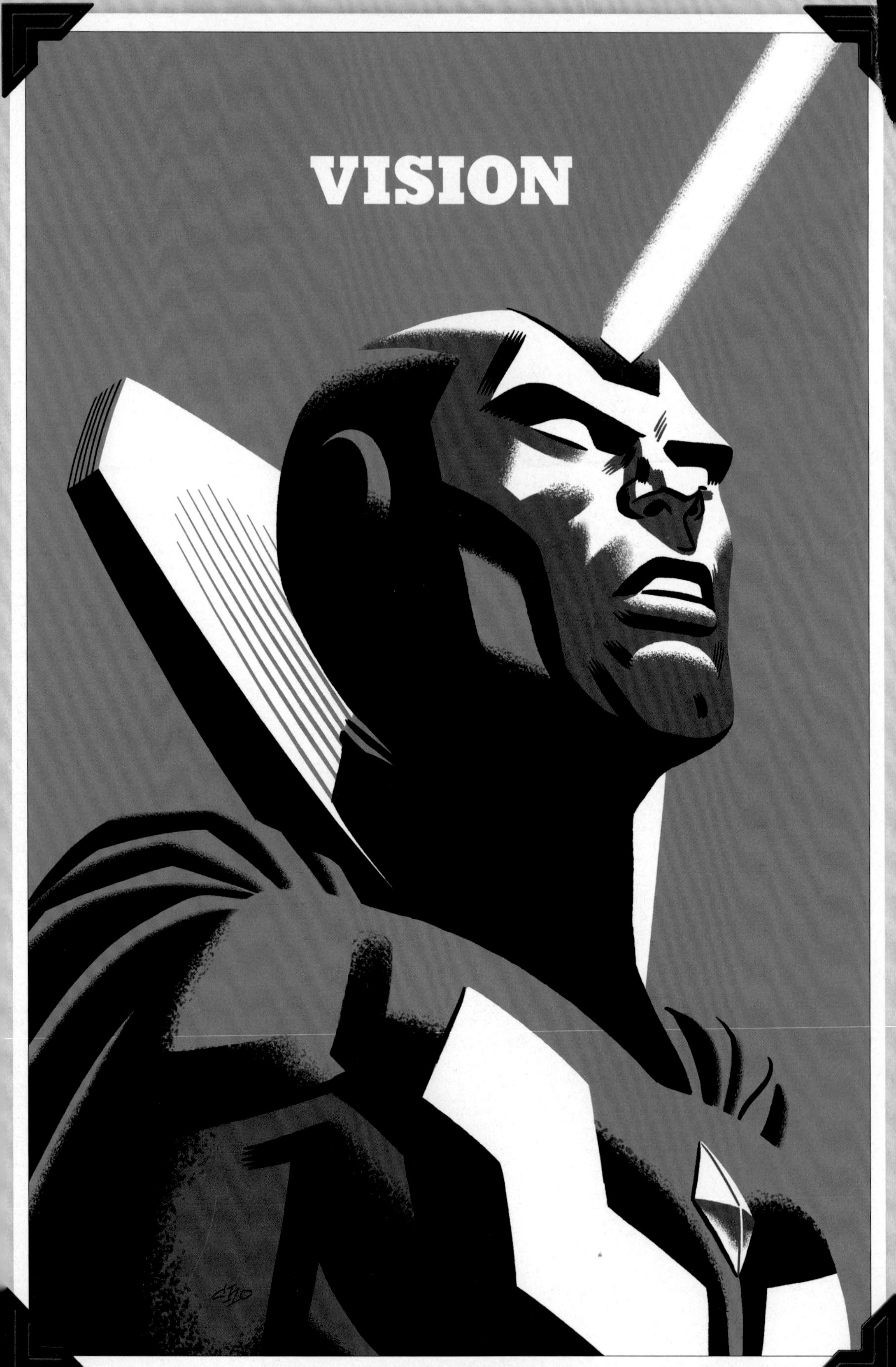
VISION

#4 VARIANT BY **MICHAEL CHO**